3/11/25

MW01256578

9 Mindsets for
Igniting Growth to
Become an Authentic Leader

SHINING
THROUGH
DISRUPTION

Praise for *Shining Through Disruption*

"Disruptive times require a new model of leadership. Our most respected leaders are those who listen first, lead with compassion, and foster a psychologically safe and inclusive culture. *Shining Through Disruption* will make you not only a better leader, but a better human being."

—Minette Norman, author of *The Boldly Inclusive Leader* and *The Psychological Safety Playbook*

"Stephanie Klein is an extraordinary thinker. In *Shining Through Disruption*, she tackles the challenge of our times: "How do we stay true and centered during upheaval?"

—Matt Church, Founder of Thought Leaders, Author of *Rise Up: An Evolution in Leadership*

"*Shining Through Disruption* is a game-changer for anyone ready to lead with authenticity and purpose. This isn't just another leadership book—it's a masterclass in turning challenges into opportunities. Essential reading for those who want to lead fearlessly and prosper in your business and life."

—Ellen Rogin, *New York Times* best-selling author of *Picture Your Prosperity*

"Powerful ideas, actionable for growth. This must-read book is for anyone who cares enough to lead better and live larger."

—David C. Blowers, Vice Chairman of Northern Trust

"*Shining Through Disruption* is an essential guide for every leader navigating change today. Stephanie Klein offers an inspiring and practical roadmap that will help you see the potential opportunities in disruption and know how to use them to your advantage to accelerate your leadership success. It's also a great read!"

—Lisa Bennett, co-author of *Ecoliterate* with
Daniel Goleman, editor of *Women Amplified*

"Klein shares intimate glimpses into the life of top leaders, complete with the fear and frustration, to help encourage the rest of us into being a bit braver and shining a whole lot brighter."

—Nancie McDonnell Ruder, Founder and CEO,
Noetic Consultants

"In *Shining Through Disruption*, Stephanie Klein masterfully illustrates how our obstacles can be transformed into opportunities for greater growth. This book is a must-read for anyone looking to lead with more authenticity, purpose, and resilience through the discomfort of uncertainty."

—Steven L. Fradkin, President,
Wealth Management, Northern Trust

"With her experience as a C-Suite Executive, certified professional coach, academic instructor, and cancer survivor, Stephanie Klein embodies how to adapt with resilience, skillfully guiding us through the art and science of mindfully leading through change."

—Meena Vetri Wehrs, Associate Dean,
Chicago Booth Executive Education

"Stephanie Klein's unique approach in *Shining Through Disruption* stands out among leadership growth books. By leading with mindfulness grounded in science and backed by real experience, she offers practical and creative strategies accessible to leaders at all levels and in every field. This must-read book empowers leaders to grow by learning new skills and unlearning habits that hinder effective connection and communication with their teams."
—Paul J. McLoughlin II, PhD, VP and Dean of the College, Colgate University

"In *Shining Through Disruption*, Stephanie Klein brilliantly demonstrates how to mindfully rewire our brains, expand our holistic intelligence, and optimize our potential. This insightful book is a transformative guide to authentic leadership growth, powered by her 4P's: presence, purpose, perspective, and progress."
—Diana Cordova, PhD, Clinical Professor and Managing Director, Kellogg Executive Education

"In this impactful book, Stephanie Klein redefines leadership growth like a masterful orchestra conductor—seamlessly integrating knowledge from diverse *instruments*, such as organizational behavior, positive psychology, modern neuroscience, ancient archetypes, and real-world experience—with true artistry. Her engaging style and vulnerability feel like a stimulating conversation with an insightful friend. Whether you're seeking fulfillment in a large organization or want to thrive faster as a free agent, this book will guide you."
—Bruce Butler, Chief Executive Officer, Samaritan Health Plans

"Shining through Disruption is an essential read for all leaders, educators, and life-long learners seeking balance, mindfulness, and high performance. Stephanie's distinctive voice energizes us to lead authentically and inspire others—elevating self-care, purpose, and connections—so we all rise together."
—Daniela B. Friedman, PhD, Professor and Administrator, Graduate of the 2022 Mindful Leadership Program - Chicago Booth Executive Education

"As a gifted course leader and executive coach, Stephanie Klein guides us through the fascinating insights that will help you get from where you are to where you want to be, all the while assuring us that where you are now is exactly where you're meant to be. This helpful book put so much into perspective for me."
—Randy Deutsch, Educator and author of *Superusers*

"Stephanie's journey is a testament to the resilience and growth that can emerge from life's most challenging disruptions. In *Shining Through Disruption*, she offers invaluable insights and practical tools for leaders navigating their paths, inspiring them to embrace change, cultivate authenticity, and achieve lasting success."
—Katie Drescher, JD, ESIA, SP, Master Certified Coach

9 Mindsets for
Igniting Growth to
Become an Authentic Leader

SHINING
THROUGH
DISRUPTION

STEPHANIE K. KLEIN
CREATOR OF MINDFUL LEADERSHIP FOR THE
UNIVERSITY OF CHICAGO'S BOOTH SCHOOL OF BUSINESS

Capucia LLC
211 Pauline Drive #513
York, PA 17402
www.capuciapublishing.com
Send questions to: support@capuciapublishing.com

Paperback ISBN: 978-1-954920-97-2
eBook ISBN: 979-8-9915156-1-0
Library of Congress Control Number: 2024919266

Author photos: Julie Kaplan
Cover Design: Klassic Designs
Layout: Ranilo Cabo
Graphic Design: Lisa Murphy
Editor and Proofreader: Simon Whaley
Book Midwife: Carrie Jareed

Printed in the United States of America

Capucia LLC is proud to be a part of the Tree Neutral® program. Tree Neutral offsets the number of trees consumed in the production and printing of this book by taking proactive steps such as planting trees in direct proportion to the number of trees used to print books. To learn more about Tree Neutral, please visit treeneutral.com.

For my mother—your love lit me up and inspired me to follow my dreams.

You live on in me and my daughters, who light my way forward.

Contents

Foreword

By Bill Carmody, PCC, Chief Coaching Officer
for Positive Intelligence, Executive Coach,
Bestselling Author

L eadership has always been a tough job, but it's getting tougher, with accelerating change being the only constant. Disruptive change wreaks havoc on the emotional operating system of teams and leaders, pushing them into fight, flight, or freeze mode, and often turning into burnout. It's safe to say that disruption affects millions of people, not in a good way.

Stephanie Klein knows this and what we can do about it. I wish I had known Stephanie Klein when I was growing up, going to college, or simply had any of her sage wisdom that you're about to read. This book is a practical and inspirational guide for leaders who are facing continual, stressful change— to stop sabotage, adapt faster, and reclaim control. Not just to survive through disruption, but to authentically and confidently shine through disruption. If I had this book earlier in my life, I surely would have approached my biggest challenges differently, realizing they were opportunities to learn and grow into my greater potential. In fact, that's what inspired Stephanie to write this book. She wished she had all this wisdom earlier in life, too, so she could thrive faster through disruptive change—without waiting for her wake-up calls of cancer and burnout. Now, she's passing on what she's learned as a former three-time Chief Marketing Officer with three decades of building Fortune 500 brands, combined with her experience as an Executive Coach and Mindful Leadership instructor. As it is, I feel incredibly lucky to know Stephanie today.

So why read this book? There are so many great books to help high achievers maximize their potential. Why listen to what Stephanie has to say? Simply put, your life will be deeply enriched in all the ways that count if you not only read this book, but also take the time to put these core principles into practice. As the late Stephen R. Covey said, "To learn and not to do is really not to learn. To know and not to do is really not to know." You can trust Stephanie. She's worked with the biggest companies, taught at the most prestigious schools, and she genuinely cares about helping you because she's walked in your shoes. Fueled by passionate purpose, Stephanie has created an indispensable guidebook for skillfully riding disruptive waves without burnout. This book is for you if you are facing emotional turbulence—from organizational change, a new position, or a crossroads. *Shining Through Disruption* will serve as a lifeboat to help you travel confidently to your desired destination, without falling overboard. Most people focus on what you need to know. Stephanie also reveals who you are meant to be, so you can light up your whole brain's intelligence—creative, emotional, intuitive, and rational—and rise to your authentic leadership potential.

I have had the pleasure of getting to know Stephanie through my role as Chief Coaching Officer at Positive Intelligence, the mental fitness company. As of the publishing of this book, Positive Intelligence was named the 567th fastest-growing private company in the US, according to Inc. Magazine, and we've trained over 55,000 coaches (about 50 percent of all coaches globally).

Stephanie and I share a passion for an individual's deep sense of purpose: to "shine authentically and trailblaze your life, fueled by deep Purpose." When you are connected to your deeper why, you can overcome just about anything, rise to any challenge, and face any disruption. When we hold the perspective that life is happening for us, not to us, we are open to accepting the many gifts life has to offer.

And purpose is just one of the 4Ps that Stephanie shares in her book. No, these are not the 4Ps of marketing. They are the 4Ps to living up to your extraordinary optimal potential: Perspective, Presence, Purpose, and Progress. Each provides a depth of wisdom that is so clear and concise, they are easily incorporated into your life with immediate benefit. Any one of them has the capacity to change your current trajectory. Put them all together, with Stephanie's FAST framework to Focus, Adapt, Stretch, and Thrive—and you're bound to experience exponential (not incremental) growth.

My one request is that you savor this work. This is not the kind of book to blow through on your next flight somewhere, even though it's a fast, compelling read. You'd miss the richness that Stephanie has painstakingly put into her masterful life's work. By slowing down and really absorbing the concepts that Stephanie puts forth, you'll experience a transformation in yourself and be well-prepared for whatever comes up next in your life. Personal transformation is tough. The focus on embracing change with inner purpose is what makes *Shining Through Disruption* such a valuable resource. This book has the power to forever change how leaders survive and thrive through disruption. I am inspired by Stephanie's work and am honored to have the opportunity to amplify her wisdom and profound insights.

Let's face it. You can't control what life presents to you along your path. But you can master your mindset, aligning your mind and heart. To build resilience to handle whatever comes your way. To be curious and hold a different perspective.

To challenge yourself to be fully present to what's happening in this moment. To live a life filled with deep purpose and true satisfaction. And to celebrate all the incredible progress along your life's journey. Isn't that what it's all about?

Finally, I want to thank you. Thank you for picking up this book. Buying this book says something about you. It says you're the type of person who chooses to shine brightly despite any obstacle or disruption you face. I know that once you've completed reading this book and put into practice what Stephanie is sharing, the world will be that much better off for your efforts. How do I know this? Because I've witnessed it firsthand. I believe in the interconnected web of humanity, of which we are all a part, and how much higher we can rise together.

When each of us is willing to do the work to make ourselves better, we not only improve our own lives, but we also improve the lives of everyone around us. For this, I thank you. Your work here does not go unnoticed. I know you are committed to living a more mindful life, and you have joined a growing population of people all over the world committed to doing this too.

Be well, my friend. Whether you're seeking to rise as a leader or inspire others at the next level, this book is the resource to help you succeed. For it is the biggest challenges in our lives that shape us and call us to who we truly are. You have answered life's call and your adventure awaits. I wish you all the best.

Introduction

Wake Up and Shine

In April 2011, I was diagnosed with cancer that could have killed me, but it woke me up to living instead.

I was a stressed Chief Marketing Officer (CMO) who thought I had no time to spare for a doctor's appointment when I found a lump, the size of a golf ball, under my right armpit. Two days after a painful biopsy, I got a call from the breast cancer surgeon that shocked me to my core.

"Your lump is malignant."

I felt the ground crumbling beneath me as I struggled to breathe, but I needed to dive in quickly and figure out a treatment plan to save my life.

The cancer scared me, but I was most terrified of breaking the news to my two daughters, aged eleven and thirteen. I'd waited until this particular day, two weeks later, since my chemotherapy was about to begin. While cancer is not an easy pill to swallow for anyone, my girls had lost both their grandmothers to cancer, so I knew this would sound like a death sentence. I still remember the pain of losing my mother when I was twenty-nine, and I wanted to protect my daughters from ever experiencing that kind of sorrow.

As I looked into their eyes, I heard my voice quiver when I told them. "I have cancer." I quickly added, "But it's not like Grammy Sue's or Grammy Arlene's. We have a plan, and I'm going to beat it."

They looked at me in shock and horror. Tears filled their eyes, and they began to cry. I felt their love and fear so acutely, and I burst into tears too. I wanted to ease their pain more than anything, and I managed to say, "I love you so much, and I'm not going anywhere. I promise you."

Of course, I knew I couldn't guarantee my recovery. Yet, I had no intention of failing. I knew with every fiber of my being that I hadn't finished what I came here to do. I was a high achiever who thrived on goals, and now I had the biggest and most meaningful one of all: to stand up and fight—for my children, for my life. I wanted so badly to be part of their lives as they experienced each milestone and became the beautiful women I knew they'd be. I could see it. Feel it. Taste it. I had love and meaning on my side. I had conviction in my soul. I was going to prevail.

With this fierce sense of purpose, and lots of support, I beat my cancer. That surprised me less than discovering I could flourish while doing it. Life was hard. Life was beautiful. Both things were true. In getting aligned with what was most important, at work and home, I was able to empower others and let go of what didn't serve me. I put myself back on the priority list and woke up to the power of compassion. Profound joy arises when we realize how precious life is in each moment. I became a better mother, leader, and human being. I mistakenly thought this must happen to everyone who experiences a huge existential crisis. I later learned it doesn't.

It would be seven years before I knew why.

I've realized that facing death wakes us up to the reason why we're alive. As the German philosopher Frederick Nietzsche wrote, "If we have our own 'why' of life we shall get along with almost any 'how'."[1] I've since realized my *big why* goes beyond my family. It includes Me. And You. We are all interconnected. And we all have a unique reason to be on this planet right now. My mission

I've realized that facing death wakes us up to the reason why we're alive.

is to help you discover your *big why*, *big who*, and the *big how* to achieve it, which starts with embracing the surprises we never see coming.

There's an old Yiddish saying my mother used to quote: *Man Plans, and God Laughs.*

It took me a very long time to really get that message. I had believed that life should unfold according to my plan because, until my twenties, it largely did. It was painful to realize that I couldn't control the disruptive waves in my life. But I woke up to accept their profound purpose: breaking me open to reshape my life and how I live it.

In my twenties, I lost my mother to invasive cancer and realized how short life can be. Her death was the first major disruption in my life and helped me see what I valued most.

In my early thirties, just after returning to work from my second maternity leave, I was laid off with two kids under the age of three, a daunting mortgage, a full-time nanny, and an unemployed husband. I was devastated. However, I discovered my life changed for the better, with greater purpose, balance, and well-being.

In my forties, as a brand new CMO, I led a global team through the 2008 financial crisis and worked crazy hours amidst constant anxiety and uncertainty. Mentally, I could handle it, but I had no idea the huge toll this *constant stress* was taking on my body—until 2011, when I got my cancer wake-up call. I'm grateful I learned how to let go and make time for everything that was truly important.

In my fifties, at the pinnacle of my corporate career, I experienced a disruptive acquisition that diminished my control, shook my identity, and brought me to burnout. After months of suffering, I realized I could reclaim my power by exiting on my own terms. From this pain, I discovered a more meaningful next act as an executive coach, leadership trainer, educator, speaker, and author.

This book is the guide I wish I'd had during my three-decade career to deal with the ongoing stress, challenges, uncertainty, and disruptions of life. It will help you live and lead with more passion, purpose, and balance. If you're a high-achieving professional, I know your pain, and I've learned the secret to transforming it into even greater purpose and potential.

It's the *Transitions Guide* I wish I'd had in my twenties when I discovered I couldn't completely control my life. It would have empowered me to move with greater ease and confidence toward what was waiting next for me.

It's the *Balancing Guide* I wish I'd had in my thirties when I struggled with effectively juggling my passion for my career and my family, so I could embrace more joy, presence, and holistic well-being across my life.

It's the *Lifeline* I wish I'd had in my forties while leading through the financial crisis of 2008 and suffering burnout, followed by cancer. It could have helped me set boundaries and prioritize self-care and self-compassion, so I could find more sustainable ways to navigate ongoing uncertainty outside my control.

It's the *Next Act Roadmap* I wish I'd had in my fifties when I exited my last CMO role, feeling untethered, without excitement for my current path or clarity on my next one. It would have helped me pause and create space intentionally to design a new meaningful life.

I took the long road to learn how to live and lead with more meaning, balance, impact, and joy than I'd imagined possible. Now I want to help leaders at all stages of life to flourish faster authentically, without waiting for the wake-up call.

Our big problem, as high-achieving professionals, is that our world is changing faster than we're prepared for, and it's scary. In the next one hundred years alone, we will experience 20,000 years of change![2,3] We all know how stressful and overwhelming disruption can feel. However, instead of backing away from it, we can learn to adapt faster. By embracing disruptions as potential opportunities, we can come out stronger on the other side, shining even brighter.

Yet, it's hard to navigate ourselves, let alone lead teams, while we're living with fear and anxiety from constant change. It's like we're being asked to build a plane and fly it at the same time. No wonder we're moving into hyperdrive and exhaustion as the new normal. In 2021, 77 percent of US professionals reported employee burnout, with half experiencing it more than once.[4]

Now I'm passionate about sharing my secrets, and those of other leaders, of how to shift beyond burnout to a better balance. You can stop the firehose of overwhelm and learn how to live and lead with greater resilience, productivity, and well-being.

While my life's disruptions felt so wrong at first, they served a purpose. I eventually saw gifts I never expected, but they were exactly what I needed to strengthen and grow to my next level.

I wrote this book to answer this question: **How can high achievers thrive through unexpected disruption to unleash more purpose and authentic growth?**

I've realized that the best leaders—those taking big risks to be happier and chase meaning amid uncertainty and change—have two big things in common:

1. They fall in the elite 10 percent of people who bounce forward with adaptive resilience in the face of ongoing, uncontrollable events. They remain immune to *learned helplessness,* knowing they can find a solution to any difficult problem.[5]

2. Through seismic change, they experience post-traumatic growth, which enables them to experience greater purpose, connections, and joy.

I learned their wisdom was often hard won, coming from an existential crisis that disrupted their view of the world, so they could recreate an even better mental model.[6] In *Life Is in the Transitions,* Bruce Feiler's research showed we commonly experience huge disruptions in a pileup of three—to get us to really pay attention and *change,* with huge aftershocks that can last for five years.[7]

As the pandemic lockdown began in March 2020, I thought I'd already experienced enough disruption and was about ready to publish my book about thriving through it. In 2018 alone, I'd survived a stressful acquisition, resigned from my Chief Marketing Officer role, become an empty nester, and started reinventing my career as a mindful leadership instructor. But I realized I had more chaos to experience alongside the rest of the world.

I know how tough it feels to lose control during a significant disruption, but I also appreciate the huge opportunity we have to reclaim it. I hope to inspire anyone who reads this book to see how you can transform adversity into your powerful advantage.

As I progressed on my journey as an executive coach, speaker, and emotional intelligence (EQ) trainer, I realized both myself and my book were still evolving. That's when I experienced a big *Aha!* moment—I learned we can intentionally disrupt ourselves to grow exponentially anytime.

Armed with this insight, I explored this powerful question: **How can we intentionally harness disruption to access more of our whole-brain's intelligence (emotional, intuitive, creative, and rational), so we optimize our potential?**

Change is the only constant, as we know. That's why the acronym VUCA, which stands for *volatility, uncertainty, complexity, and ambiguity,* never goes out of style. While VUCA can be a useful management tool, it often leads us to react from fear instead of creativity. To succeed in our rapidly changing world, our logical, rational left-brain thinking isn't sufficient and is often compromised. We have a great opportunity to operate at a higher level and dial up our right-brain's emotional, creative, and intuitive intelligences. Becoming more holistic and authentic leaders, we can solve seemingly intractable problems with greater connectivity, insight, and innovation—reframing VUCA as *vision, understanding, courage, and adaptability.*

Accessing more of our authentic potential is simple, but not easy. It's led me to live with more purpose, passion, presence, and progress. It's changed who I am and given me the inner confidence to be more unapologetically myself—trusting my voice, heart, and gut intelligences. While I will always be a work-in-progress, I've created new habits and practices that have catapulted me forward into a meaningful career and life that feels more balanced and impactful than ever.

I've been privileged to help thousands of professionals transform into more authentic, mindful leaders who inspire and motivate, starting with themselves. Their growth ignites teams and organizations to lead at the next level, with positive ripple effects in the world. My holistic approach lives at the intersection of emotional intelligence and brand leadership. It's based on my thirty years of insight and experience with clients, senior-level leaders, teachers, and collaborators around the globe, including the courageous leaders in my *Mindful Leadership* Executive Education course at the University of Chicago Booth School of Business. With a proven roadmap of nine mindsets, you will light up more of your innate superpower to shine authentically across your life. You'll learn how to dance with whatever disruption you face, with greater awareness and mastery, moving confidently forward even if you can't clearly see what's next. If that sounds good to you, I hope you'll join me, because the world needs what you can uniquely bring.

Wherever you are, you are exactly where you are meant to be right now. But change can feel uncomfortable until you get comfortable again. Know that you're not alone and that this bold adventure is worth it. I appreciate the encouraging words of Fred Rogers:

"Discovering the truth about ourselves is a lifetime's work, but it's worth the effort."[8]

I used to think that courage was required in larger proportions when unexpected disruption fell in our path. Now I realize that the courage to create our own disruption is the biggest game changer. The choice is ours.

Shining through Disruption is the big promise of this book. Unleashing your brilliance to shine with boundless potential starts one step at a time. I've done it, and I've worked with so many others who've done it too. Let's dive in!

PART I

Embracing the Four Elements of Potential

In Part I, we'll learn to embrace our Four Elements of Potential—Emotion, Energy, Essence, and Experience—by drawing inspiration from the Four Elements of Nature: Water, Air, Fire, and Earth. Just as these natural elements are fundamental to the world around us, our Four Elements of Potential are essential to our being, helping us operate more consciously across our heart, mind, spirit, and body with whole brain intelligence. At the mastery level, we power up the 4Ps of optimal potential: *Perspective, Presence, Purpose,* and *Progress.*

Optimal Potential—Fear and love are the most powerful emotions, so we begin by illuminating and catching them. Fear strikes like lightning—energetic, unpredictable, and fierce—to correct what's imbalanced. It can paralyze or spread fast and furiously, interfering with the other elements, which limits us. Fortunately, love conquers fear—rapidly expanding and rebalancing all elements to restore equilibrium and power the 4Ps. Like capturing lightning in a bottle, love's magic creates rare, extraordinary success. When we can transmute fear into love, we unleash infinite possibilities to optimize potential.

Emotion of Heart (Water)—Just as water flows naturally and has the power to carve valleys, our emotions flow through us, carrying powerful insights. The best leaders possess emotional intelligence, enabling them to understand their feelings and those of others, fostering deep growth and connection. We all have the capacity to enhance self-awareness to create more ease and flow in our lives and relationships. At the mastery level, we cultivate deeper wisdom for heightened *Perspective.*

Energy of Mind (Air)—Energy, like air, cannot be created or destroyed, only transformed. When we are mired in doubt and negativity, our energy feels heavy, as if we are carrying the weight of the world. Learning to lift our energy allows us to rise with inner confidence and creativity, positively impacting others. At the mastery level, we inspire through elevated *Presence*.

Essence of Spirit (Fire)—Your essence is your core, radiating warmth and light like fire. It's the distillation of your best self, as unique as your fingerprints, yet it's often buried under protective layers that dim your luminance. Igniting your inner flame creates boundless potential and massive momentum. At the mastery level, you shine authentically, trailblazing your path fueled by deep *Purpose*.

Experience of Body (Earth)—In life's marathon, we face challenging relationships and circumstances that seem like immovable obstacles. Just as the earth's landscape is filled with unexpected terrains, life's twists and turns can take us to surprising and often difficult places. Learning to accept reality grounds us so we can adapt and grow through all situations. We experience less stress and more resilience, empowered to reshape our journey. At the mastery level, we move forward with sustainable *Progress*.

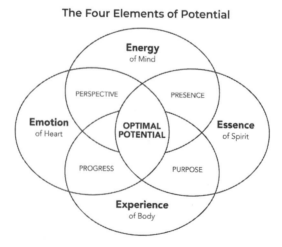

The Four Elements of Potential

Chapter 1

Transmute Fear into Love
(Optimal Potential)

I learned that courage was not the absence of fear,
but the triumph over it.
—Nelson Mandela

Diving into Fear

In 2019, at age fifty-three, I found myself in Queenstown, New Zealand, where commercial bungee jumping originated, so I figured, *Why not?* I like a good adrenaline rush and pushing myself to my edge. But once I stood at the top of the gorge and saw the water 141 feet below, I questioned my sanity.

I'd never bungee jumped before and had received no instructions yet, even though I was less than ten feet from the cliff's edge.

I'd expected to feel excited, but instead felt overwhelming *fear*—I had a knot in my stomach, tightness in my shoulders, and my heart was beating so hard, I could feel it coming out of my chest. The voice in my head wasn't helping either, as it kept saying, *What were you thinking? You are too old for this!*

I walked towards the company guide standing at the end of the plank and waited for words of wisdom to take my terror away. But he simply said, "Okay, jump!"

Shocked and suddenly anxious about doing it *wrong* and becoming seriously injured, I asked, "How can I make sure I don't throw out my back?"

He replied, "Oh! Then you'll want to *dive* instead. Aim for that far away bridge in the distance."

What? I'd been scared just to walk off the plank with my eyes closed, and now I had to dive! My fear reached new heights.

The Biology of Fear: The Amygdala Hijack

Fear helps protect us from harm, which is how we've survived as a species over generations. Given our powerful survival instinct, I don't believe anyone with a strong will to live has no fear when diving off a bridge for the first time.

Whenever we experience a threat, whether it's perceived or real, the part of our brain responsible for the *flight, flight, or freeze* response, called the amygdala, is activated like a fire alarm. It lives in our limbic, emotional brain, warns us of impending danger, and activates the body's stress response.

This floods our body with adrenaline and cortisol to boost energy, heart rate, and blood pressure in the short term. That's why you're able to swerve quickly to avoid getting hit by a car when it moves into your lane, even before your rational brain can say what's happening.

Our higher rational, executive thinking center goes offline for a few minutes, on average, so we literally cannot make the best decisions. How long this lasts depends on the level of threat and our innate ability to recover, but we can recover faster with mindfulness practice.

Modern Day Overrides: From Autopilot to Aware
Once we recognize the signs, we can learn to shift from our
pre-programmed autopilot reactions of flight, fight, or freeze
to take a more calculated response. For example, in my bungee
situation, instead of being frozen in my tracks, I knew I had a
secret go-to practice. So, I looked at the guide and declared,
"I need a minute to breathe."

Three Breaths Practice
In just three deep breaths, you can feel immeasurably calmer.
According to the American Lung Association, we typically
take between twelve to fifteen breaths a minute, or 17,000
to 22,000 breaths a day automatically. However, we have
the power to slow down our breathing rate and breathe
mindfully, with intention and attention. This restores the
balance across our mind, heart, and body so we can operate
at our best. Depending on how stressed we are, we may need
several minutes of slow breathing, but we can feel calmer in
just one breath.

On the plank, I took three deep breaths:
- First Breath: I noticed my body. *Relax those tight shoulders!*
- Second Breath: I noticed my feelings. *Still scared... but getting calmer.*
- Third Breath: I noticed my thoughts and asked myself, *What's most important now?*

My answer came through loud and clear: *I can do this. Just dive!*
Maybe, I hoped, I'd even get an adrenaline rush and enjoy it.

So, I dove. I was completely aware of every moment, as if time itself slowed down. Fear disappeared, while excitement and curiosity took over. I was surprised I didn't feel scared in the moment or experience an adrenaline rush when the bungee cord swung me from high to low and  back again. I just felt present and connected. When I saw the boat emerge below me, I felt myself being lowered, so I could reach for their pole and get pulled on board. Moments later, relieved and emotionally spent, I looked up at the sky with a big smile on my face.

While I don't plan to repeat bungee diving anytime soon, I received benefits that will outlast the experience. When I face fear now, I often remind myself: *You bungee dived. You can do scary things.* I also know in my heart that I can always take a moment to pause and breathe.

Fear Outside Our Control

Fear often arises from disruptive factors outside our control, threatening us mentally, emotionally, physically, or socially. We've all faced some big disruptions together, such as the Covid-19 global pandemic, the financial crisis of 2008, and 9/11. Merriam-Webster defines disruption as "a break or interruption in the normal course or continuation of some activity, process, etc." So it

Fortunately, facing your fear makes you FEAR LESS.

feels like the world is shifting beneath us, which leaves us feeling shaky and untethered, lacking equilibrium. Fear can strike in ways that paralyze us or cause harmful reactions. Fortunately, facing your fear makes you FEAR LESS.

Facing Fear

Whether or not we choose the fear-inducing situation, you can always choose to face your fear, prove you can do scary things, and grow your confidence and courage. When you embrace challenges that push your fear button but deeply align with what you want, *good stress* results. Examples may be public speaking, interviewing for that next promotion, saying "No," or leaping into your next thrill-inducing adventure.

Facing fear makes you better at dealing with it. Confronting fear, either proactively or opportunistically, strengthens us for next time—similar to when we stress our muscles by going to our edge on a workout.

Fear boosts performance, but panic causes paralysis, so learning to dance on the edge of our own line has evolutionary advantages for higher performance. From a young age, we experience thrill intermingled with fear, like when we ride a roller coaster and plummet with butterflies, ski down a mountain, or bungee jump. As we gain skill at thrilling activities, we find we can do them with excitement versus freezing. I may have been terrified on my first black diamond ski slope, but with experience, I gained the confidence to ski any mountain, even if I need to take it slow. Interestingly, the energy of fear and excitement is the same, but our mindset is different.

Staring My Worst Fear in the Face

It was May 1993. I was twenty-seven years old and my life had gone mostly according to my plan. Naturally, I thought I was in complete control. I'd married my business school

SHINING THROUGH DISRUPTION

sweetheart, started my dream marketing career in Chicago, and had just moved into our new townhome. Then, my worst fear came calling, when my father phoned with the most devastating news of my life.

"Your mother has cancer, and it's incurable."

With those seven words, my life changed in a heartbeat.

A lightning bolt of fear struck me like I had never known before. Time slowed to a standstill. My heart started racing. I felt my face flush and heaviness take over my body. I felt strangely terrified and numb at the same time. A flood of other emotions washed over me: confusion, sadness, anger, helplessness.

My mom, Arlene, had just turned fifty-three. She was diagnosed with Carcinoma Ex Pleomorphic Adenoma of the Parotid Gland — a rare disease not even well understood by her doctors, who simply deemed her case hopeless. Anyone who saw her could tell something was very wrong, as her once beautiful smile that lit up every room she entered was now permanently lopsided. She could only muster a smile on one half of her face, with the other half stuck permanently in a frown. The effect was so unlike my mother that I would look into her eyes to find the warmth I knew was still inside.

I couldn't bear losing my incredible mother, the beating heart of our family. I was overwhelmed with questions, the most important being, "What do we do now?"

Our Reactions to Fear and Stress Are Unique and Universal

Our DNA/biology of fear is hardwired, but how stressed we become and how it impacts our bodies is as complicated as we are.

While we react differently to stress, I love how author Elizabeth Gilbert writes in *Big Magic: Creative Living Beyond*

Fear: "... everyone's song of fear has exactly the same tedious lyric: 'STOP, STOP, STOP, STOP!'"[9]

I have found that hope transmutes fear. Fear is normal, but when we kindle hope, we are inspired to keep moving towards a better reality. I appreciate Nelson Mandela's wise words:

"May your choices reflect your hopes, not your fears."

How Leaders Endure High-Stress Situations

Sometimes we *choose* change (e.g., getting a promotion at work or moving locations) and sometimes *it* chooses us (e.g., loss of a job, death of a loved one, work or health crisis). Either way, change is inevitable—and often invokes fear, even if we are excited and unaware of its presence.

Leaders in high-stress situations often get very good at managing mental stress and are even better at *not listening* to the signals from their emotions and body, so they can persevere through the chaos. They say, "I'm fine," because they feel they have to be.

As a new executive leading a global financial services team through the 2008 financial crisis, I prided myself on handling the constant barrage of mental stress. I didn't realize my mind was ignoring the amygdala's continuous alarm signals. It was as if I were playing loud music to avoid hearing the fire alarm, but that didn't mean that my house wasn't really burning inside. My recipe to drown out my alarm bells was being *completely driven* at work and *completely off the grid* when I took vacations to recuperate. Looking back, I'm not surprised that three years later I got my severe cancer wake-up call.

I'm not alone. Professionals seek short-term pleasure boosts to numb the pain, such as vacations, alcohol, comfort food, and shopping. Or they may take medication, sleeping pills, and other diversions that, when used excessively, can often lead to severe health problems.

While we can ignore what's going on at a cellular level, our stress leaves its indelible mark on our bodies, as Dr. Bessel van der Kolk wrote in his bestselling book, *The Body Keeps the Score*.[10] With trauma, our rational brains are very good at denial, but the survival brain is not. It can reactivate at the slightest hint of danger, get our stress hormones pumping, and hasten unpleasant emotions and impulsive reactions. I've been to massage therapists who can actually give me a map of the stressors in my life based on touching various areas of my body. We can fool our minds, but never our bodies, or skilled practitioners!

Fortunately, we can find a better way that's sustainable and healthy where we can experience the reality of how we feel with awareness—and expand our capacity for joy. It's simple, but we need to dig deep.

The Leadership Gap: Overestimating Self-Awareness
Emotional Intelligence (EQ) is an *inside job* rooted in self-awareness.[11] Research shows 95 percent of people think they're self-aware, but only about 10-15 percent actually are.[12]

EQ accounts for nearly 90 percent of what sets high performers apart from their peers with similar technical skills and knowledge. It enables outstanding leadership, stellar performance, and well-being instead of burnout.[13] With EQ, we can effectively inspire and motivate teams to ever higher performance, which is the skill leaders need most.

Awareness of Fear: Unroot to Transmute
Mindfulness is at the root of self-awareness and critical for unrooting fear. We can define mindfulness as simply *being aware* in the moment of how we feel in our bodies, hearts,

and minds. Importantly, it's about taking judgment off the table and accepting whatever shows up—with an attitude of kindness and curiosity.

My original bungee thought of, *What were you thinking?* was based on fear and kept me frozen in place. During my Three Breaths, I illuminated what was real, without judgment, and captured my new, empowering thought of *I can do this*, energizing me to dive into action. Being present without judgment is like adding the warmth of a hug. It melts our inner critic soundtrack, which icily states, "We can't," and empowers us to believe, "We can."

Awareness Model: Above or Below the Line
I like the way The Conscious Leadership Group has created a simple paradigm to think about when we are in modern-day fire alarm mode, as being *below the line*.[14] At any moment, we can ask: "Are we above or below the line?"

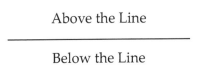

When we are *below the line*, we feel fearful, stressed, immobilized, in scarcity mode—fiercely defending our position to protect ourselves. When we're *above the line*, we're operating from a place of safety and abundance. We're able to expand our thinking, innovate with flow, and be curious, creative, and open to learning.

Fear lives *below the line*. You can't see the big picture clearly or make sound decisions because blinders narrow your focus on physically dealing with the scary situation. Until we handle the fear, we can't recover and regain a state of equilibrium. It's as if we are pushed underwater, with fear rapidly filling every cell of our body, so we must fight to breathe.

Below the Line: What Pushes Us Down

In today's world, it can be difficult to know when we're being hijacked, because we're often triggered by subtle or sneaky events that either don't threaten our existence or don't have a neat ending. For example, on a macro level, we face ongoing socio-political injustices and racial inequities; on a micro level, you may be in a complicated relationship with a relative or co-worker, living in an increasingly toxic work culture, or have unrealistic expectations for your team with never-ending work demands. Sadly, research shared at the World Happiness Conference in 2022 and 2023 showed many people report their most miserable moment of the day is when they are with their boss.

The bottom line is that no matter what pushes us below the line, we can't see options for how to get out. Fear pushes us into a victim mentality where we feel we lack control.

Negativity Bias

What's more, it's hard to let go of what feels wrong, which keeps us *below the line*. We're literally wired with a negativity bias, which biologically primes us to avoid danger, so we survive and pass our DNA to the next generation.[15] We latch onto negative events like Velcro while letting positive events fall away like Teflon. For example, we remember exactly where we were on 9/11, but we wouldn't recall what we were doing two days before. It's also why we gobble up gossip or the story about what didn't go right. The media preys on this knowledge, feeding us scary, negative information we feel is vital to our survival and safety within our community, which spreads quickly like lightning.

But we also overestimate threats, even when the situation is positive or neutral. Have you ever gotten a performance review that is 99 percent positive, with 1 percent focused on something constructive to change? When this would happen to me, I would immediately stop thinking about the glowing remarks and latch onto the constructive feedback. I couldn't stand the dark realization that my boss could see I wasn't perfect, and I piled on negative judgment.

Fortunately, we can neutralize the negativity bias with positivity, but it's not a one-to-one ratio. We need to focus on at least three heartfelt positive emotional experiences to override one negative.[16] In dark times, marking progress can be a beacon of hope. Research shows that making progress in meaningful work is the single most important thing you can do to boost happiness and motivation.[17]

Channeling Fierce Anger

Anger is also a form of fear. It's the fear of losing what you love and value deeply, so you want to protect and fiercely fight for it. The energy of anger propels change; yet, the most effective, emotionally intelligent leaders know how to channel their anger productively by responding from *above the line*—versus lashing out *below the line*. Dr. Martin Luther King Jr. experienced deep pain and anger around social injustice and discriminatory voting practices, but he channeled it into peaceful protests to make the black right to vote a reality.

Before my mother was diagnosed with cancer, we were told her tumor was benign, and we were so relieved. Several months later, when her face became paralyzed, she got more scans and learned the scary truth: her cancer was malignant.

I don't ever remember feeling angrier in my life. I wanted the doctors and hospital to pay for losing months of treatment, even though they said it wouldn't have mattered. The truth was that no amount of blame was going to fix what was really wrong. My anger was in response to the depth of my pain when the person I loved most was in mortal danger. My father helped me see I could channel my actions into hope and love instead.

Pain and Stress Pushes Us Down

In her healthy state, my mom was an eternal optimist who wore rose-colored glasses throughout life. It helped her and our entire family move forward with alternative treatments, hoping to cure her. However, as her illness progressed, she faced continual disappointment on top of acute, chronic pain. This forcibly pushed her *below the line* and held her down, mired in fear. My mother felt at war with her fear and journaled about its harmful effects one year into treatment:

> Fear—how destructive
> How distinctly painful
> A hell-like war
> A holocaust to confront
> Who survives?
> Must one have no doubt that survival will be?
> It is said that this belief is the link.
> Is this what frightens me?
> Do I not have confidence that I am a chosen one
> To succeed…without Question!

Physical Repercussions

To complicate matters, a health crisis or toxic situation may drag on for months or years, without a clear beginning, middle, and end. These ongoing stressors wreak havoc on our bodies because the amygdala keeps firing, thereby causing destructive hormones to continue flooding our bodies. Since we're not deployed into physical action (i.e., escaping from the tiger), we don't complete the stress cycle and return to equilibrium. When this happens, we experience harmful cumulative physical effects, which can turn into chronic pain, cancer, heart disease, and disabilities. It's not surprising that 75-90 percent of doctor's visits are due to stress.[18]

To shift from a hijack situation, we need to recognize we're *below the line* and take responsibility for rising above it. How? The first step is to *reveal what's real*, listening to fear across your mind, heart, and body.

Recognizing Stress and Fear in Your Body

Nearly all executives I survey before my workshops state, "I experience tension in my body due to stress," but they don't know what to do about it.

- When I endured the toxicity of my post-acquisition situation, I experienced debilitating back pain, tied to my feelings of weakness around my threatened core identity.
- Rachel's lungs collapsed when she felt she couldn't use her voice to be heard.
- Cheryl experienced heart palpitations when she realized she didn't have the heart for what she was doing anymore.
- Stephen experienced heart arrhythmia after being demoted by his boss for being compassionate in their toxic, fear-based work environment.

Left unaddressed, fear can take its toll on our bodies in unbelievably laser-targeted ways. So, what do we do?

Once we're aware of where and how our stress and emotions are manifesting in our body, we can acknowledge what the fear is revealing. Like a person, we need to allow fear to be felt, seen, and heard for it to release its tight grip.

The Power of Your Beliefs

Recent neuroscience shows we can reduce our time in amygdala hijack by changing our beliefs around fear. How cool is that? I'd already been cultivating a mindfulness meditation practice to recover faster from stressful triggers when I heard this incredible bio-hack from esteemed neuroscientist Dr. James Doty:

"Fear is not about the event itself; it's about how you process it."[19]

For example, we know our body's natural response to fear and stress is biological—it's a simple fact. But when you reframe these physical changes in your body and interpret them as getting you energized, preparing you to meet this challenge, you transform them from stressful to helpful, like transmuting ice into water.

Reframing our stress can even help us live better and longer! In her illuminating TED Talk and book, *The Upside of Stress*, Stanford Professor and researcher Kelly McGonigal shares a compelling study that changed her view of stress. The study tracked 30,000 adults in the United States for eight years and asked two key questions:[20]

- How much stress did you experience in the last year?
- Do you believe that stress is harmful to your health?

Then the researchers used public death records to find out who died. The results were unexpected.

People who said they experienced a lot of stress in the previous year had a 43 percent increased risk of dying. However, that was only true if they also believed that stress was harmful to their health.

It turned out that people who experienced a lot of stress but *didn't* view their stress as harmful were no more likely to die. In fact, their risk of dying was the lowest of anyone in the study, including people who had relatively little stress. Over the eight years they tracked deaths, the researchers estimated that 182,000 Americans died prematurely—not because of stress, but because *they believed their stress was bad for them.*

What does this mean for you, as a leader, balancing your own stress-success cycle? How you perceive your situation is critical. For example, if you're feeling stress that fuels your adrenaline and drives you to perform to your edge—with excitement, creativity, and other positive emotions—carry on! You're experiencing *good stress*. However, if you are feeling negative emotions, such as anxiety and overwhelm, pay attention. Even if you think you're handling it, think again. You are likely experiencing (but ignoring) harmful effects in your body that could have severe repercussions, like when I woke up to cancer after navigating the financial crisis of 2008.

Heidy, a Senior Vice President, was fearful when she needed to do big presentations on behalf of her company at conferences. However, she reminded herself that she didn't feel fear once she was doing the activity, only leading up to it. So she transmuted her stress into action, which turned into healthy confidence.

Embracing Fear Like a Friend

Fear is uncomfortable, so we often push it away to feel comfortable again. But treating fear as an enemy is not as helpful as *tending and befriending*. Like a difficult person, once we understand what's behind the behavior, we can empathize and create a good versus adversarial relationship. When we listen and understand, we shift *above the line* and see new possibilities. We're not tamping down on fear and blocking out its information, or letting it take over by running, fighting, or becoming immobilized. We're listening and learning. Fear tries to protect us, so leaning into our vulnerability allows us to see the cracks and let light in.

Nancie, the CEO of a marketing consulting firm, had a difficult client issue she knew was her team's fault and wanted to dig in and fix the problem. So, she led off her team meeting with vulnerability, owning up to her failure in not seeing the situation sooner. She created safety for the team to relax and shift from *below the line* feelings of fear of blame, so they could also be vulnerable and creatively find a solution from *above the line* together.

My Fear of Failing: Leaning into Vulnerability

Two years into my mother's cancer journey, I received the dreaded call from my father. "Your mother can no longer walk... prepare yourself for the end."

Time stopped. Fear struck again and obliterated the last rays of hope, which had been my beacon for so long. My mom's days were numbered, and she needed care around the clock so she could remain in the comfort of her home. While my dad was with her, nurturing wasn't his strength; he was a surgeon who fixed things. Thankfully, she had the best caretaker in my cousin, Joyce, who loved her dearly and would remain a fixture by her side. But I couldn't help wondering: *Was it time for me to take a leave of absence to be with her?* My heart wanted to get on a plane, but I had a fearful knot in my gut that I couldn't untie to move forward.

I was twenty-nine and had kept to my aggressive timeline of achievement that seemed laid out for me at every stage. My high-achiever tendencies had paid off with a promotion to brand manager in record time and stock options. I was competitive and had no experience with *getting off the moving train,* not to mention the implications for my personal life, leaving my husband behind in Chicago.

But there was more to it. I knew how to be the daughter who was a sunny breath of fresh air, sprinkling optimism on each visit, then returning to my *normal life.* I was scared I didn't know how to be the daughter who nurtured her mother and faced suffering each day, and I didn't want to fail her. I vulnerably shared this with my cousin, Joyce, who gave me this timeless wisdom, "We regret the things in life we don't do."

Still terrified, I faced my fear and took a three-month leave of absence.

Vulnerability is scary because we are showing up as our raw, tender selves; yet that's what makes it such a powerful antidote to fear. The paradox is that we believe we'll lose control by facing our messy emotions, but it's the opposite. When we acknowledge our truth, we take control of fear by reducing its potency.

From Fear of Failing to Mindful Growth

During my leave of absence, my love and compassion kept me showing up *above the line,* and I overcame my fear of failing as a caregiver. As I took small steps, fueled by love, I was unknowingly weakening my fear's power and strengthening my belief and confidence that I could be someone who can handle whatever suffering I'd face.

It is moments such as these that I find comfort in this perspective by Anaïs Nin: "Life shrinks or expands in proportion to one's courage."[21]

Facing my fear with vulnerability changed our relationship and allowed me to grow. I didn't do what fear told me to do, which was to continue with my life as it was currently unfolding. Instead, I trusted myself to face my mother's suffering and my own, and I expanded my capacity to love, create, and experience joy. No wonder Tenzin Gyatso, the fourteenth Dalai Lama, says, "The opposite of fear is trust".[22]

The Paradox of Fear

Fear lives in our anxiety about the future, or our rumination over the past. Fear is stripped of its power in the present moment.

When my mother was diagnosed with terminal cancer, I couldn't imagine a scarier villain than death. Yet, as her condition worsened, and I knew how much pain she endured, I no longer feared it. I wanted what she wanted—the end of her physical pain. When my mother asked me, "Is it okay to let go now?" I held her hand and replied truthfully, "Yes."

> **Fear is stripped of its power in the present moment.**

Again, *Man Plans, and God Laughs*. It's a timeless truth I understand more every day.

We plan and plan, thinking we can control our lives, and then something comes along that knocks the wind right out of us—because it is absolutely not part of our plan. We fear death—for ourselves and others. And this is healthy to a degree, as we fight valiantly for our lives and loved ones when survival is at stake. Yet, once we are in the eye of the lightning storm, living in the moment, fear doesn't seem to have a place anymore.

When I stopped fearing my mother's death, I could more fully embrace life.

During our last days together, I was able to be present with my mom and let go of the stress from not knowing which day would be her last. More than any other time since childhood, I was able to just *be*. At the moment she died, time seemed to slow down. I took in every detail, knowing life would never be the same. It had been cold and cloudy all day, but now the sun shone through her window and slowly started to set. I felt as if she'd found the light and stood in the heart of it. I savor sunsets now, knowing their beauty is precious and fleeting, just like each day. Just like my mother. Just like each of us.

Grief and Fear

I think grief and fear often walk together. When our life is disrupted by loss, we fear the change it brings. We need to find a new way forward, and it's dark, murky, and scary. We've all experienced grief in different ways at various points in life.

For me, my mother's loss felt like a hole in my heart. I'm comforted by Jamie Anderson's view that "Grief is just love with no place to go."[23]

After the global pandemic, we all collectively grieved our old way of life, even though we didn't realize what we were losing and when. We experienced grief with no place to go. We are still facing the fear of continual change as the waves of uncertainty keep rolling in around us.

Grieving is important for all of us when going through big changes. We must allow ourselves to move through our emotions of loss, and gain comfort and compassion from others. We have funerals and rituals to commemorate and celebrate loved ones so we can move on. But we are lacking rituals for the ongoing change we face, with no clear ending. *What ritual can you do to mark the change you are grieving and fearing?*

Disruption Forces Action

During crises, we rarely have the luxury of sitting on the sidelines to figure out the perfect plan. Instead, we are forced to act quickly amidst chaos—and notice that our fear disappears more quickly too. With each step, we adapt and learn more of what's possible to keep flowing forward.

With the financial crisis of 2008, my team quickly made a huge shift from delivering monthly communications to daily—to address client anxiety. During the pandemic, many shifted to remote working and realized productivity remained high.[24] Higher education shifted to online models overnight that would have taken years to test and approve. I now work with top business schools that have improved their pre-pandemic business models to offer a greater range of virtual options that significantly impact their profitability and growth.

How Leaders Can Stop Fear from Stopping Them

The Power of Choice

In high-fear mode, we often freeze, feeling powerless and immobilized. Fortunately, we can choose to respond differently. This profound wisdom is from the teachings of Viktor Frankl, Holocaust survivor, psychotherapist, and author of *Man's Search for Meaning*.[25] In the foreword of *Prisoners of Our Thoughts* by Alex Pattakos, Stephen R. Covey summarized, "Between stimulus and response, there is a space. In that space is our power to choose our response. In our response lies our growth and our freedom."[26]

Choosing Action

A powerful way to stop fear is by choosing action. This shifts our thoughts and feelings, helping us reclaim a sense of control.

Leaders often put the brakes on taking action when they experience fear from uncertainty and change. When we have perfectionist and controlling tendencies, we fear being wrong and lack confidence. We tell ourselves we're being prudent—we are waiting to get the plan *just right*. We don't realize our hesitancy is rooted in fear.

Garnering outside support can be a lifeline to pull us up from victimhood or fear when we need it most. Other people can help us see when our fear is smartly disguised as caution with much-needed *above the line* perspective and compassion.

During my coaching training, when we were way past the point of being qualified to coach, I still wasn't taking on paying clients. I told myself I needed more skills: "I wasn't ready yet." However, with coaching, I realized my caution was actually a lack of confidence rooted in fear. In reality, holding myself back kept me from helping people and becoming the best coach I could be. With this awareness, I acknowledged the fear and let it go. Then, I could shift *above the line*, build my client base, and grow my confidence based on real results. When I look back at my first client, I'm blown away by her progress in growing her business exponentially while also creating greater balance and joy personally. For any leader who serves others, remember that our inaction prevents others from receiving our gifts.

Nora wanted to become the leader of her team, but suffered from imposter syndrome. She believed she wasn't ready to take on this big leadership role, so she almost didn't interview for it. We worked on her mindset, helping her see she had the technical competence and emotional intelligence to become a stellar leader, as long as she took action. She interviewed for the role and got it! Now she gets to build her leadership muscles even further—and aspires to become CEO.

Shifting Mindset Above the Line

In many situations, we're not immobilized by fear, but we're hijacked by it—feeling victimized or angry. Give yourself space to shift *above the line* before responding to your *below the line* fear or anger-based narrative. When you accept responsibility for your own thoughts, feelings, and actions, you shift *above the line*—feeling better, increasing productivity, and improving relationships. For example, maybe you receive an email from a colleague that sets you off. You're angry, or upset, and want to respond right away with a piece of your mind. Instead, first *stop* and *pause*. A few breaths or a little break may be all you need. Or if you're really upset, take a bigger pause. Then, focus on your mindset: what if you release judgment and give that person the benefit of the doubt, knowing you can explore the issue later with them?

Importantly, this isn't about glossing over negative emotions with toxic positivity. It's about meeting the moment with your awareness and attention and choosing how best to respond to minimize harm to yourself and others. We can call out behavior that's upsetting to us, but it's better to do it *above the line*, where your energy is calm instead of blaming. Nobody ever regrets doing that, but we almost always regret it when we don't.

Situation: Upset over an email you received at work

Above the Line
Thoughts: *They didn't realize how their message was coming across.*
Emotions/Feelings: *I can help them better understand me and my project.*
Actions: *Focus productively and strengthen the relationship.*

Below the Line
Thoughts: *They are being rude and insensitive.*
Emotion/Feelings: *I don't feel respected/valued as a person.*
Actions: *Stew in negativity or lash out and harm the relationship.*

While some situations are more triggering than others, we can often shift from *below* to *above the line* in the span of a few minutes or less. Practice shortens our recovery time.

In March 2019, I began a twenty-minute daily meditation practice as part of my mindfulness teacher training. In early June, about twelve weeks later, I noticed a profound change in how I responded to a circumstance that would have seriously triggered me before—getting unfairly blamed. I was visiting a scenic overlook with my father in the hills of San Francisco, and a man screamed at us for inadvertently bringing in dust as we parked near his vehicle. I felt as if time slowed down so I could respond with a better choice. Instead of reacting defensively to the man's angry tirade, I felt compassion for this man whose anger over dust outside our control prevented him from enjoying the beautiful view.

Now I recover faster from most road bumps, big and small, with fewer triggering me. Any mishap motivates me to rewire my brain with new neural pathways to serve me better next time.

Using Fear to Grow as a Courageous Leader in Life

Leaders and humans crave control. So, in uncertainty, it's natural to feel scared, angry, frustrated, blaming, lonely, fatigued, overwhelmed, frozen, weighed down, powerless, threatened... and many more *below the line* emotions. However, the key to great leadership is recognizing this state of fear and catching it before it spreads out of control. Then, we can respond from a place of equilibrium and higher positivity, so we can bring our best energy and creative thinking forward.

While we are often tested in life, I believe courage is required in a larger proportion when we face challenges. Words often attributed to Joseph Campbell resonate with me: "The cave you fear to enter holds the treasure you seek." Courage begins by facing fear, uncovering what you need, and deciding what you want. Embracing fear—with love, compassion, optimism, and acceptance—helps us shift *above the line* and builds greater resilience to face even scarier situations. Each small step forward helps us see with more clarity what comes next. When you're low, reach for connection to help you see the light ahead.

Fear doesn't go away, but it loses its destructive power and transmutes into the power we need to grow in extraordinary ways. We learn that being uncomfortable isn't the problem. Diving into discomfort with vulnerability is the necessary state of flux before we feel comfortable again.

Your Chance to Practice

At the end of each chapter, you'll find exercises to help you practice what you've learned so far and build new skills, including one of my favorites: journaling (expressive writing).

Expressive writing is when we journal about a topic that triggers strong emotions. It's a wonderful way to illuminate our fears, so it's a practice worth cultivating. Since the age of eleven, this practice helped me endure tough times. I've amassed over eighty journals so far, writing three to five times more frequently during adversity. Transformational growth occurs when we have an experience and reflect so we can take new actions. I realized intuitively that expressing emotions through writing is powerful for converting pain into meaning. It helps us to see through the fog.

Did You Know?

Studies have shown even small amounts of expressive writing go a long way. Journaling emotions for five days resulted in laid-off professionals finding jobs at much higher rates than those who didn't—68 percent versus 27 percent.[27]

In another study, just two minutes of writing on two consecutive days led to higher rates of improving mood and well-being. Meta-analysis outcomes include lower medication use for chronic illness, fewer PTSD symptoms, and decreased anxiety.[28]

Groundbreaking research shows it can even improve the immune system and lung function, diminish psychological distress, and enhance relationships and social-role functioning.[29]

Chapter Mindset	From: Burned Out Leader	To: Shining Authentic Leader
1: Transmute fear into love, and power up *optimal potential.*	Remains *below the line* in 'fight, flight, or freeze' mode with blinders on.	Chooses to rise *above the line* with self-awareness to see exponential possibilities.

The Four Elements of Potential

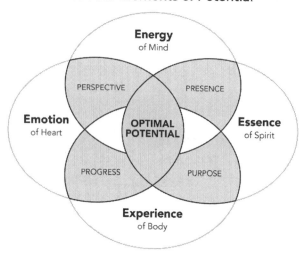

Exercises: You can do these exercises on your own, or go to www.ShiningThroughDisruption.com/resources to access the workbook and guided practices.

1. Try the Three Breaths micro-practice on page 21.
2. Journal prompts for expressive free-writing: Don't lift your pen—just free-write for two minutes on each of these prompts. This invites and encourages your thoughts and emotions to flow onto paper. If you have nothing to say, then just write, "I have nothing to say." Keep your pen on the paper and keep writing. You're just opening a channel and seeing what comes up.
    o   What would you do if you couldn't fail?
    o   Reflecting on your life, what's an example of how you've faced your fear and prevailed in a powerful way?
    o   What lessons can you pull from your experience to help you embrace fear in the future?
3. Take action: Do something this week that you are afraid to do.

Chapter 2

Channel Your Emotions (Water)

It's not what you are that holds you back,
it's what you think you're not.
—Denis Waitley

My Moment of Discovery: The Tug of War between My Two Voices

It was June 2019. I'd left my Chief Marketing Officer role one year earlier, following a nearly three-decade career and one disruptive acquisition. I never envisioned I'd be where I was right now—three days into a seven-day silent retreat.

I had a thirty-minute window before our next meditation session to hurry up this mountain and relax in my *perfect place* (I realize that's an oxymoron). I'd discovered the idyllic spot on my first day, at the top of this mountain with a bench overlooking the picturesque valley. I'd excitedly returned the next day, only to find a man meditating with eyes closed on *my* bench—not even soaking up the view! I felt a keen disappointment and vowed to beat him there next time.

Yet, while rushing to my destination, something unusual caught my eye. I nearly stepped on two lizards mating in my path, which completely captivated my attention. I felt pulled to stay in this moment and just *be*, but the voice in my head was saying, *Keep running! We need to get there first!* I'd felt this tug of war inside of me many times, thinking about what to do *next*, which took me away from the joy *of right now*.

That's when I had an *Aha!* moment of clarity. I could choose to make what *feels* right *be* right. I felt as if I had just woken up on the right side of wrong. Or found a secret power I had all along, like Dorothy's magical ruby slippers that could whisk her home. In that precious moment, after three days of silence and fifty-plus years of believing every voice in my head, I realized my inner soundtrack was not always to be trusted.

> **My win/lose story wasn't the truth, even though I'd been believing it my whole life.**

The win/lose story I was telling myself was not a higher truth, even though the soundtrack had been playing on repeat throughout my life. Now I realized I could change my tune, and I could win anytime I desired with this new *right side of wrong* mindset. These stories had been frozen in my brain, but I could melt them and create new neural pathways of thoughts that better served me now, like a waterfall feeding new streams trickling down the mountain.

Suddenly, it became so clear that *wrong* was simply my ice-cold *judgment*. But I could choose to let it go anytime, just as I'd intuitively done that day. By shifting my mindset, I listened to my heart and connected to the bigger picture. I realized I could win *and* slow down, having enough time for what I wanted, while also experiencing more joy.

Later, I learned that the *hyper-critical, overly competitive, hyper-achiever* voice in my head was my *left* brain talking.

The part of me that knew, deep down, how magical and perfect this precious moment was, came from my *right* brain, which is wise beyond words. Our brains are divided into two hemispheres, each with its own responsibilities and preferences.[30] I'm oversimplifying a bit because our brains are complex and interconnected, but we will all benefit from building our right brain capabilities.

Your right brain is a superhighway to light up the greater power of all three of your brains (mind, heart, and gut), so you achieve more *whole-brain* potential and can lead more powerfully across your life. It's the way to build mindful emotional intelligence (EQ), which is what the greatest leaders possess.

Right and Left Brain—How We're Wired

My left brain is invaluable. But it's not enough. It helps me analyze data, communicate with others, reflect and share about my past, and plan for the future. It's the little voice that reminds me I need eggs from the grocery store and remembers to follow up on emails and RSVP to events. It knows how to drive my car and get myself dressed, so I can do these things efficiently and on autopilot. It helps me decide how to prioritize my time based on relevant experience and data.

Sometimes, though, it's rigid, like ice. It gets stuck ruminating over what I wish I'd said or done, holds onto guilt, and judges myself, others, and circumstances. It thinks it knows the truth, but it's usually filling in the gaps with negative narratives. Basically, it's doing what it can to protect me at all costs.

We tend to overuse our left brain as the commander-in-chief of our big *thinking* mind-brain. However, it's really not cut out for that. It's an incredible worker, and we are fortunate to have it on the team, particularly when it works interdependently with our right brain. But putting the left brain in charge is like giving the keys to the kingdom of whichever artificial intelligence model is currently in vogue. Our left brain is a productive, efficient tool that helps us see what's critically wrong, but it lacks the wisdom, humanity, and heart to realize all that's right. That's where the right brain comes in.

> ### Did You Know?
> Jill Bolte Taylor, neuroanatomist and PhD, wrote the inspiring book *My Stroke of Insight*,[31] based on her rare stroke at age thirty-seven, where she completely lost access to her brain's left hemisphere and power of speech. Yet, she remembers feeling a surprising sense that all was right and beautiful in the world when her right brain took the helm. Watch her incredible 2008 TED Talk here: https://www.ted.com/talks/jill_bolte_taylor_my_stroke_of_insight/[32]

Our Metaphorical Bag

Beyond our right and left brain's wiring, we all come into this world with our unique DNA that mixes with our experiences and leads to how we react to stress, how we interpret life, and who we become. Whether or not we realize it, we are shaped strongly by a complex interplay of multiple factors—including our upbringing, cultural influences, and personal experiences, which impact our identity, beliefs, and the stories we tell about ourselves. They come from our family of origin, our friends, and the context of the times in which we're raised. It's widely accepted that a great many of our core beliefs are established in childhood, particularly before the age of seven, since this is the critical period for cognitive and socio-emotional development.[33]

Whether you had an idyllic childhood or a traumatic one, you started assembling a metaphorical bag as a child that you keep filling up into adulthood. Your bag becomes quite heavy with things that you believe are protecting you. Unfortunately, you don't realize your power to examine the bag and toss out what doesn't serve you anymore. Just like my closet, though, it's hard to see through the clutter to what's inside.

Your bag is filled with stories, assumptions, limiting beliefs, and deeply rooted gremlins of insecurity, that have helped you cope with life. These impact how you interpret and react to situations in a very different way than someone else. For example, with the threat of layoffs in my early career, I reacted with calm given the story that I told myself: *layoffs don't happen if you work hard and do a good job* (in other words, *I'm safe*). Others reacted with intense fear and worked hard to protect their positions, perhaps driven by insecurity or their experience that layoffs can happen to anyone at any time. Once layoffs occurred, and I was one of the casualties, it cracked open my false story and caused me to change my perspective based on my lived experience. This was one belief I could toss out of my bag. In its place, I created a new belief that *layoffs aren't personal*, which helped me lead with more

SHINING THROUGH DISRUPTION

empathy as I rose in my career and needed to lay off people periodically. The more we question the beliefs we've been given, the more we can discard and lighten our load—and thoughtfully create new beliefs that serve us even better.

Dangers of Strengths on Overdrive

Typically, we lean into our strengths as children to protect us. They stretch into overdrive during times of stress, turning into unhealthy response habits that weigh us down.[34] For example, I'm a high achiever who prides myself on delivering high quality on time; failure is not an option. In stressful times, when faced with a lack of resources and an encroaching deadline, my response pattern was to do whatever it took to deliver, working around the clock if necessary. No wonder it was always tough for me to garner additional resources on my teams because I compensated by filling in the gaps, instead of setting firm boundaries on what was reasonable. I'm not saying this to brag, but to prove my point. When I left my position as Director of Communications to begin a new role, the company had to hire six people to replace our team of two. It was a recurring pattern for me.

We think our stress comes from the big challenges outside us, such as delivering our project by the deadline. But it's mostly from listening to the critical voices in our heads that feed us lies, such as, *You're not good enough, You need to work harder than everyone else*, or my personal favorite, *It's not perfect yet.*

I have had hundreds of conversations over the last few years and heard a wide spectrum of stories. I've met people who grew up with extreme wealth and privilege who were carrying around shame and guilt, feeling undeserving of all they had. I've also met people who experienced abuse and trauma and somehow rose above it to break the chain and create better circumstances for themselves. In every situation, as adults, they are waking up to realize the inner critic soundtrack they've been listening to all these years isn't the *real* story after all.

It all starts by opening our bag and re-examining our stories inside it with fresh eyes. Here's a taste of what was in the bag I began filling in childhood. I've found my tendencies match those of many of the high-achieving leaders I teach and coach. I hope my story will light up some awareness about your own situation.

My Origin Story—Birth of Stress Responses

I was born in 1965 in Cleveland, Ohio, the oldest of three, and the only daughter of well-educated parents who loved us but were overwhelmed with stress in our early childhood. My father had just left running a family business to follow his dream and take the long road to becoming an orthopedic surgeon. My early memories were of my father being an overworked, exhausted new medical student I rarely saw, and my mother being an overwhelmed homemaker single-handedly raising us three kids under the age of five.

Birth of Over-Giver Syndrome

By the time I was eleven, my two younger brothers, who were fourteen months apart, had knockdown fights that were sometimes violent and scary. They were also very clever and had figured out how to lock babysitters in the basement. Since the role of babysitter was becoming increasingly hard to fill, my parents needed me to step in. I loved feeling like the perfect daughter who could save the day and please them.

In adulthood, I leaned into my strength of giving in my marketing career by meeting everyone's needs: customers, bosses, teams, and colleagues. Soon, this strength became the

Trojan horse that took my energy. I gave too generously of my time, craving external validation, without prioritizing myself or sleep. When I started a family, I really lost my balance, becoming an over-giver to my family and my work. I felt expressing my own needs or taking time for self-care was selfish since my parents were paragons of selflessness. So, I worked on being a mixture of them without complaining or asking for help. Along the way, I gave away my power to others, and I stopped knowing what I really wanted and needed.

Not surprisingly, I struggled with work/life balance even at companies known for it, not realizing that it all starts with me.

Birth of Hyper-Achiever

I was also very driven and goal-oriented, which I learned early on gained me respect, attention, opportunity, and validation. But as soon as I achieved one goal, I set a bigger one, and I never stopped moving. I was competitive, comparing myself to others and also setting ever higher standards for myself. My belief was that working hard led to my success—and not pushing myself fully would lead to my failure. I believed short-term pain was part of the deal, not realizing I was running a marathon that never ended. When I was under big-time pressure, I went into overdrive to get it *right*, striving for perfection to avoid criticism. When my husband disrupted our life to follow his dream—buying an orchard to grow fruit—I became the primary breadwinner. Suddenly, my achiever-instinct went into hyperdrive, concerned with saving for college and providing our girls with all the opportunities I felt they deserved.

I didn't realize how much of my stress was created by me.

I used my childhood strengths of empathy, vision, and achievement to succeed at all costs. I didn't realize how much of my stress was created by me.

My soundtrack was *I must work harder to achieve—and give more to be loved*, so that's what I did. I thought any senior executive was supposed to work long hours, feel stressed, carry the weight of the world on their shoulders for their team, and feel *not good enough* at work or home. So that's exactly what happened. I didn't realize there was another way where we could drive even greater connection, productivity, and satisfaction while eliminating burnout.

Just like Henry Ford is often attributed as saying, "Whether you think you can, or you think you can't—you're right."

What's inside the Head of High Achieving Leaders

Our limiting beliefs are powerful and persevere because, unfortunately, we think we need them to succeed in the future, since they helped us succeed in the past. The truth is, they helped you succeed, but at a huge cost. In the famous words of thought leader/coach Marshall Goldsmith, "What got you here won't get you there."[35] Letting them go enables you to grow into your higher, optimal potential.

I've conducted quite a few workshops with leaders who share similar Over-giver/Hyper-achiever sabotaging beliefs that are triggered during stressful times.

Do any of these resonate with you?
- *It won't get done without me.*
- *I'm the only one accountable for the results.*
- *I know the right way and wrong way.*
- *I need to get it done perfectly, or it's not worth doing.*
- *If I achieve more, I will be worthy of respect.*
- *I need to move quicker to what's next—how do I make "the paint dry faster"?*

- *Pushing myself harder leads to success, so I must keep pushing.*
- *Asking for help or admitting vulnerability is weak.*
- *Taking time for myself is selfish.*
- *I need to make this work because failure is not an option.*
- *I'm overwhelmed with stress because I don't have enough time or resources.*
- *I can't say No.*
- *I need to take on more work myself so my team doesn't burn out.*
- *If I don't rescue people, who will?*
- *I'm not good enough... as a parent, professional, etc.*

With these beliefs, it's no wonder so many executive leaders feel stressed and burned out or continue along paths that don't feel right anymore.

We all carry sabotaging thoughts. But we don't see how the negativity prevents us from making better decisions, improving our relationships, and experiencing sustainable well-being. No matter how they arise—from nature, nurture, or a combination—we give them power each time we listen to the critical voice. Worse, they drown out our underlying feelings, which always provide valuable information—if we listen.

If you don't like your thoughts, it's time to change them.

Pro Tip: Whenever we feel negativity or that feeling of *This is too hard*, it's an invitation to shine a light on our emotions and expose the feelings under the surface. When we acknowledge them with warmth and acceptance, we can flow forward.

Self-Fulfilling Prophecy

The simple truth is that whatever we tell ourselves comes to pass. For example, when we think *It won't get done without me*, it becomes a self-fulfilling prophecy. We take on more work and don't empower others, so they aren't incented to work as hard, and the work comes right back to us. We get exactly what we're afraid of. When we elevate awareness, we can choose healthier beliefs that work better for us and others.

Shattering Our Societal Limiting Beliefs

While we all carry around our own limiting beliefs through our personal life experiences, our society creates limiting beliefs that can unknowingly hold us hostage as well.

Breaking Free—Roger's Story

Since 1886, many people had tried and failed to break the four-minute mile record. Experts believed it was physically impossible unless you trained in a certain way, had perfect weather conditions with no wind, a hard, dry track, and a huge crowd to inspire the best-ever performance.

But Roger Bannister broke the record with none of those conditions on May 6, 1954. It was a cold day on a wet track in a small meet in Oxford, with barely anyone in the bleachers cheering him on. Interestingly, he trained under his own special scientific method, which also included visualization.

Just forty-six days later, Roger's record was broken and soon thousands followed[36].

Whether we're running on a track or running an organization, we don't need permission to do things differently to make breakthroughs. What we need is to shatter our limiting beliefs.

Change Beliefs by Listening below the Surface

How do we change our beliefs and self-sabotaging thoughts? We start by noticing them and calling them out! Whenever we hear these negative voices in our heads, based on stressful triggers, we're *below the line*, hijacked by fear. They lead to emotions such as stress, anxiety, self-doubt, frustration, and restlessness. While the thoughts aren't true, the feelings behind them are. The trick is to stop believing the *below-the-line* negative thoughts. Instead, start listening to what the emotions are telling you, for they contain valuable information.

However, most of us dwell on the negativity for far too long, like keeping our hands on a hot stove. We only need to pay attention long enough to know what we're feeling (e.g., heat!), so we can quickly remove our hands and not get burned.

Overcoming Imposter Syndrome

If your inner critic is saying you're not ready for the next level position, you may be experiencing imposter syndrome. This is the phenomenon where high achievers have skills, accomplishments, and credentials but haven't internalized them and worry about being exposed as a fraud. Even though the story isn't true, the underlying fear is real and holds them back. Get curious. *What's really going on? Why is this situation bringing up some insecurity about my self-worth now?*

In a workshop (of super high achievers), a participant once asked me if *Fake it until you make it* is a good empowering thought to overcome imposter syndrome. I personally prefer a more empowering belief, like *I can do hard things*. However, the best empowering belief is the one that empowers *you*.

Imposter syndrome is prevalent in high-stakes situations or transitions, such as upleveling to a new role, new career, or entering a competitive program, where you are comparing

58

yourself to others. Interestingly, it was attributed more to women in the past, since early research focused solely on highly successful women. Later, research showed it affects both men and women. However, they have different expressions to counter the phobia. Women tend to live with it and do what scares them anyway, while men will engage in less threatening experiences to avoid feeling imposter syndrome, going where they can be high performers.[37] No matter how you respond, imposter syndrome is likely to affect you at some point, for high achievers never want to fail. Raising awareness of your sabotaging tendencies and reframing your mindset with more empowering beliefs, such as *I win or learn from everything that happens*, will help you raise your confidence in overcoming this syndrome.

Emotions Drive Decisions
Even though we often don't pay close attention to our underlying emotions, they are really driving the reputed 35,000 decisions we make in a single day.

While we have a myriad of emotions, psychotherapist Natasha Sharma states that love, hate, and fear will drive your decisions more than any other emotion.[38] If that's the case, only love is capable of driving well.

What power we have to wake up and realize what our emotions are telling us, so we can make more conscious choices! Start by noticing triggers in your body. When do you feel a knot in your stomach? Or that feeling of dread? Paying close attention to your feelings of resistance or angst will clue you in to your underlying beliefs and emotions. We need to find them to deal with them or they will not go away. Remember, *reveal what's real*. Sometimes these scary feelings are rightly protecting us, but more often, they are keeping us stuck until we acknowledge and validate them.

When Emotions Are Pushed Down

Have you ever held back a strong emotion for a while and then exploded? When we ignore our emotions and suppress them, it feels like we're pushing a beach ball below the water's surface—it's exhausting and unproductive.

Like many executives, when I was asked to do the impossible and felt great stress, I pushed down my emotions to cope. In my last CMO position, post-acquisition, I was told to cut my staff by 20 percent, cut spending by more than 50 percent, and grow our topline revenue and productivity by 20 percent. I knew rationally that the math didn't work. But I kept telling myself that I would keep showing up every day and deal with it. I realized many people couldn't endure that kind of pressure (or were too sane to want to!), and I knew I could mentally handle the stress. Yet, I used so much energy to push my emotions down until my back felt like it was breaking. I had literally taken on too much pressure and needed to let it out.

Digging up Limiting Beliefs: Anger as Bad

In my coaching practice, I've worked with clients who grew up in homes where negative energy caused them to tamp down their anger. For example, at one extreme, their anger or sad emotions weren't tolerated; on the other, they witnessed anger being out of control and didn't want to emulate that. So, they judge anger as *bad* and repress it. On the outside, they show up in the world as *happy* and *everything-is-fine* people, but inside, they are masking their underlying feelings, which takes significant energy and hides the full picture of what really matters to them.

When we emotionally judge our feelings as inappropriate at a subconscious level, we prevent them from physically being expressed as *energy-in-motion*, like crying when we're upset.

Over time, negative hormones accumulate underneath the surface and take their toll on our bodies. We start thinking it's normal to feel weighed down and eventually experience physical pain, such as back issues, cancer, and more.

Carrie's Story

Carrie grew up in a home where anger was scary, so she had a lot of judgment around expressing it. During the Covid-19 pandemic, she faced extreme pressure to do more work with fewer resources. She became upset and resentful and experienced back pain, fatigue, and burnout. Since she believed it wasn't appropriate to face or express her anger, she planned to resign, even though her organization and position were a great fit for her strengths and aspirations.

We brought her anger to the surface so she could see what it was telling her: "It's time to protect your sanity and well-being." When she acknowledged it, she could shift *above the line* and see new possibilities beyond resignation—such as recommending and getting additional support. Carrie was able to not only stay in her organization but also grow as a leader.

When you explore your own limiting thoughts, beliefs, and stories, how much sense do they make for you anymore? Dig into your beliefs:

- Where did they come from?
- How are they serving you now?
- What do you want to believe instead?

Stress Responses: Managing Burnout

Like me, most senior level executives and professionals I coach are high achievers who have a tendency to shift to hyper-achiever mode under pressure. They are highly motivated to accomplish and control the situation and win against all odds. While accomplishment is good, hyper-achiever mode can result in burnout for them and their teams. They also reach for the next milestone before celebrating this one, working non-stop, like the *never-satisfied* Alexander Hamilton syndrome. It's ironic because they rarely achieve the satisfaction that drives their underlying desire for achievement.

Many high-achieving leaders are also giving, caring people who shift frequently into *over-giver mode* too. Over-givers often lose a sense of their own boundaries and needs, burn out faster, and suffer negatively in their careers.[39] Many of the women I coach fall into this category, for they have been conditioned to carry it all—and that self-care is selfish.

Interestingly, Adam Grant's research shows that givers are found at both ends of the success spectrum.[40] The difference is that those who rise to the top of their fields learn how to stop over-giving. Warren Buffet, who is definitely at the top end, is attributed to have said, "The difference between successful people and very successful people is that very successful people say 'No' to almost everything." Therefore, they strike the right balance between giving and self-care. They set healthy boundaries and ensure that their generosity is sustainable. I love poet and author Jeff Foster's positive reframe: "A boundary is not a NO to someone else's existence. It's a YES to yours."

Current State: Burnout vs. Balance

I have great empathy and understanding for these Over-giver and Hyper-achiever syndromes and want to illuminate a better way to beat the burnout they cause.

According to the World Health Organization (WHO), burnout manifests as a combination of three distinct dimensions or symptoms:

1. Exhaustion/ energy depletion—which impacts physical, cognitive, and emotional resources
2. Cynical detachment—which erodes engagement
3. Reduced professional efficacy—which leads to a lack of achievement and productivity

It's good to diagnose your specific symptoms so you know how to best address them. I've found high-achieving leaders tend to fall overwhelmingly into the first symptom of exhaustion/energy depletion, although some experience all three. While situational factors are the biggest contributor to burnout, new research shows that individuals can help influence their recovery by prioritizing re-energizing acts of self-care, including rest, nutrition, exercise, meditating, journaling, enjoying nature—and compassion. Self-compassion remedies exhaustion by helping you let go and replenish your depleted resources. Interestingly, the best antidote for cynicism and inefficacy is rich interpersonal social connections—and giving others compassion.[41] We'll cover more on compassion in Chapter 9, as it's an EQ superpower we all need to improve for greater leadership, relationships, and well-being.

I created the Burnout Balance Beam model (pp. 64-65) to expose the dangers and lies of the Over-giver and Hyper-achiever syndromes, which give us the opposite of what we really desire and typically take the exhaustion road to burnout. Their *below the line* storyline is devoid of compassion.

Burnout isn't new, and neither is mindfulness nor self-compassion, but it's time they got together.

Take a look. What resonates with you? Nobody is a perfect fit, but our tendencies and patterns are pretty recognizable. We've spent a long time creating these habits, so we need to spend some concerted mental energy to stop them. Growing our self-awareness helps us pause and choose what serves us better.

Burnout Balance Beam

GIVER
"I unconditionally deserve to prioritize myself."

OVER-GIVER
"I need to help others to feel worthy."

SABOTAGING LIE: People will give me respect and acceptance if I please and rescue them.

RESULT: Gives constantly and resents when others don't reciprocate or appreciate them enough; loses sight of their own needs and boundaries, which leads to burnout.

OPPOSITE OF WHAT YOU WANT: Feeling underappreciated harms vs. strengthens their relationships with self/others.

Burnout Balance Beam

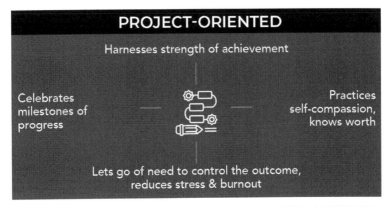

PROJECT-ORIENTED

Harnesses strength of achievement

Celebrates milestones of progress

Practices self-compassion, knows worth

Lets go of need to control the outcome, reduces stress & burnout

HIGH-ACHIEVER
"I am unconditionally worthy
no matter what I do."

HYPER-ACHIEVER
"I must be the best to
feel worthy."

SABOTAGING LIE: I will be satisfied and respected by achieving results, so I need to do more and never fail.

RESULT: Pushes to achieve next milestone without celebrating their current accomplishments; overstresses themselves and team members, which leads to burnout.

OPPOSITE OF WHAT YOU WANT: Continually chasing what's next means they miss satisfaction of current achievement.

> **Pro Tip:** If you're interested in delving deeper into your specific stress response tendencies, I recommend you check out Shirzad Chamine's Saboteur Assessment, from the Positive Intelligence (PQ) program (https://www.positiveintelligence.com/saboteurs/) which scores you on ten sabotaging factors.

Shifting our Story: Shatter Left-Brain Limits

A good place to begin is to ask yourself: *What story am I telling myself now?* We often think our story is 100 percent true, but it's rarely the case (even for me!). Let go of thinking you know all the answers and focus on some powerful questions instead. Whenever you are feeling negativity, chances are your left-brain critic is at the wheel. Here are some questions to challenge the story you are telling yourself:

- How do you know your story is true?
- What else might be going on?
- What would someone else (your spouse, your friend) say about what happened?
- What is the kindest, most positive thing you could assume?

For example, when someone fails to respond to an email I sent, I could tell myself they don't care and feel disrespected — end of story. But I've learned the email recipient typically has a good reason, such as "I was on a holiday," "I got completely buried at work," or "I thought I replied and never hit send!" I've learned to suspend judgment and realize I only see one part of the story. In fact, when I follow up with kindness, I find they are often grateful and want to engage. But letting go of the story allows me to let go of stress either way.

> **Pro Tip:** People's actions say more about them than they do about you!

Power of Neuroplasticity: Rewiring Our Brain

Fortunately, we can intentionally change our stories. Modern neuroscience debunked the myth that we are "fully baked" in early adulthood. With the power of neuroplasticity, we now know we can change the structure and function of our brains by *what we think, do, and pay attention to—at any age.*

With focused repetition, we create new neural pathways, just as we create deeper grooves in the snow by traveling the same path on a ski slope. *Neurons that fire together, wire together.*

We practice whatever we want to cultivate:

- Empowering beliefs lead to empowering feelings, actions, and outcomes
- Meditation leads to mindfulness as an outcome
- Focused attention helps promote calm and clear thinking in challenging situations
- Self-compassion helps us grow into more compassionate leaders and replenish our depleted resources

Our natural biological wiring is incredible; we are supercomputers that can continually rewire to operate at higher levels, and even make our brains younger.[42] If it seems sci-fi, I agree, but it's real.

> **Did You Know?**
> With consistent meditation practice, we can see dramatic effects in our brain's structure within eight weeks.[43]

Paying Attention—from Autopilot to Aware

Yet, we're often on autopilot, basing our actions on past habits and assumptions without paying attention to what we're doing. Why? It saves us energy and time and prevents us from falling into decision fatigue.[44] For example, I don't have to remember each day how to brush my teeth, or what to drink in the morning (coffee, of course!). Habituation saves us time, but it can make us complacent if we take it too far. The challenge is to wake up to what we're thinking, doing, and paying attention to more often. With greater awareness and attention, we can design our desired life versus living our default future. We can also listen, learn, and keep growing.

I appreciate Dr. Amishi Jha's research that attention is a superpower we should get smarter at using, since it's a finite resource.[45] She explains we can more intentionally shift between our three modes of attention, so we are able to:

- Focus when we need to—like shining a flashlight
- Notice the breadth of what we need to—like shining a floodlight, and
- Plan and organize our behavior when we need to—like juggling to overcome distractions and accomplish our goals

The kryptonite to our attention is distraction. We're distracted nearly 50 percent of the time in our monkey minds— by life, negative media, interruptions, external demands, or emotional conflicts. But when we increase awareness and train our attention with meditation, we can notice them more easily, redirect our attention faster, and recover quicker from stressful situations. Like riding a bike, we can make many micro-shifts that start to feel smooth and continuous, leading to our desired destination.

Mindfire® Mindshifting Model

I've created a model called Mindfire Mindshifting to intentionally and positively shift our thoughts and emotions (a.k.a. energy in motion), so we can catapult forward with momentum. I named my company Mindfire Mastery because I passionately believe peak performance arises when we harness the *power of our mind* aligned with the *fire of our heart-driven purpose*. By disrupting your limiting beliefs, you can shift your mindset to create more powerful outcomes you really want.

If we're not making progress on something we say we want, the culprit is likely our underlying thoughts or emotions. Our thoughts, feelings, and actions are linked, so changing one will have a domino effect on the others. We can start in any order, but since we have many untrustworthy thoughts, I like beginning with them.

According to research by Dr. Fred Luskin from Stanford University, humans have around 60,000 to 80,000 thoughts a day, and a whopping 90 percent of those thoughts are playing on repeat each day.[46] That means we only have a 10 percent chance of coming up with something new if we don't mindfully intervene.

Clearly, we have many opportunities to intercept our thoughts and rewire our brains. With intention and practice, we can make tremendous progress on our big goals. Over time, we're also able to recover faster from negative reactions in the moment—and we become more productive, creative, collaborative, and even happier.

Here's how the mind-shifting model works in these eight simple steps that conveniently spell MINDFIRE. Steps one to four are the MIND portion, which is about intercepting our negative thoughts and feelings, so you can reframe them in empowering ways. Steps five to eight are the FIRE portion, which is about putting your new thoughts and feelings into action, so you can create the outcomes you desire—and reflect and learn for true transformation and sustainable success.

1. **M**indful awareness: When triggered by stress, think *SOS*: *Stop* and *Observe* the *Situation*. Probe for what's really happening with an attitude of kindness and curiosity.

2. **I**dentify your *thoughts* and *beliefs*: What story are you telling yourself?

3. **N**otice all your *feelings*: Tune in, acknowledge, and accept them. (If you are really upset, just stop at this step for a while—maybe walk, exercise, journal, sleep, talk it out.)

4. **D**isrupt yourself: Decide on a more positive, empowering thought that aligns with your goals and values. (This is a critical step when you're ready! When you commit to a new belief, you rewrite your story and rewire your brain.)

5. **F**ocus forward: How does your new thought change your mood and feelings?

6. **I**gnite intentional action: Proceed with more ease and flow *above the line*.

7. **R**eflect and reshape: How did this work for you? Test, learn, and adjust.

8. **E**mbrace change with self-compassion: You're

creating new neural pathways, which doesn't happen overnight. Give yourself kindness and celebrate progress, fostering a growth mindset.

Micro Mindshifting in the moment becomes easier when we have a dedicated meditation practice. We start to create space between what triggers us and how we respond. Yet, we can also use this model for Massive Mindshifting, where we shift core limiting beliefs into more empowering ones. It begins with: What do you believe now—and what would you rather believe?

This model provides maximum momentum because you intentionally align your left-brain *rational mind* with your right-brain *emotional mind*, so you integrate what you really want across your thoughts and feelings. Balancing our heart and mind is the stepping stone to creating balance from the inside out. Then, you are intrinsically motivated to act, propelling you to achieve the outcomes you desire. We become truly unstoppable.

Work/Personal Life Balance: The Impossible Dream

Let's use the Mindfire Mindshifting model to improve our work/personal life balance. This topic has always been an important one for me, as I strived to balance my passions for family and career. For the Over-giver and Hyper-achiever syndromes, this tool can help swing the pendulum in the right direction.

Let's start by examining my *limiting beliefs* on balance, as they may resonate with you. I used to think *Balance is impossible, but I'm going to try anyway.*

My personal beliefs about balance were born from childhood. As a product of a workaholic overachieving father and a stay-at-home over-giving mother, I wanted to be the perfect balance of both, with no roadmap on how. When I came out of business school in 1991, I wanted to *have it all*—an exciting career and a loving family. Yet, the women I saw rising to the top were often single or childless, having made a clear choice on their priority. At first, I believed balance was impossible for me, since I saw no role models to back it up. Eventually, I found women who were paving the way and became beacons for me and others. But for a long time, it's no surprise that I found balance elusive, even when I moved to companies that were voted *Best Place for Working Mothers*, fourteen years in a row.

How did my limiting belief around balance serve me?

In my professional life, not believing in balance furthered my workaholic tendencies, particularly because the corporate playbook rewarded me for my higher levels of achievement and I never calculated the cost. Since I grew to believe hard work was my path to success, I jumped on a non-stop stress-success cycle, where I was *never enough* at work or home, even though I tried to ace both roles. Sound familiar?

It turns out I'm not alone. Many of the executive women I coach are classic over-givers who don't prioritize themselves and attain the balance they desire. As leaders and mothers, their superhuman efforts are focused on others, at their own expense. They lean towards being dangerously overextended and depleted, if not already at burnout. Maintaining a semblance of balance became even more challenging during and post-pandemic, with boundaries blurring significantly between work and home, and burnout levels rising. During the Covid-19 pandemic, research found women stepped up in bigger ways as they juggled work, homeschooling, and anxious teams with even more compassion and empathy, yet received no added recognition or support.[38]

But it's not just women who struggle with a lack of balance and burnout. Balance is elusive for many high-achieving men too. I've coached and led workshops with male leaders who are professionals in business, law, and medicine. They're often surprised to learn that balance starts inside, even though their challenging and stressful environments contribute greatly to burnout syndrome. For emerging leaders and MBA students, I'm seeing a great openness in learning mindful new ways to succeed in business on their own terms.

Empowering New Beliefs: From Impossible to Possible

What Do We Want to Believe Instead?
How about: I can passionately lead my life with better balance around my priorities!

This is huge—the first step to empowering change is believing something big, audacious, and meaningful is truly possible. Now we feel differently, so optimism and hope can emerge. We take new actions—like setting priorities and boundaries and believing we will succeed. If we keep testing, learning, and deciding, it will happen.

Here's how we begin the process with Mindfire Mindshifting:

M	**Mindful Awareness:** Stop and Observe the Situation (SOS)—without judgment. *Life feels overwhelming, stressful, and out of balance— with an aggressive work deadline looming.*
I	**Identify** your thoughts, beliefs, and story. *Balance is impossible—I have too much to do and not enough resources, which hurts my personal life and well- being.*

N	**Notice** all of your feelings: acknowledge and accept them. *I feel out of control — 'not good enough' at work or home. I'm worried I'll fail since I can't keep carrying the weight of the world on my shoulders.*
D	**Disrupt** yourself and **Decide** on a new, empowering belief. What if your limiting belief wasn't true? What would you rather believe instead? *Balance is possible if I think of it like a verb, not a destination. I can be agile, keep adjusting and lean into NO. "When I say NO to someone else, I am saying YES to me!"*
F	**Focus Forward:** How does the new belief make you feel now? *Optimistic, hopeful, and inspired to set boundaries and prioritize exercise and my family.*
I	**Ignite Intentional Action:** Proceed with ease and flow on the next step(s). *Block off time in my calendar for key priorities (focused thinking time, workouts, family). Empower and delegate more to my team by letting go of what's not mission critical for me.*
R	**Reflect and Reshape:** How did it work? Test, learn, adjust. *I am getting more done in less time; I can set firmer boundaries for the future and be clearer on what can and can't happen with our existing resources.*
E	**Embrace Change with Self-Compassion:** Use kindness and celebrate… *I made progress, but I fell back into some old patterns, so I wouldn't disappoint others. I realize it takes time to create new habits. I'll keep showing up and celebrate interim milestones!*

Okay, I hear what you're thinking. *But what if I don't really, really believe my new thoughts and beliefs are true? Will this actually work for me?* Great question. Even now, I don't truly believe that balance is viable for very long, but I do believe that, just like my yoga tree pose, I can get better at sustaining it for longer periods.

At first, you may not accept your empowering belief. But if it inspires you, and you commit to it, then say it out loud. Repeating it gives it power, which eventually makes it real, just like in *The Velveteen Rabbit*.[47] Write lists of why that belief is true or will be true. Look for role models who show you what more is possible. Start to do what they do, adapting it for you. When you start to say it's true, feel it's true, and act like it's true—guess what? It becomes true! I swear this is true.

The truth is that we never really know we can do something if we haven't done it before. But when we decide to envision a new belief (Step D), we make different choices that lead to new outcomes. Recall the story of Roger Bannister. We need to create impossible new beliefs to break through our current limits—on our way to boundless brilliant potential.

Chapter Mindset	From: Burned Out Leader	To: Shining Authentic Leader
2: Dive into emotions and find treasure in *perspective*.	Relies on their harsh inner critic who limits and drains—riding the *stress-success cycle*.	Replaces limiting beliefs with empowering, energizing ones—accessing deeper wisdom.

The Four Elements of Potential

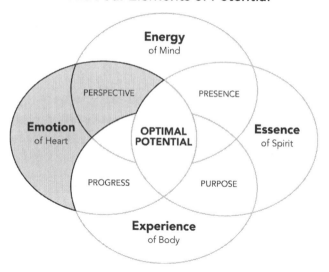

Exercises: You can do these exercises on your own, or go to www.ShiningThroughDisruption.com/resources to access the workbook and guided practices.

1. Do expressive journaling on these two prompts for three minutes each:
    o   What limiting beliefs are no longer serving you?
    o   What empowering beliefs would you rather believe?
2. Rewire with neuroplasticity: What one new step can you take this week to create more balance in your life? Start small to ensure success and repeat to build new neural pathways. (e.g., Set new boundary, saying "No" as a complete sentence, blocking time for exercise and mindfulness).

Chapter 3

Lift Your Energy (Air)

Listen to the wind, it talks. Listen to the silence,
it speaks. Listen to your heart, it knows.
—Native American Proverb

The Silent Apology That Struck the Right Tone

Have you ever said or done something that was taken out of context, and the more you try to explain, the deeper the hole you dig for yourself? Silence can cut through like words never could—*if* we choose the appropriate energetic response. Let me explain how.

My most impactful apology happened in silence—with a stranger during a silent retreat. I had accidentally taken another woman's meditation bench, thinking it belonged to the retreat center, when I saw it on her seemingly abandoned mat after our first morning. The next day, I discovered she'd returned and reclaimed the bench, just as the teachers were announcing to everyone, "Please don't take anything off anyone else's mat." In that instant, I knew their instruction was directed at me, and I swear I could feel the heat emanating from her back, which was all I could see. Even though we committed to silence all week, I knew I needed to convey a heartfelt apology—without words.

When we finished meditating, I directed all my energy toward her, so that when she turned around, I could capture her attention. I looked up at her eyes and saw coldness, and I knew without her needing to say a word that my actions had hurt and angered her.

I put both hands on my heart, and with every fiber of my being, I energetically transmitted what I was thinking and feeling in that moment: *I am so sorry. I had no idea it was your bench. Can you please forgive me?*

I naturally found myself bowing my head to show my humility. When I lifted it again, I could see her eyes had visibly softened. They were brighter, glistening with tears, and a smile was forming slightly at her mouth. She bowed back to me, and I knew she'd forgiven me.

Moments before, this woman had been a complete stranger whom I'd inadvertently made an enemy. But with energy and body language, we'd transformed the situation; we'd communicated in silence, using the universal language of our hearts which connected and lifted us. As someone who had greatly relied on words throughout my life, I was surprised I didn't need them.

The Impact of Heart-Centered Communication

After a short break following our silent reconciliation, I returned to my mat. As I picked up my shawl, I discovered a note hiding underneath. Knowing it was verboten to exchange even written words, I felt that old familiar surge of excitement, like passing notes back in high school. I scanned the room to make sure no one saw me discreetly pick up the paper and scan its message. I quickly realized it was from *her*—and my heart began to melt at her kindness.

Hi,
I'm happy to share my meditation bench with you.
I'm a commuter, and will not be using it at 9 p.m. or 6:30 a.m.
sits. Just please return it after you are done using it. I brought it
from home.
Warmly, Taryn

I had already felt her forgiveness before her note spelled it out in forty words. Emotional energy speaks volumes.

> **The power of silence doesn't mean the absence of anything else.**

Listening to the Sounds of Silence

The power of silence doesn't mean the absence of anything else. It means we make space to hear what's really going on, paying close attention to other cues. Silence also gives us space for emotions to come through with crystal clear clarity. Words aren't needed and sometimes even get in the way.

Composer John Cage premiered his silent piece, 4'33" at the Maverick Concert Hall in Woodstock in 1952 and quietly inspired the audience and generations of musicians to expand their thinking of what music could be, by not playing standard instruments at all. Rather, in his four minutes and thirty-three seconds of silence, he created a space to listen carefully to the sounds that evening. Could people hear birds chirping outside? The sound of wind rustling the leaves? A car driving by? Maybe they heard sounds of people shifting in their seats, a cough or sneeze, or breathing in and out. He opened up the idea that the world has infinite possibilities of sound that we can tune into anytime, by being silent and just listening. Instead of escaping from the outside world, Cage opened a portal to drop into it.

The Language of Energy

Research shows we have five broad emotions that are universally recognized on our faces: anger, happiness/enjoyment, sadness, disgust, and fear.[48] Yet, emotions can be quite complicated, for each of these core emotions can cascade like a waterfall into a myriad of streams and rivulets. And emotions aren't binary either. They can be subtle and complex, mixing in various shades just like when light is refracted through molecules of moisture, creating a rainbow spectrum. For example, sometimes we feel excited, nervous, happy, and tired all at the same time, like when we are traveling to new places.

If we're not aware, these emotions can sabotage us like a stealthy enemy, depleting our energy. That's why The Dalai Lama commissioned Dr. Paul Ekman to create a map, *The Atlas of Emotions*, to become more aware of all the states that can arise, so we calm our mind and create more peace in the world. If we can name them, we can tame them. Check out the interactive tool at atlasofemotions.org/#introduction/. More recently, Brené Brown published *Atlas of the Heart*, which outlines the eighty-seven emotions that define what it means to be human, all of which resonate at different levels of energy.[49]

I'm encouraged by knowing the more we tune into our own awareness, the better we get at recognizing our own emotions and those of others. This allows us to access more of our energetic potential.

However, it's important to realize that Emotional Intelligence is like another language to be learned cross-culturally, something leaders should be aware of with their global teams.[50]

I experienced this cultural confusion firsthand when I was in Japan for business early in my career. During our workday, my Japanese colleagues weren't very expressive in our meetings and I couldn't read them. Once we left work, though, I discovered our Japanese leader came alive at dinner and put me to shame singing karaoke. Emotional bonding didn't occur at work, but in the many hours outside of it. The good news is that over my three decades of global business, I've found when we show up authentically as human beings from the heart, and invest time in relationships, we realize we have more in common and can deeply connect.

How to Shift Energy
We know that energy can be neither created nor destroyed. However, it can be shifted, so we use it more wisely.

We have two main types of energy:
1. Catabolic energy—this is *below the line*, destructive, and repels. Think of the toxic leader who is often agitated and creates stressful tension in the workplace.
2. Anabolic energy—this is *above the line*, constructive, and builds. Think of your favorite leader who inspires you to greater heights.

The Seven Levels of Energy Model
(This piece contains my interpretation of the copyrighted work of Bruce D Schneider and the Institute for Professional Excellence in Coaching (iPEC).)
There are seven levels of core energy or consciousness. Just like the stock market, our energy fluctuates throughout the day as our thoughts, feelings, and actions change.[51] The seven levels cover a spectrum of emotions from catabolic to anabolic, ranging from apathy/victim (Level 1) to absolute passion for creation (Level 7). While we don't stay at just one level, we do have primary and secondary levels that we tend to hang out in, which filter how we see the world.

For example, my primary level is 5, *Collaborator*, which is about creating win-win new ideas and opportunities. My secondary level is 6, *Connector*, which is why I love teaching, coaching, and collaborating since I'm energized by deep, meaningful relationships.

Here is a snapshot of the seven levels and their dominating mindset and emotion.

Level 7: Creator—Oneness.
Level 6: Connector—Intuitive.
Level 5: Collaborator—Open.
Level 4: Giver—Caring.
Level 3: Rationalizer—Responsibility.
Level 2: Antagonist—Anger.
Level 1: Victim—Apathy.

No level is *good* or *bad*. However, the lower two levels of Victim (Level 1) and Antagonist (Level 2) are mostly catabolic and will not lead to the best results. They feel heavy, weighing us down in apathy, fear, and anger, so we don't want to stay there long. While being in a catabolic state is perfectly normal and human, it means we are compromised. We're in protection mode, wearing blinders, to deal with our stressful situation. That's why emotionally intelligent leaders quickly recognize their negative emotions and shift to higher, anabolic levels before responding to them.

Each type of energy has its purpose and can be harnessed to help us achieve our goals. For example, while anger isn't a place to linger, it's telling us something feels wrong and needs addressing.

With practice, we learn how to recover quicker from catabolic energy—and use our finite energetic potential more productively. When we tap into *above the line* anabolic energy, that attracts and builds, we create positive connections to motivate and inspire change. This is how great leaders, such as Martin Luther King Jr. and Ruth Bader Ginsburg, drove social justice.

RISE Map: Rise in Self-Awareness and Energy

By raising our emotional self-awareness (EQ) and mastering how we energetically respond to triggers, we can intentionally rise from one energy level to another. We can make conscious choices that shift us through the seven energy levels. When we resonate higher energetically, research shows we experience higher satisfaction across fourteen areas of our life, including financial success, leadership ability, relationships, level of engagement, communications, productivity, time management, work/life balance, health and wellness, and spiritual connection.[52]

RISE Map
Rise In Self-Awareness and Energy)

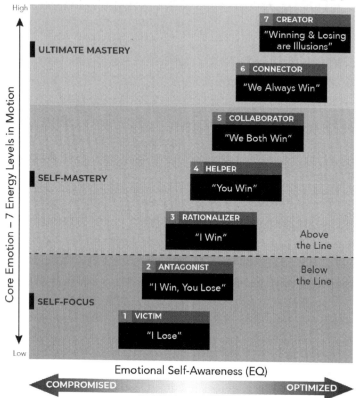

Adapted from ©2020 Institute for Professional Excellence in Coaching (iPEC)

Pro Tip: When we spend more time in the higher ranges of anabolic energy, we can more easily move between energy levels at will.

Managing the Energy in the Room

How can you show up with the right energy at the right time? Ever walk into a room that feels electrically charged, like something wrong just happened? As a leader, you can change the room's energy by managing your own. Whether your meeting room is virtual or in-person, your energy is critical. Post-pandemic, many leaders found employees were reticent and anxious about coming back into the office, which made reading energy more of a challenge.

As a leader, you can create positive intentions and explicitly outline norms for engaging in richer communications where you benefit from hearing what's said—and not said. For example, it can be as simple as stating upfront in Zoom calls for attendees to activate their video and why. Or it could involve breakout groups for large meetings so everyone's voice can be heard. The key is to create ways to ensure people feel seen, understood, and heard. This stops Zoom fatigue and creates deeper connections, engagement, and positive energy!

I attended a three-day online facilitator training via Zoom with a heart-centered group called XCHANGE (xchangeapproach.com). Their mission is to unlock the collective wisdom in groups at scale. At the end of each eight-hour session online, I was amazed at my high level of energy, and how many of us stayed and kept communicating. Even virtually, we were lit up with the power of level 6 energy connections.

Reflect Practice

In this simple Reflect practice, after someone speaks, encourage others to respond in a way that acknowledges and/or validates what the speaker communicated. For example, it could be as simple as "Thank you for that perspective, Nancy," or, "I'm inspired to think about this in a new way, Mike," or "I hear the passion in your voice, Dave," or "I appreciate you sharing why this project is important to you, Amanda." As a leader, you can model this warmth in behavior and explicitly encourage it from team members, positively lifting the team's energy.

If someone communicates with you on an emotional level, try to reflect on an emotional versus thinking channel so they feel you are tuned into them. For those of us who live in our heads, this doesn't necessarily come naturally. For example, if your direct report confides, "I feel anxious about this project," responding from a thinking channel may sound unfeeling—i.e., "You don't need to worry. You have plenty of experience." Instead, acknowledge their scared feelings with empathy and compassion. "It's understandable that you're feeling anxious because you've never done this before. How can I support you?" Can you feel the difference?

Energy Is Contagious

All energy is contagious, negative or positive. When people feel negative energy, it can spiral, so pay attention to your own energy as a leader. Instead of focusing on *what* you will say to begin a meeting, focus on *how* you will say it. Are you coming across as serious or stressed? Lighthearted or fun? How might you shift to being more empathetic and kind, curious, and open?

As a leader, intentionally conveying positive energy can positively shift *others' energy* toward greater outcomes. When we're *above the line*, we and our teams do our best work, get more done in less time, see more possibilities, and improve relationships.

My favorite health club trainers have positivity that's palpable—and Julie stands out. She tore her Achilles tendon, but never lost one drop of her enthusiasm. She even biked one-legged in spin class and dared us to beat her—motivating us even more.

If you can't be authentically positive, lean into what you do feel with vulnerability. Being real will create deeper trust and allow others to share vulnerably as well.

Story: Presence and Positive Contagion

During the Covid-19 pandemic, I joined a group coaching program to help stretch myself as a new coach and business owner, while dealing with extreme pressure and continual uncertainty. Our mindset coach, Lisa, was masterful. We were all facing fears that popped up like a Whac-A-Mole game, and she listened and met each person where they were, completely transforming the energy of individuals and the group dynamic. You could literally see the Zoom chat catch fire with the energy of positive contagion.

When I asked her how she did it, she said, "Nobody wants a fried coach! I take care of myself with sleep and nourishment, remove distractions, and always show up being 100 percent grounded and present." She exuded positivity and inspired us to greater heights too.

Guess what? Nobody wants a fried leader either. While life will get in the way at times, be intentional about how you're showing up with a grounded presence. It will change the energy of your team and yield exponentially better results. Simply ask yourself before each meeting, *What's the energy I want to bring today?* I often lean into empathizing, compassionate energy in my workshops and coaching sessions, striving to create space for participants to speak their truth bravely by modeling it myself.

> **Pro Tip:** Ask people to check-in at the beginning of the meeting with two words. It helps to gauge the energy in the room immediately, so you can meet people where they are.

Communication: Energy Speaks Louder than Words

I spent Winter 2021 working from Maui, Hawaii. Towards the end of my trip, I decided to treat myself to a Qi Gong class at the Lumeria Educational Retreat Center. Before the class, the teacher passed around a surprising note: *I will be conducting the entire class in silence, due to overextending my vocal cords by singing loudly for the last couple of days.*

I was confused. How was I going to learn something new if she wouldn't speak?

I didn't realize she could lead without saying a word. As she moved her body, we watched and followed her actions. We are hard-wired to each other's brains through *mirror neurons*, which automatically fire both when someone acts and when someone observes the same action performed by another. That's why we feel happy when someone smiles at us and why we feel pain when we see them stub their toe.

I could feel the teacher's energy by reading her facial expressions, which were supportive and encouraging. I appreciated how she gently created eye contact with me when I wasn't following her correctly, so I knew to look more closely and adjust. I left feeling more energized in my body and inspired by her effective use of non-verbal communication.

The Science of Nonverbal Communication

There's a famous study on nonverbal communication conducted by renowned behavioral psychologist Dr.

Albert Mehrabian, which essentially states that in a rich communication environment where we can see your body language and hear your tone of voice, your spoken words matter least.[53] Knowing this, it makes sense that I could follow the Qi Gong teacher, since nonverbal communication accounts for about 55 percent of communication.

It's not that words don't matter. If that were so, I'd be wasting a lot of time writing this book! But *spoken* words are influenced greatly by tone of voice, which conveys more meaning.

Just think about when our words, tone, and body language don't match up. What do you pay more attention to? For example, imagine I say, "I can't believe you did that!" My voice and tone could come across in a variety of ways: angry, disappointed, delighted, or surprised. My body language could be rigid and confrontational, or relaxed and playful.

When in doubt, body language and tone of voice will override the words we say every time.

When in doubt, body language and tone of voice will override the words we say every time. Again, *what* you say is far less important than *how* you say it. I shudder to think how many times I said something seemingly innocuous to my husband, and upset him. Whenever I was confused and asked why, his answer was always, "Your tone!" I didn't think I should be judged on tone, but guess what? It's not up to me. We are judged based on our communication's impact versus our intention. When we are upset or stressed, our energy speaks more loudly than words.

As leaders, we need to be aware of what energy we bring, for it's not only contagious, but it also affects how others feel around us in their bodies. If you want to create a sense of safety through chaos, bring calm energy. If you want to create connection, bring empathy. Think about someone sitting in a meeting you are running—they're slumped over, looking disengaged. Even if they aren't saying, "I'm not engaged," how much meaning are you getting from how they are showing up energetically? What if they are sitting up, leaning forward, and nodding at your words? How much different do you feel? As an audience member, I'm always nodding and engaging as a friendly face. I'm very aware of what a difference it makes when I'm the one speaking in the front of the room.

Remember these wise words often attributed to Maya Angelou:

"People will forget what you said, people will forget what you did, but people will never forget how you made them feel."

Unleash More of Your Listening Potential

In my emotional intelligence workshops, I love sharing the science and practice of how to unleash more right-brain optimal potential, beginning with better listening. Being able to harness the power of our whole brain is the greatest superpower emotionally intelligent leaders can use to unlock deeper empathy, connection, and potential. Leaders tell me repeatedly how this practice increases awareness of themselves and their relationships. They're also surprised that when they just focus on listening, they actually remember more of what the speaker said.

Most business leaders are rewarded for overusing the left brain, so they naturally continue to do so in conversations, which is detrimental to great listening. At work, we may listen just long enough to analyze what's happening, so we can fix problems and offer perspective and advice.

Yet, when we ignite our right-brain, which is non-verbal, emotional, and creative, we can connect and inspire others more deeply. By giving our silent rapt attention, we learn what they *really* want and need.

When I launched my Mindful Leadership Executive Education course at The University of Chicago Booth School of Business, participants said *Mindful Listening* was a game changer. One leader said it saved her from interrupting a colleague and solving the wrong problem! Daniela astutely noticed, "It is amazing how all we are learning [about EQ] can be implemented into a five-minute conversation."

The Powerful Practice of Mindful Listening

Mindful Listening is giving our full quality of attention to the person speaking without interrupting. While simple to do, it's not often done. Yet, its impact is magical, for people feel fully seen and heard—in a matter of minutes. The key is ensuring the attention stays on the speaker because talking often diverts it away when we say things like, "That reminds me of my experience when…" or, "I have an idea to solve your problem." We mean well, but our impact can be to grab the driver's wheel, which leads to disconnection versus connection.

As a listener, it doesn't mean you must sit stoically with no response. You can use natural facial expressions and body language, which we know are extremely effective in communication.

Think about how it feels when someone makes eye contact with you and smiles and leans in when you're speaking. How do you feel? For me, I'm fueled to tell the best story of my life. What about when you're speaking and notice they're looking at their watch, or looking away from you? I feel my energy draining and now realize I should stop talking and let them attend to whatever is on their mind. Since I know how powerful eye contact is, I practice really focusing on someone's eyes when they speak, so I connect to their spark and stay grounded in the present moment.

> **Pro Tip:** Build on mindful listening with *generous listening* where you still keep focus on the speaker, but you may clarify or ask a question. Also, try *empathetic listening* where you listen at the feelings level. We do this intuitively, but tuning in with more intentional awareness enables us to validate their feelings verbally.

Tuning in with Empathetic Listening

In 2019, I leaned into generous and empathetic listening with my eldest daughter, Kaela, who was a junior in college. I called her the day after my first emotional intelligence training ended. Kaela sounded busy, trying to balance her new leadership role in her service fraternity and her academic workload. When I asked how she was doing, she replied, "I'm drowning but handling it."

In the past, I may have applauded her for keeping it together, since I knew that juggling balls is a life skill of successful people. And yet, her stressed tone made me pause since I'd just come from an intense few days of tuning into feelings and being more empathetic. So I responded differently. Instead of my typical reaction of, "Good for you!" I asked, "How are you, really?"

That was all she needed to open up the floodgates to me. "Sad, overwhelmed, and not sure how I'm going to keep it all going."

I asked how I could help her. She responded, "Can I speak to a professional?" This important opening led us to discover her bipolar disorder. Thankfully, we were then able to get her the support she needed. I am so grateful I learned how to deepen my empathy to hear her pain and offer compassionate support, as she now does each day for herself.

Accessing All Three Brains — the Power of Magical Thinking

In our *mind*-brain, with nearly one hundred billion neurons, both our left brain and right brain hemispheres work interdependently. However, certain brain cells dominate and inhibit the use of other cells, so it's in our best interests to create a better balance. Most professionals have tended to lean left and over-think, so we have much more potential to access the *right side*. This not only neutralizes other stressors in our body, it opens greater connections to the neurons of our *heart-brain* (forty thousand neurons), and *gut-brain* (one hundred million neurons).[54]

The three brains are like an orchestra, with billions of neurons that can cooperate to produce a harmonic symphony. When we amplify the intelligence of our three brains, we make better decisions, align with our authentic genius, and enhance our effectiveness and happiness.

Learning to access our right brain with agility provides us with deeper wisdom and insight from our heart brain and gut brain. I'm mindful that it's my left brain that writes over sixty thousand words for my book to engage you in the topics, while my right brain knows to focus on how you feel (heart brain) and to unlock deep truths (gut brain).

Our life begins when our heart beats and ends when it stops. Our right brain, with its direct connection to our heart, is the superhighway for listening to its valuable information.

Yet, we tend to favor our left-brain's verbal centers, which don't connect to what our hearts are saying. This may be why cardiovascular heart disease (CVD) is still the number one killer worldwide every year.[55] With risk factors including poor sleep, stress, and high blood pressure, mindfulness could be a viable lifestyle strategy.

Did You Know?

Growing research shows how music (which is processed in the right brain) can help retrieve memories and create new ones. Listening to music can also create new neural pathways to the left brain, where speech is controlled when the brain has been damaged. This means that our brain is extremely adaptable and, by trying new and creative methods, we can create new neural pathways in all areas.[56]

Holographic Thinking

When we blend the power of all three brains (Mind, Heart, Gut), we expand our possibilities with *holographic thinking*. Using all our brainpower—thinking (analytical, creative), emotional, and intuitive simultaneously—or as close to it as we can, creates complete, big-picture thinking. When we access higher energy levels, such as level 6, we create more potential for this type of integrated thinking.

Holographic Thinking
The Three Brains Triangle

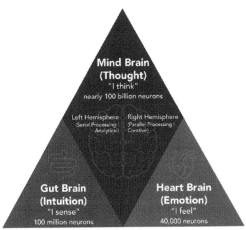

When working together, the three brains lead to higher truth. The left brain, which we rely on most frequently, does not.

The Right Brain's Untapped Brilliance to Solve Complex Problems

We intuitively know that our right brain has much untapped potential, but we often lean into and overuse our core left-brain strength—language, rational/analytical thinking, linear processing—to try to solve complex, wicked problems. We forget to unleash our right-brain's brilliance with its creativity and parallel processing power, which has a direct line to our emotions and intuitive *knowing*. It's as if we are operating with one hand, one eye, and one leg, and not using our full wattage of whole-brain power.

As I was nearing my deadline to submit my manuscript to the publisher, I was falling into left-brain overdrive, for

I saw my key challenge as cutting words. I am a prolific writer, and given I'd been writing this book for several years, I had piles upon piles of words. I was becoming overwhelmed, finding it challenging to discern which ones mattered most. Fortunately, I was participating in a coaching program that focused on right-brain mastery at the same time. I was reminded that we can view the same picture through different lenses.

My Block Print — Tapping into My Three Brains

To solve my big word count problem, I set an intention to unlock more of my full-brain potential. I quickly came across an image of three trees, a block print I'd created a couple of years ago (my one and only), and stuffed in my desk. Now, I was struck by how I could look at this image of Three Trees with my three different brains for different insights and solutions.

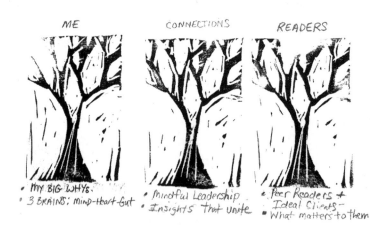

ME   CONNECTIONS   READERS

- my BIG WHYs.
- 3 BRAINS: mind-Heart-Gut
- Mindful Leadership
- Insights that unite
- Peer Readers +
- Ideal Clients —
- What matters to them

With my analytical, logical left brain, I critically view the elements, analyze, and plan. *I counted three trees, and the number of branches, analyzed all the imperfections, and planned what I could improve next time.*

When I viewed it with my emotional right-side heart-brain, I gained information and wisdom from my feelings. *I felt proud of the artwork—and experienced positive feelings from the beauty and majesty of trees. They reminded me to stay grounded and present to what really matters.*

But what surprised me most was my right-sided gut-brain's power. It immediately knew the answer to my complex question: *how do I know what to cut?*

My intuition sensed that each of the three trees represented a different aspect of my mission:

1. Me and my big *why*s
2. My readers, and what matters to you, and
3. The human connections and insights that unite us

Under each tree, I put some notes to ground myself on how to stay connected to each one of these tree's roots, and I posted them next to my computer while I edited. It gave me confidence and trust that I would know what to do if I stayed grounded in these trees and their meaning.

The metaphor energized and inspired me with anabolic, positive energy to focus on what I was building—instead of fixating on the negative catabolic energy of what I was losing. I solved my complex problem and raised my energy level at the same time. I stopped pushing myself and felt more balanced and confident, bolstered by the clarity and wisdom of my whole brain's intelligence.

The answer lies in awareness.

With greater awareness, we ignite our whole brain brilliance to unlock the answers we seek.

By the way, my logical, rational-brain figured out that the word *answer* literally lies within the word *awareness*. My gut-brain knows this truth without needing the words to spell it out. My heart-brain is smiling at this entire paragraph.

Attention and the Five Senses

The right brain, connected to our heart-brain, gut-brain, and our five senses, is the powerful gateway to mindfulness and Emotional Intelligence (EQ).

Did You Know?

Meditation is a way to awaken the right brain and grow mindfulness—meta-analysis shows major benefits of greater attentional control, emotional regulation, and self-awareness.[57]

We can engage any of our five senses (sight, hearing, smell, touch, taste) to focus, calm our minds, and activate more of our right-brain creativity and possibility. Meditation is one way I highly recommend, but we can strengthen our right-brain muscles in many other ways (see Exercises at the end of this chapter!). Ultimately, our goal isn't about getting better at meditation; it's about getting better at life. So practicing mindfulness as part of our daily lives can strengthen our sensory awareness. One of my favorite ways is mindful eating—where I savor a beautiful meal.

Mindful Eating: Multi-sensory Experiences

A joy that lights me up is creative dining experiences that engage all my senses. Years ago, my husband planned a magical dinner at Heston Blumenthal's The Fat Duck restaurant, located in the charming town of Bray, outside of

London. The Sounds of the Sea course is indelibly etched in my memory because it uniquely lit all five senses. I felt as if fireworks were going off around me, and every cell in my body was jumping up and down with joy. The seafood was a feast for the eyes, served on a glass plate of edible sand, floating above seashells I could touch. As I smelled the salt and brine of the sea, I inserted earbuds that peeked out from a conch shell and listened to the sound of waves crashing on the beach and seagulls screeching overhead. I savored each morsel's taste and texture, so much so that time slowed down. I even took notes with the pencil and paper provided to capture my thoughts in the moment, but I'll never forget my delicious memories.

Ironically, I felt this same way dining at the SingleThread restaurant in 2023, when I was in Healdsburg, California for my birthday. I discovered that the owner/chef, Kyle Connaughton, was the same chef who created that memorable Fat Duck dish years before.

Lest you think mindful eating is an expensive proposition, it doesn't need to be. We often savor more thoughtfully during a special expensive meal, but we can savor anytime—and I do. One of my favorite daily meals is avocado toast with multi-grain bread, a fried egg, market fresh tomatoes, and chives from my garden. So yum! I don't multi-task, so I can slow down and focus. I smell the aroma, take in the vibrant colors and unique texture of the ingredients, and chew slowly and mindfully, feeling joy and nourishment in each bite.

Achieving Mind-Heart-Body Coherence

Our heart-brain operates at its best when we are taking ten-second breaths (five seconds in, five seconds out), which enables us to think and feel optimally. With this *balanced breathing*, we experience an even heart rate variability (HRV) and access more heart intelligence. However, since it's not easy to count our breaths intentionally all the time, we can also achieve this state of balanced breathing by simply shifting to positive emotions. This brings us greater mind-heart-body coherence and access to deeper intuition.

For example, think about when you're frustrated by someone. You feel stressed. Your breathing becomes shallow. Your heart's rhythm is irregular. You can't see past a narrow window.

In contrast, when you shift to appreciation, you generate positive emotions, and you naturally breathe more evenly and can see, feel, and know new possibilities. It seems like magic, but it's very much backed by science.[58]

While we are all motivated by different things, accessing more positive energy in our lives is critical, for we're able to operate at our best, mentally and physically. We feel calm, balanced, energized, creative, able to respond more effectively to whatever happens, and positively influence others.

Tuning into More Right-Brain Positive Energy

Our right brain is all about love and emotional connection. When we're feeling *below-the-line* negative energy, awareness allows us to tune into emotions with greater clarity, like getting a clear signal on a radio station. We can then tune into a different channel if desired. Like a person, our emotions just want to be recognized, acknowledged, and validated—so *see them to free them.*

When I change my emotional frequency to a more positive channel, I raise my energy to higher levels. I don't tamp down on my emotions. Instead, I transmute them, like melting ice into flowing water. For example: with the negativity of competitive comparison, like when someone comes out with a book that's so well written and I wish it were mine, I can fall into the negative comparison spiral of *I'm less than*. After realizing this doesn't serve me, I can tune into feelings of appreciation and celebration of their uniqueness and mine, so I can lift my energy higher.

Trusting Our Intuition: Gut Brain

Have you ever sensed that something was wrong just by feeling it in the air? Or have you woken up and felt you shouldn't get in your car? Information can come at us from unexpected places, as our bodies are like computers that take in information through the neural receptors in our mind, heart, and gut. Research shows we know when things aren't right in our gut-brain before our thinking-brain. However, most of us don't listen to our intuitive reptilian brain's valuable information because we don't know why.

How do we know when we are feeling our intuition? Have you ever felt the hair on the back of your neck stand up or goose bumps all over your body? That's intuition. Our gut brain knows something is true in our bones, even if we don't know *how* we know. It connects to our right-brain's emotional power, but not to our left-brain's verbal centers, so we lack words to translate its meaning. What about those situations where your hands go sweaty? Your palms react to stress before your brain even registers that you are nervous or anxious. Your body knows before your brain when something is wrong, which is information that can benefit us—but only if we pay attention.

The Iowa Gambling Study

This study shows the dramatic connection between our physiology, emotion, and decision-making.[59] Imagine you are a participant—you walk into a room and are shown four decks of cards, two red and two blue. Each card will either win or lose you money. Your objective is to turn over the cards, one at a time, and maximize your winnings.

What you don't know is that the red cards will always lose, and the blue cards are necessary to win. How long does it take to figure it out? *Most of us start to form a hunch after turning over fifty cards, but we can't explain why. By eighty cards, we know the trick.*

What's fascinating, though, is that the scientists literally went deeper with this study. They hooked up each gambler to a polygraph machine (lie detector) which measures the activity of the sweat glands under the palms of our hands. While most sweat glands respond to temperature, those in our palms react to stress. The scientists discovered that the body's stress response started at the *tenth* card! This occurred *forty cards* before people even formed a hunch. What's even more important is that when their palms started sweating, their behavior changed too: they started favoring the blue, winning cards—without consciously realizing it.

When we're in alignment with our three brains—heart, mind, and gut—we can better access our deeper intuition and understanding. Einstein knew this was the source of true genius. He's attributed as saying: "The intuitive mind is a sacred gift and the rational mind is a faithful servant. We have created a society that honors the servant and has forgotten the gift."

Listening to My Emotion and Intuition

I was a poster child for ignoring my emotions and operating like my head wasn't attached to the rest of my body. Even so, I know my heart and gut have saved me from some pretty bad situations. For any major decision, I've listened to my inner-knowing voice, my gut, which knows when something feels wrong or right, even if I don't know why.

When I left Corporate America in 2018, I had a good exit package and didn't need to take another job right away. However, when consulting opportunities arose quickly, I couldn't help thinking *Maybe I should take them, because they may not appear later.* That was my rational, fearful left brain talking. But my heart and my gut just wouldn't let me say, "Yes." It was as if they were physically pushing on the brakes, even though, "No," was a foreign word to me. Thankfully, I got sage advice to listen to my heart and intuition, which gave me the confidence to lean into *No.* I learned that *No* lives in the land of *Yes,* for eventually it made space for me to find my current path with more purpose and meaning.

Many of us operate with this sort of gut-level thinking on the important stuff, and we bring in data and rational thought to support our decisions. But what if we embraced all our brains more consciously, realizing they work best together?

From Right Brain to Whole Brain: Amplify Creativity

The myth is that right-brain thinkers are more creative and naturally born that way—and others aren't. If you entered a more analytical line of work, you may believe *all the creative people are in marketing.* While we all have our zones of genius, creativity is a skill that can be honed and strengthened, like anything else. For breakthrough creativity that leads to paradigm shifts, we need our whole brain.

Tapping into our right-brain is important for creativity, but it's only half the picture. It quiets the left-brain's critical judgment and allows us to generate more ideas and wisdom through our senses with a pure, unvarnished *beginner's mind.*

The *educated* left brain is where we form our perceptions and store our great knowledge. Tapping into this treasure trove while also accessing the right brain is key! In positron emission tomography (PET) scans where people are engaged in creative thinking, it is clear that both their left and right brains are active at the same time.[60]

Power of Visual Thinking

We all know the saying, "A picture is worth a thousand words." While some people are more visual, auditory, or kinesthetic learners, we know and feel how visuals quickly convey emotion and meaning. Just think of Nike's swish, Coca-Cola's dynamic stripe, Disney's Mickey Mouse ears, and Hallmark's crown. These visual icons quickly capture our emotional connection to the brand, like a photo of a trusted friend.

In 2017, when I was leading the global rebranding of our company, we started with creating a big unified purpose (with words); then, we focused on how to bring it to life (with a new visual identity/logo). We knew there was great power to align the left-brain's words and the right-brain's visuals to tell the evolving story of our new Fortune 500 brand—and connect more emotionally with our stakeholders.

We'd hired a great rebranding consultancy for the strategy and creative design, yet I give huge credit to our CEO, Ed Tilly, for bravely contributing his creativity. Early in the process, Ed said, "I'm not creative." I've heard this from many senior executives, particularly in my fifteen years in financial services where rational numbers are king. Ed had a highly developed logical left-brain which led to his enormous success, so it made sense he wasn't nearly as confident in his less-used creative right-brain muscles. What we forget is that we were all artists in kindergarten and traded our crayons for calculators as we entered middle school.[61]

But as we began logo creation, Ed could see the possibilities for bringing our purpose to life visually. One morning, he rushed excitedly into my office with kid-like enthusiasm, and he pulled out a drawing he'd scribbled on note paper.

It was crude, yet clear enough to see a creative new way to integrate our two companies. His drawing was an integral input to creating our final, unified visual identity.

The hardest step is simply moving past our fear and judgment, which keeps us from creative experimentation. Ed was a unique, fearless leader who got out of his own way and dived into action. This allowed him to keep learning and growing his already powerful toolkit with right-side visual and creative brainpower.

Drawing comics can help us tap into emotions through our right-brain's visual channel. Marek Bennett shows how to use comics to draw out our emotions and their story, providing us with greater awareness, perspective, and insight.[62] See my personal example below (access template on p. 111).

Energy of Music

Music is a gateway to a new emotional frequency. When we are sad and dealing with difficulties in love and relationships, we can find plenty of songs to make us feel less alone. And when we need energy and confidence, we can use music to lift our mood.

During the pandemic, I created a Spotify playlist called *The Soundtrack of Awesome*. It was designed to perk me up on tough days, and I still use it for that purpose. In fact, Spotify called me a *Repeater*, which is not very sexy, but it speaks to how often I tap into the power of my key songs to tune my mood. (I preferred Spotify's wrap-up genre for me, Happy Confident Theatre Kid, which provides more insight into my song preferences.)

Flow Is Balancing Your Brains

When we're in a Flow State, we have balanced right-and-left-brain synergy. Flow is a state of peak performance when all aspects of your brain are connected and firing on all cylinders. It's similar to when athletes are *in the zone* and perform at their best, and we do too. You are so absorbed in what you're doing that you lose track of time. (More on how to flow in Chapter 6)

Powerful Storytelling: Words and Energy Communicate Together

Whenever I saw a great speaker in my firm, I always noticed how they began with a story to warm up the crowd. We know intuitively how good it feels, but do you know why?

Good storytelling lights up both our left and right brains; it powerfully conveys emotion, which impacts how people feel. In his TED Talk, *The Magical Science of Storytelling*, David JP Phillips explains how we can intentionally tell more powerful stories that release hormones and neurotransmitters for different outcomes.[63] It starts by bringing together the full power of left-brain language and right-brain energy to create motivating, inspiring communications.

For example, we can use empathy and vulnerability to release oxytocin, which fosters trust and generosity; or use humor, which releases endorphins, to improve focus, memory, and creativity. Or we can tell stories with suspense, which releases dopamine, leading to more focus, motivation, and improved memory. Great communication taps into the power of our whole brain, and it's a vital, underutilized superpower for connection. Take a look at Brené Brown, Dr. Jill Bolte Taylor, or anyone you think is a great storyteller. You will hear, see, and feel how they intentionally communicate in ways that inspire, educate, and entertain your mind, heart, body, and soul. With intention, you can do this too! The best leaders communicate at the next level by knowing how to use the right energy, at the right time, in the right situation.

Chapter Mindset	From: Burned Out Leader	To: Shining Authentic Leader
3: Shift and lift energy, elevate your *presence*.	Gets stuck in *catabolic* energy that repels and destroys—harming self and relationships.	Rises with *anabolic* energy that attracts and builds—inspiring creativity and collaboration.

The Four Elements of Potential

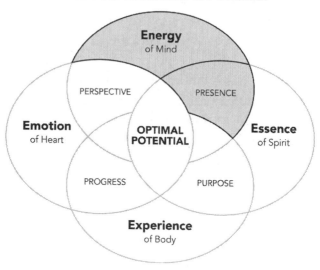

Exercises: You can do these exercises on your own, or go to www.ShiningThroughDisruption.com/resources to access the workbook and guided practices.

1. Build your right-brain's muscles by drawing your emotions to access their wisdom, using Marek Bennett's comic template: https://marekbennett. com/2020/03/23/diary-comic-4panel/
2. What five songs uplift your energy?
3. Try these suggested practices to engage your five senses and light up your right brain in everyday life. Feel free to create your own.

   o *Touch*—feel the steering wheel of your car, feel the soap in your hands as you wash, feel your fingertips with exquisite attention or those of your child's.

   o *Taste*—mindfully savor the first three bites of a meal, slowly sip your coffee or tea in the morning, and taste the saltiness of your lips.

   o *Hear*—be still for two minutes, listening to sounds you hear. Hear the furthest sound, then listen for the closest sound. Pay attention to the sound of your own breathing.

   o *Smell*—smell the fresh scent of your clothes, smell the aroma of your food, take a walk and smell the flowers and nature.

   o *See*—look deeply into the eyes of the person you're talking to, look at a picture you enjoy and notice all the details, and watch the sunset and how it slowly changes.

Chapter 4

Ignite Essence, Fuel Purpose (Fire)

Don't ask what the world needs. Ask what makes you come alive and go do it. Because what the world needs is people who have come alive.
—Howard Thurman

Lighting the Way to My Childhood Essence

When I left my CMO job in 2018, I was burned out and had forgotten what it felt like to be truly free and on fire. I'd been climbing the ladder since 1991, and I felt like I'd lose my spot if I stepped off. I'd been focused for so long on pleasing others and achieving more that I didn't remember what I needed to light myself up. So, I started searching.

As I followed my right-brain's intuition and heart, I attended a transformational mindful emotional intelligence program in December, called *Search Inside Yourself* (SIY). In two days, I unlocked the door to more empathy and vulnerability than I'd ever experienced as a leader, and I saw an immediate impact on my relationships. I applied to teach the SIY program, wondering: *What more is possible for me and other high-achieving leaders?*

By March 2019, I was midway through my first week of teacher training in Berkley, California—the start of my nine-month journey. A couple of days earlier, we'd been divided into four-person groups, or pods, which would become our *safe space* to grow together. Now, we were asked to put trust on the table fast by being openly vulnerable about some areas we wanted to improve. I was terrified, but I felt an inner tug to raise my hand and go first.

I'd noticed over those last couple of days how it was important for me to get people's approval. As a former A student and C-level executive, I'd been rewarded for coming up with the *right* answers. But now, when I spoke, I wasn't getting the validation I needed, and I wasn't sure what I was doing *wrong*. I shared this fear with my group—and waited for their wisdom. Nobody told me what to do, or gave me constructive feedback that I should be more emotional or vulnerable. Instead, they unlocked my own wisdom and perspective by asking me powerful questions, such as "What do you need to resolve?".

I remembered the inner child I'd abandoned long ago. She'd been shy, quiet, seeing, and soaking up the world around her, often going unnoticed. At age five, she sat silently on the bus when the bus driver missed her stop, curious to stay and see where her schoolmates lived. Soon after, she realized how easy it would be to lock that part away and start speaking up to get attention and appreciation, so she did.

It worked, and I never looked back, thinking how easy it had been to become the new, vocal, confident me. But now, with greater awareness unlocked, I realized I'd left an important part of myself behind.

My pod-mate, Cheeyon, gently looked at me and said, "What if your two sides play together now?" With that simple invitation, I felt an opening for me to embrace both my quiet stillness and my extroverted spark. And, I kid you not, my energy changed that day. People who knew me could tell something was different when I returned to Chicago. My presence altered. I'd typically come across as confident, bold, with an urgent energy, for I felt the need to use my voice for acceptance and validation. Now I had an inner acceptance of all of me: my intuitive, introspective child and the extroverted, enthusiastic adult. Both are true.

With this shift, I stopped relying solely on external validation for my self-worth. I revealed more of my true essence and grew as a passionate creator who embraces time for quiet reflection and meaningful connection.

I also realized the powerful magic of vulnerability, and I really leaned into it. Instead of worrying about what I was *doing wrong*, I began voicing what *felt wrong* to the people I trusted. They never fail to open me up to new awareness and perspectives. With vulnerability, I grew faster in the next few years than I had in the decades before.

Importance of Essence

What is *Essence*? It's the DNA of you that is unchanging at your core level. There are eight billion people in this world, and not a single one of them is just like you. Never underestimate why you are here at this moment in time. You are made from stardust: truly unique on the one hand and inextricably connected to everyone

You are made from stardust: truly unique on the one hand and inextricably connected to everyone on the other.

on the other. When we discover our essence, we play more in our *zone of brilliance,* where we show up authentic, confident, and agile.

Great brands and great leaders know how their essence fuels their distinctive, meaningful purpose. It enables them to propel forward authentically, emotionally connect to others, and reap extraordinary success. During the nineties, I worked for one of the best advertising agencies in the world, Leo Burnett. We grew iconic brands such as Kellogg, Kraft, Hallmark, McDonald's, and many more. We always began with essence, discovering the brand's true core, so we could grow authentically to where we aspired to be.

As individuals, we know that each of us comes to this world with unalterable individual fingerprints that create our distinct essences—anyone with multiple children can see this. No two kids are exactly alike, even identical twins. However, our fingerprints only tell part of our unique story. The other key to deciphering us comes from our hands—hand *shape* and hand *lines*—which keep evolving over time, depending on how we live our lives. Unleashing our full potential is about understanding the DNA we bring and the potential baked into us to keep evolving on *purpose.*[64]

To be an authentic leader of your life is to shine with your innate brilliance. When you know your essence and align with your purpose, you can take meaningful actions to bring it to life. Yet to survive, we learn what's acceptable and hide pieces of ourselves to fit in. One day, we wake up and forget the beautiful being hidden under layers of protection, so we need to get a shovel and start digging. It helps to bring friends along, as I did with my SIY pod-mates, because we may have a lot of shoveling to do.

Vulnerability: Brave Launching Pad for Growth

I'd always thought of myself as a brave person. However, I defined bravery as facing fear with bold action in the face of external challenges, like showing up for my mother's cancer battle and my own, leading through organizational change, or reaching for higher levels of success and achievement, even if I didn't feel ready inside. And let's not forget bungee jumping.

I hadn't realized there is a soft, yet strong bravery that comes from facing fear with vulnerable action, fueled by psychological safety and trust. Facing my internal fears and voicing them boosted my courage. Essentially, it removed the powerful, invisible inner blocks that usually held me back, since I wasn't trying to hide my imperfections anymore.

Brené Brown has certainly shined a much-needed spotlight on vulnerability, saying it goes hand in hand with courage. I believe vulnerability is the key lever that leaders like me have long avoided. When we stop using our energy to present a façade of perfection, vulnerability becomes the game changer to leap to the next level. Because at the top of your field, people are rarely telling you how to keep growing. They assume you've *arrived*, and focus on external challenges — meeting growth targets, attracting and retaining talent, and adding shareholder value. The way to truly accelerate as an emotionally intelligent, authentic leader is by going inside and revealing the emotions getting in your way. Nobody really knows how to help you get it right unless you tell them what feels wrong. Being authentic and vulnerable is how we expose the cracks, let light in, and build deeper bonds of connection with ourselves and others.

Why We Forget Who We Are: Leaning Left

We rely on our left brain to function in our world and make sense of how we relate to it. This can cover up clues to our essence from our right-side's heart and intuition. To know our *true* essence, we need to access both our right and left brains, ensuring our souls feel safe enough to show up. Then we can see the balance of everything we truly are.

I thought I knew my essence and purpose. But I had been leaning too much on my left brain, which loves credentials and compares my differences to others, which is only half of my picture. The right-brain's side holds the hidden heart of my story—and yours—that unleashes our whole greatness.

Left Brain Story

Our left brain is where we focus on the fact that we are distinct human beings who need to protect our ego to survive, so we communicate how we're valuable and compete to succeed in rational ways.

My left brain told me I was Stephanie Klein, Chief Marketing Officer and mother of two, who was in control, and who always strived to grow to the next level. It formed my distinct identity as a working professional, mother, partner, daughter, sister, and friend.

My left brain was a junkie for achievement and pushed me to get credentials, go for the win, and avoid failure at all costs. It remembers the past and files away all facts for retrieval, like that I graduated from Duke University with an AB in psychology, got my MBA from the University of Chicago Booth School of Business in marketing, and held multiple marketing roles in my three-decade career. It compared me to others as I progressed in my career in brand management, advertising, brand consulting, and became a CMO in financial services. It kept driving me to raise my game and set new milestones for achievement, even before the paint was dry on what I'd just completed.

As I moved into my next meaningful act, it compelled me to accumulate more credentials for credibility, so I became certified as an Emotional Intelligence teacher and Executive Coach with more letters behind my name, before founding my company, Mindfire Mastery.

Right Brain Story

Our right brain is all about love and connection. It knows we're perfect just as we are and evolving constantly as we interdependently connect with others. Instead of competition, we see our common humanity and feel safe in knowing we're not alone. We feel gratitude and warmth across our personal and professional roles. We know the world is beautiful, that everything is a gift, and who we really are. It's the part that lights up when we play and feels joyful from the inside out, like when I swam with elephants in Thailand with my two daughters or launched my company's new brand with my CEO.

My right brain knows I have enough time to do whatever I need to do, that I am worthy of putting myself back on the priority list, and everything is unfolding as it's meant to be. No matter what I achieve, it knows that I'm always worthy of unconditional love.

TRUE Essence Model

To unleash our magic as authentic leaders, we need to bring both our left (l) and right (r) brain superpowers together to complete our TRUE Essence model and reveal our core essence:

- Trusted Authority—what credentials we bring (l) and why people trust us (r)
- Role—what we do (l) and what lights us up (r)

- Uniqueness—how we are unique from others (l) and how we are peerless (r)
- Expression—what's our personality (l) and what really motivates us (r)

TRUE Essence Model

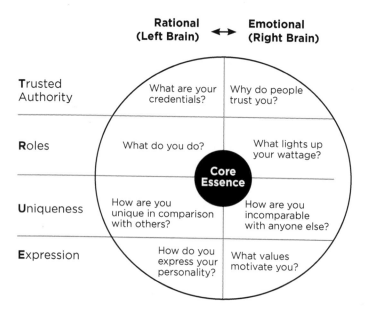

Rational (Left Brain) ←→ **Emotional (Right Brain)**

Trusted Authority
What are your credentials? | Why do people trust you?

Roles
What do you do? | What lights up your wattage?

Core Essence

Uniqueness
How are you unique in comparison with others? | How are you incomparable with anyone else?

Expression
How do you express your personality? | What values motivate you?

Your unique essence forms the basis for how you'll make your mark on the world. You are brilliant now and ever-evolving. As Amy Cuddy said so succinctly, "You are a verb, not a noun."[65] Once discovered, our essence guides us through life like a north star, illuminating our purpose. Do we light up by connecting with people? Are we drawn to knowing how the world works? Do we have a strong drive to create passionately?

How to Reveal Your Essence

We start by filling in the left and right brain sides of the TRUE Essence Model. The left side is more straightforward and easily visible than the right because it's what we typically focus on and show the external world. To discover who we are on the right side, we need to peel back the layers. It helps to dig for clues, like a fascinated anthropologist, exploring your many facets with a mindful attitude of kindness and curiosity. Let's begin!

Right Brain TRUE Essence Clues

T—Trusted Authority: What Gives You Credibility and Why Do People Trust You?

You know your credentials, so digging into your emotional appeal is key. The best brands and leaders know trust is foundational to creating an emotional connection. They also know which levers dial-up trust or diminish it. They build Trust by building Credibility (competence), Reliability (doing what they say), and Intimacy (vulnerable connection), while dialing down Self-interest (their agenda).[66] Extraordinary success comes from leaning into intimacy, by displaying vulnerability and deep understanding.

Hallmark's Essence and Trusted Connection

Of all the brands I had the privilege to grow, my favorite was Hallmark, because I was a passionate consumer of cards and loved how we could creatively show how cards can deepen connections. If I cried at a creative pitch, we'd struck gold.

Hallmark's essence was *Caring Shared*.

Around the globe, Hallmark's essence was the same, but that didn't mean our commercials didn't look and feel different in various countries and evolve over time. In the US, they made you cry. In the Netherlands, they were edgier; in Australia, funnier. Yet the DNA of *Caring Shared* united them all, and it was underpinned by vulnerability, the feeling of being emotionally exposed which nurtures trust by increasing Intimacy (I). With a Hallmark card, you could express your feelings in just the right way and make the impact you desired, without having to figure out the perfect words on your own.

Just like great brands, everyone has qualities they are known for that create a trusted connection and are integral to who they are.

- *How do you convey trust?*
- *How do your clients/colleagues/team benefit from working with you?*
- *How do you make people feel psychologically safe?*

R—Roles: What Roles Do You Play and What Lights up Your Wattage?

What Lights You up (Past)

When it comes to looking at the roles we play, it's worth reflecting on how these have changed over time. Our childhood is typically when we were creatively free and more likely to express our true selves. Sometimes it can be useful to look back and remember what lit us up because it can serve to light our way forward.

What Did You Stop Doing That You Loved to Do as a Child?

For me, it was musical creative expression. I started playing piano at the age of nine so I could sing along to any music I loved. I found great joy and connection from singing and eventually accompanying all our high school choirs. I even performed my senior piano recital at a concert hall to an audience of hundreds. I knew I'd never be a professional pianist, but I felt internal satisfaction, pride, and accomplishment. Unfortunately, as I strived to balance work with raising a family, my musical pursuits of singing and piano fell by the wayside.

Now I realize music was a creative and emotional outlet for me that I shut off in adulthood. I particularly grieved my loss of singing, since I'd enjoyed peak experiences performing with my high school choir. Yet, my left-brain hyper-achiever critic judged my voice as *not good enough* beyond casual karaoke as a young adult. It took me a while to realize I could use my voice to connect and express my emotions in a new way, as a writer, speaker, and instructor. I even rekindled my musical spark at my daughter's twenty-third golden birthday party on the twenty-third day of April in the year 2023. Joyfully, I played piano and sang *Piano Man* and could feel my childhood essence shining through with unbridled passion and joy. Two weeks later, I found a place to sing karaoke again with my daughter and friends at a neighborhood bar.

What gives you joy that you've lost touch with? How can you rekindle that light in your work or life today? What new possibilities could unfold when you do?

What Lights You up (Present)?
Here are a couple of questions to ponder:

- What endeavors and activities light you up most in your life right now?
- What do you feel fascinated by and drawn to?

Make a list of ten to fifteen things that light you up and give you joy. Then look for golden threads or themes that let you know what's important to you.

As an example, my top things are:

- Smiles/Big belly laughter
- Multi-sensory meals
- Soulful music
- Meaningful connections
- Travel adventures
- Riding my bike in flow state
- Connecting dots/Solving puzzles
- Playing in the ocean
- Sunshine
- Writing/Creating
- Savoring sunsets
- Flowers/Beauty

Three Golden Threads That Emerge Are:
1. Connections (people, nature, puzzles, humor, smiles, flow)
2. Creative expression (writing, music, multi-sensory meals, flowers/beauty)
3. Unexpected joy (the ocean, big belly laughter, travel adventures, sunsets)

It's not a coincidence that these threads or themes that light me up align with the work I love, which plays at the intersection of:

1. Authenticity—deepening real *connection* to self, others, and world
2. Mindful Leadership—expanding our capacity to lead and live with whole brain balance, flow, and *creative expression*

3. Embracing Disruption—finding joy and *upside through the unexpected*

What Lights You up (Future)?

Imagine it is one year from today, and you have just awakened from a long sleep. As you look around, you see yourself doing what you have always wished and dreamed of. What is happening? What is different? What have you accomplished that gives you the greatest sense of pride, meaning, and fulfillment? Your answers are clues to your essence and how you'll bring it forward into the world with purpose.

It's also helpful to uncover what energizes us to our bones—and what drains us. These are vital clues to who we really are, and they tend to stay consistent throughout our lives.

Clue: Energy Enhancers

From a young age, I loved creating and performing. As a CMO, I expressed this by developing and delivering presentations to our partners around the world or speaking on panels for conferences. I was completely alive and energized on stage, in flow, happy, and being my highest self.

While important, public speaking was only a small portion of my CMO role. Yet, this joy served as a powerful clue to help me realize what I wanted to dial up in my next act. Now, as a speaker, author, and educator, I get to play in this area more than ever.

Clue: Energy Drains

My entry-level job out of college was in accounting. While I could do it, I watched the clock tick. After business school, I shifted into marketing, and for three decades, time flew by—I never watched the clock tick again. Yet, each marketing role helped me hone in more on what I loved to do—and didn't.

My first job in new product development and brand management was the perfect blend of left-brain strategic and analytical skills with right-brain creativity, and I thrived overall. However, once a month, my responsibility included submitting our financials to management. It was an all-day project to complete our profit-and-loss financials, budgeting, forecasting, and reconciling. I knew I was competent, but the work felt heavy, with high stress around getting the process and the numbers *exactly right* (which isn't even possible for forecasting). I felt anxious, stressed, and sick to my stomach all day.

I used this information to choose my next marketing position in advertising, so I could lean more into my strategy and creative chops and leave more of my energy-draining stress around financial management behind. As a creative idea person, I was energized and rewarded for generating new possibilities for our brands. I also learned more clues about what I wished to change for my future.

U—Uniqueness: What Are Your Unique Differentiators in Comparison to Others—and What Makes You Peerless, Incomparable to Anyone Else?

To find your incomparable uniqueness, start with: "What is the *one* thing you cannot *not* do?" What's magnetically drawing you in? That's a clue about what you really love and are destined to share.

For me, it's expressive writing. Good times and bad, I cannot *not* journal. Even on my silent retreat, where we were told not to journal, that was the *one thing I could not stop* (even though most people thought talking would be most difficult!).

Writing is an extension of me, like breathing or thinking. It helps me process what I think and feel. I get into a zone, and time flies. As a passionate creator, this is part of who I am.

In 2011, I leaned into my love of writing during my cancer journey. Every two weeks, I wrote a *Project Recovery* update—where I briefly shared my progress and reflections with my friends, family, and colleagues. For the first time in my life, I shared vulnerably with others, in ease and flow, leaving perfectionism and judgment behind. I was surprised by the joy it brought me, and even more surprised to hear my updates inspired others and resonated deeply—and that I should publish my story.

But my left-brain's judgment and rationality held me back. It saw all the cancer books in the hospital library and decided *I'm not unique or original enough*. My left brain also told me *I'm not good enough*, for it set an impossibly high bar, comparing me incessantly to writers I admired. I'm not a beautiful writer like Ann Patchett or Pat Conroy. I'm not as entertaining and expressive as Elizabeth Gilbert. I'm not a PhD researcher like Brené Brown, Adam Grant, or Angela Duckworth. Fortunately, my right brain woke up years later and knew it was part of my soul's purpose. It knows I have my own unique style and story which will resonate if I'm authentic, because that's what makes me incomparable to anyone else.

What's Your Superpower?

Every one of us has a unique mixture of skills that forms our superpower, and we may tap into it differently as we evolve through life. My superpower is connecting the dots in an authentic, creative way—bridging the gap from where we are now to where we aspire to be.

Sometimes, we don't appreciate we have this superpower, simply because it comes so naturally to us. When we're in our zone of genius, we find flow, where our left and right brains work in tandem—and time seems to fly.

What Do Others Appreciate about You?

Often, it's our colleagues, friends, and family who see and appreciate our special ability. What skills and abilities do you take for granted that others admire? What comes so easily that you don't appreciate it?

When serving as Chief Marketing Officer in an asset management firm, we had a crisis when a key investment leader departed suddenly—and did a *lift out*, taking his entire team with him. Overnight, we lost a key capability that differentiated our firm. As we sat around the conference table in our executive team meeting, we discussed how to communicate this disturbing news to clients. Our Chief Financial Officer (CFO) wanted to communicate transparently, telling clients *exactly* what had happened. That would mean sharing that we were blindsided and going to restructure quickly to fix the problem, which would likely stir up anxious client reactions.

While I admired his integrity, I could see how to tell our story truthfully and strategically at the same time. We had planned to restructure later, so this news was only accelerating our timetable. I said, "I can tell our authentic story in a way that will convey calm and confidence if you give me an hour." None of the rational, analytical senior finance executives in the room could see how this was possible, but they agreed to let me try.

One hour later, we reconvened, and I shared my written communication. I sat with bated breath until I saw their nods of approval. Then the CFO smiled and said, "I didn't think it would work, but it does." It thrilled me to have contributed with such an impact that day, but I discounted its value since it came so easily to me. Therefore, I was completely surprised when my contribution was rewarded with a generous bonus at year-end. We often believe we need to work harder to do our best work. I've come to realize we simply need to work in our zone of genius.

E — Expression of Self: What Is Your Personality Like, and What Motivates You?

Childhood Picture Exercise

In Chapter 2, we talked about how we started accumulating baggage at an early age in the form of limiting beliefs, assumptions, and stories that we create and carry with us into adulthood. We usually begin this hardcore protection behavior around adolescence. So, when you look at a picture of you before age thirteen, it's amazing how clearly your essence shines through. What words describe you, if you were to create a statement: "I am…"

In my Positive Intelligence (PQ) group coaching program, when we do this exercise, I clearly see people's energetic expressions of personality, even in baby pictures. They appear in clearer resolution because the masks haven't accumulated yet on their personalities — and unfiltered joy shines through.

One of my clients, Laurie, a consummate high-achiever, looked at her photo and created this statement: "I am joyful, fun, playful, and connected." She told me it's always been there, although she'd never seen it before. I call it the golden thread that's tied her life together.

What Do Your Five Favorite Songs Say about You?

Music has the power to touch our emotions and connect with our hearts and souls. So, the music we love provides a clue to our essence. I love how research professor Brené Brown asked her *Unlocking Us* podcast guests for their five top songs—and what their song list said about them. Personally, I find it challenging to create my list, which speaks volumes about me already. However, I will commit to creating my Top Five list if Brené ever asks me for them! Two songs that have stood the test of time for me are *Defying Gravity* (from the musical, *Wicked*) and *Make your Own Kind of Music*. They inspire me to live authentically and unapologetically, to reach for the stars, and to inspire others to do the same.

What top five songs could you not live without? Or, just pick five songs you love, if that's easier. What do they say about who you are?

What Motivates You: Values

Values feed into our motivation for coming to work each day. What really motivates you? Our values are deeply held beliefs and ways of being, but they're often not articulated.

For many executives, I find it helps to categorize values in buckets, such as family, personal growth, and relationships. Of course, these may shift over time. For years, I had strong values for ensuring financial security for my family, including funding my daughters' college educations. Now that they've grown, I can step more into my values of courage, growth, and freedom—taking more risks, learning new skills, and creating new paths of meaning.

When you look at what's driving you, the values you hold dear shine through. The opposite holds true as well. When you feel angry and upset, chances are your values have been violated. Why are values so important? When we're in alignment with our values and know our *big why*, we have a clear roadmap of what makes sense for us to do—and abundant energy and resilience to do it. It's magic fuel to make us unstoppable.

When Values Are Violated

Think about a time you felt like life was terribly unfair. What feelings and emotions did it trigger? Chances are, something you valued was being threatened.

Early in my career, I discovered a core value this way. When my mother came to Chicago for a six-week experimental treatment at the onset of her cancer journey, I wanted flexible hours to spend time with her. However, my company didn't allow it. I learned how much I valued freedom and family as core values, and how strongly I desired a company that supported work/family balance. After she died, I immediately found a new organization whose values better aligned with mine.

Look At the Values of Role Models

I find it helps to look at the attributes of people we admire— and the core values they hold for themselves. We can then ask how they resonate with us.

Ruth Bader Ginsburg is one of my role models, and she valued family, courage, challenging the status quo, and growth, which I hold dear as well.

Outside-In Perspective

As we complete our expression of self, it's helpful to fill in our blind spots with an outside perspective from those we trust. People see you in different lights and can reveal aspects of you that may be hidden from your view.

Core Attributes and Gifts

Ask three to five people you *trust* to describe your attributes and gifts.

In 2019, when I went through coaching training, we were asked to get feedback from five people on our top attributes/gifts. I heard some overlap in words with my own: strength, fearless, creative, passionate, optimism. And I also heard things that resonated but which I'd neglected to include: intellectually curious, joyful, change agent, inspiring, tenacious, blossoming.

Note: even though we're asking people for good feedback, it's normal for it to feel scary because we're being vulnerable. Face the fear—know that it will give you more clarity and confidence to be the most authentic you!

Illuminating Blind Spots: Guiding Career Choices

After the 2008 financial crisis ended, my institutional marketing team was divided between two business units, and I needed to choose between two very different CMO positions. The safe bet was the well-oiled machine where I would lead a large global team already in place. The higher-risk option was building out a new team in the smaller business unit with bigger upside growth potential. Both bosses were terrific, and the compensation was the same, so my choice was, which position to take? I made a pros-and-cons list, using my left-brain rational thinking, and the safe bet won by a landslide. Even so, my heart leaned towards the high-risk option. So, I asked my former boss and mentor, David Blowers, for advice. He said, "Stephanie, you're a change agent." I'd never seen myself that way, which explains why I didn't realize why the harder road beckoned me, while the easier road was staring me in the face. As a marketer, I was fabulous at figuring this out for others, but I had blind spots myself. I took the riskier role and never regretted it. And I did it again when I was recruited by a firm with higher stakes and even higher rewards.

I highly recommend the value of feedback along any self-discovery process, since each of us sees the world through our own filters and others can reveal and articulate our gifts in different ways.

Pulling TRUE Essence Together

We build our deepest expression of ourselves through self-awareness, which these clues help you uncover. Once you complete the left and right sides of the TRUE Essence model, look at everything and take it all in.

Distilling Core Essence

Then, use your three brains—mind, heart, and gut—to come up with your essence, finding two to three words that capture your core essence with an emotional feeling. Aim to keep it brief, so that each word is essential. Taking out just one word would lessen its meaning. Does it resonate with you at a gut level? Consider drawing a picture to bring it to life.

My Essence (Who You Are): Passionate Creator

Importantly, your essence should emotionally resonate with you, but it doesn't need to be shared with others. My words have shifted a bit but are always in the realm of creating and connecting—whether creating stories, brands, inspiring experiences, insights, or meaningful relationships.

Bringing Essence and Values Together to Power Your Leadership Purpose

There is huge power in knowing our *essence* and how it comes to life with *values* and *purpose,* so we can make our distinctive mark as a leader. It empowers us to break through barriers and eventually soar to our highest potential.

Your essence is the vital DNA at your core. Your values are your roots, which ground you in what's important, and your purpose is your motivating statement that propels you forward. When you pull them all together, you can communicate and inspire greatly as an authentic leader.

Who you are (essence) +
How you do it (values) +
What you do (purpose) +

= Authentic Leader

Your purpose is a short and sweet statement that describes:
- What are you driven to achieve?
- What strengths and passions do you bring to the table?
- What's important to you and gives your life meaning?

It answers the questions, *What makes you great?* and *What makes you compelling?* and it *aligns with your essence and values.* It's what you're driven to do, even if you are not being paid for it—it's the magic that winds you up. You may express your purpose in different ways at different stages of your life, but when you say it out loud, everyone would say, "Heck yes! That's so you."

My Purpose Statement: With passionate artistry, I create opportunities for authentic growth.

It aligns with my Essence (Passionate Creator) and is fueled by my Values (Courage, Growth, Freedom, Authenticity, Optimism, Connection, Balance).

Expression of My Purpose

As a CMO, I expressed my leadership purpose by helping brands and businesses drive authentic, profitable growth. Now, as an author, speaker, executive coach, and educator, I help high-achieving professionals and organizations grow authentic, sustainable success—so they lead with greater brilliance, balance, and boundless ripple effects across their lives (i.e. remarkable ROI and impact on teams, organizations, families, and communities).

When you've created your purpose, ask yourself: on a scale of one to ten, with ten being highest and one being lowest, how much does it motivate you? If it's not at least an eight, what would make it more compelling for you?

Give Yourself Time

It takes time to excavate and discover our truths because it's not a linear process. But it's well worth the effort. I'm inspired by Hopi Elders' wise prophecy: *We Are the Ones We've Been Waiting For.*

You make time for what matters. And sometimes what matters takes more time than you think.

The Value of Being Ready

When I was working remotely in Maui during the winter of 2023, I remember returning home from a late afternoon snorkel, smelling the salty sea air and feeling the breeze on my face, to find an unsolicited meeting had appeared on my calendar. The next morning, I'd be meeting with The American Bankers Association (ABA) who needed a keynote speaker for their upcoming annual conference.

They were seeking a Mindful Leadership expert and had found my course at the University of Chicago Booth School of Business. They asked, "Can you teach what you do in an inspiring and entertaining one-hour keynote, with a few key takeaways?" I confidently replied, "Absolutely." Their audience would be 600 banking industry leaders dealing with disruption: the run on banks, challenges with remote working, and no separation between work and home. They needed immediate, practical ways to reduce burnout and stress so they could grow as influential leaders.

I was ready, honored, and happy to be receiving my full speaking rate. I smiled, feeling the positive impact of living with greater purpose and balance, in ease and flow. It felt so easy, but I knew this opportunity arose from being persistent, passionate, and aligned with my essence, values, and purpose.

Prosperity on Purpose—Ellen's Story

Ellen Rogin was a financial advisor, a Certified Public Accountant (CPA), and a registered Certified Financial Planner (CFP®) with her own firm. During the 2008 recession, she experienced an epiphany about her unique purpose when she asked a very different question than other financial advisors: "How can I help people feel better about money?" She realized her purpose was to use her empathy and generosity to "create prosperity on purpose" instead of protecting security, as most financial advisors did. Embracing her purpose, she prospered.

While the market went down 17 percent, her business increased 39 percent. Learning about her purpose led her eventually to sell her financial advisory firm and become the Abundance Activist® and *New York Times* best-selling author of *Picture Your Prosperity*. She followed this with another book, *Messages from Money*, and now offers mentoring, speaking, and courses to inspire financial advisors to use generosity and empathy to prosper.

When leaders unleash their authentic purpose, they motivate, inspire, and light up the world.

Fast Track to Purpose

On May 31, 2019, I met Richard Unger, founder of the International Institute of Hand Analysis and author of *Lifeprints: Deciphering Your Life Purpose from Your Fingerprints*.

Despite all my essence and purpose work over the past twenty years, Richard blew me away with his astute analysis after taking just ten minutes to look at my fingers and hands.

My fingerprints were simple, revealing my purpose as passionate artistry. However, like any good story, I have a big life challenge getting in my way—my tendency to *block feelings and emotions* which are essential for artistry!

Since I used to think all my problems could be solved rationally, my big disruptions in life (e.g. losing my mother, losing my job, and fighting my aggressive cancer) were essential to jolt me awake to feeling my emotions. While I paid a high price for not being in touch with my emotions earlier, my resilience enabled me to grow and shine through disruption. I became inspired to help other high achievers melt their emotional blocks more quickly than I did, without waiting for the wake-up calls.

I learned I have an internal tug-of-war inside of me. I want to be so good that I can avoid criticism, and yet criticism is unavoidable when we vulnerably share our ideas. This explains why I found it easier to face my fear and bungee dive off the Kawarau Bridge in New Zealand than to share early previews of my book in progress.

I learned we all have special markers on our hands that show our potential, but they aren't a prediction of what will be. It's up to us whether we step into our greatness. For example, Richard showed me my *lines of genius* markers, which he sees in only two out of every one hundred people, typically for authors and thought-leaders. As of 2019, these lines were faint in me and would remain that way if I didn't start delivering content consistently with the outside world. I was writing my book, but keeping my content hidden until it was ready for prime time.

Richard warned me I would pay a severe penalty if I didn't start moving past my fear and towards my purpose, sharing my emotions with vulnerability. His reading created more urgency for me to share my content even sooner, starting a bi-monthly newsletter and delivering my *Mindful Leadership* course for The University of Chicago's Booth Executive Education, so hundreds of leaders could benefit in advance of my book's completion.

Sharing Your Purpose Is Critical

No matter how you arrive at your purpose, it's critical to articulate and share it with others. If you don't define who you are and what you want, others will. Also, others help you clarify your message and move forward faster, aligned with your desires. While I am thrilled that the University of Chicago asked me to create an Executive Education course post-pandemic, it sprung from them knowing my passionate purpose, which I had shared with them two years prior.

This work can be challenging to do on our own because high achievers are so busy *making everything work* they don't have the mental energy or space to see what more is possible for their boundless future. But I promise you, having people in your corner, whether at work, home, or in a professional capacity, helps you skyrocket faster.

The Importance of Small Wins

A big purpose can seem daunting. Our goal is simply to keep learning and make steady progress, as if we're headed towards a lighthouse shining through the fog. We will never quite reach it, and that's okay. We will be growing into the authentic leaders we're meant to be, making progress, and feeling happier. And if that weren't enough, studies show happier people can live ten years longer, so we have more time to make progress![67]

Chapter Mindset	From: Burned Out Leader	To: Shining Authentic Leader
4: Ignite your TRUE essence, fuel your unique *purpose*.	Leans on the left brain which hides the whole story—dimming their light.	Reveals the hidden pieces of their story— illuminating authenticity and meaning.

The Four Elements of Potential

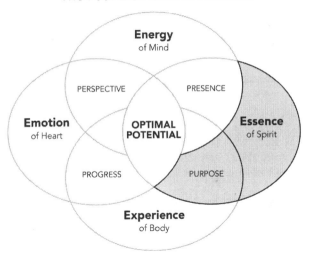

Exercises: You can do these exercises on your own, or go to www.ShiningThroughDisruption.com/resources to access the workbook and guided practices.

1. Create a *Brag Book* where you write down all the great things you've done. Go back as far as you like and list all your successes, striving for at least 100, and keep adding to it. This collection builds positive emotions, which elevates your mood when needed, and provides clues to your incomparable essence.

2. Scroll through pictures on your phone and lock screen. Which ones resonate and why? What does this tell you about what you value?

3. Journal for five minutes on this prompt (use freewriting style): What would you do even if nobody paid you to do it?

Chapter 5

Dance with Disruptive Experiences (Earth)

Life isn't about waiting for the storm to pass.
It's about dancing in the rain.
—Vivian Greene*

(*During my 2011 cancer journey, I received weekly cards from my Aunt Sandi to bolster my spirits. Whether she realized it or not, three cards had this "dancing in the rain" quote—and I think it's because it was a key message I needed to hear.)

The Unexpected, Non-linear Path

When we lived in Maui in the winter of 2021, I loved The Makamaka'ole Falls 13 Crossings hike, where we followed a riverside path that ended unexpectedly— you guessed it—about thirteen times. Each time it stopped, we needed to cross the rushing river on a path of stones to continue on the other side. We knew, somewhere at the end, we'd find a waterfall.

On my first time on the hike, I crossed tentatively at the start, worried about falling in the water. But by the fourth or fifth crossing, my confidence rose, and I stepped more quickly over the rocks. I realized I had better balance and momentum when I didn't come to a complete stop.

However, finding our waterfall destination was elusive. Given the path veered so much, we never saw it beckoning in the distance. Suddenly, the river ended, and we faced a hill of rocks. Unclear if we'd find anything rewarding on the other side, we decided to veer left and start climbing. Eventually, around a final bend, we arrived at a lovely waterfall with a refreshing bathing pool awaiting us!

We were hooked and returned. Ironically, on the second hike, we were halfway along the path when we passed hikers on their return trip back. They cautioned us: "Always stay right if you want to find the waterfall." I smiled, realizing that our success veering left last time wasn't luck. The truth was, you can veer right or left; both choices will lead you to a rewarding waterfall.

It was the unexpected adventure—where one path suddenly ended and we had to find a new one—that made this hike so enjoyable. Where to cross? Which path of stones to take? Sometimes, I took a different path than my husband and daughter. Sometimes I took a bamboo pole along for balance, and sometimes I enjoyed the daring rush from jumping quickly across on my own.

When one path suddenly ends, you eventually find a new one begins.

The thirteen crossings are a great metaphor for navigating disruption and showing us we can always transform obstacles into exciting new opportunities. You're disrupted often, challenged by changing conditions. We often can't see our destination, but we can find the next best step. There is not one clear, linear path to get to your destination. When one path suddenly ends, you eventually find a new one begins. If we keep moving forward with resilience, we will succeed eventually—and be rewarded for our accomplishments.

Life Isn't Linear

We seem to have this idealized vision that life should travel in a linear, upward trajectory. But where did that come from? We know that the shortest distance between two points is a straight line, but why would we want our life to be short and efficient? No, thank you. I'm here for a long, interesting adventure. It seems most of us experience twists and turns, even if we don't expect it. On the *Dare to Lead* podcast: *Grit and the Importance of Trying New Things*, professors and researchers Brené Brown and Angela Duckworth share that they both took the long, circuitous paths to their careers, which they felt was necessary to arrive where they are today.

How different does life feel if we don't perceive *disruption* as *interruption*? Instead, it's an array of crossings, where we can take whichever path feels right, and cross however we like—slow, fast, sooner or later. Wherever we go, we learn and grow. I like that feeling a lot better. How about you?

Research backs this up—showing we go through thirty-six transitions in the course of our lives. While uncomfortable at first, we're pretty good at navigating and crossing over to find a new path forward for most of them. Yet, one in ten of those disruptions becomes a massive change, with something big and new waiting to emerge around the bend. Just like an earthquake, some consequences and aftershocks last for up to five years.[68]

For these huge transitions, it feels as if a mountain of rocks has stopped us and we can't see a path on either side. We may feel like we're lying in the rubble, so it's daunting to proceed. Even if we're told we will find our version of a waterfall, it can be scary, difficult, and seemingly impossible to take that first step.

These situations are what I call *Dramatic disruption*, as if a seismic upheaval has shaken our lives, so they will never be the same. They may be voluntary, like changing careers or religions or leaving your marriage. But more often, they are involuntary and unexpected, like your spouse cheating on you, losing your job, undergoing stressful organizational change, being involved in a terrible accident, or facing a dire health diagnosis. No matter how the situation occurs, you have the opportunity to navigate through it with more skill, so you can recover faster and reshape your life and leadership at the next level.

Shining through Disruption Assessment

Take this brief assessment to discover where you are on the path of transforming disruptive stress into extraordinary success – and the steps needed to ascend. Read each sentence and check off the box that makes the most sense. Don't overthink the question—just think about how you typically show up. You can take the assessment online and find out your personalized next steps at ShiningThroughDisruption. com/assessment:

	Not at all like me	Not much like me	Somewhat like me	Mostly like me	Very much like me
1. I have conquered scary, life-shaking challenges that positively changed the trajectory of my life.	1	2	3	4	5
2. I usually don't pause before reacting to stress.	5	4	3	2	1
3. I can let go of negative thoughts when I become aware of them.	1	2	3	4	5
4. I have a strong sense of purpose.	1	2	3	4	5
5. I use creativity and intuition to foster new possibilities.	1	2	3	4	5
6. I have difficulty bouncing back quickly after an emotionally challenging situation.	5	4	3	2	1
7. I typically find the gift or growth opportunity in anything that happens.	1	2	3	4	5
8. I have envisioned my desired future.	1	2	3	4	5
9. When I fail to meet my high standards, my inner voice is usually *harsh judgment* instead of *kindness and compassion.*	5	4	3	2	1
10. When in conflict with someone, I take time to fully understand what is driving their perspective.	1	2	3	4	5
11. I don't set healthy boundaries to balance my own needs with those of others.	5	4	3	2	1

	Not at all like me	Not much like me	Somewhat like me	Mostly like me	Very much like me
12. I can let go of control over outcomes.	1	2	3	4	5
13. In general, I find benefit in being vulnerable, where I share mistakes, fears, and insecurities with others.	1	2	3	4	5
14. I am more likely to respond to opportunities that arise than to push for change on my own.	5	4	3	2	1
15. I don't engage in daily somatic mindfulness practices, e.g., meditation, yoga, or journal writing.	5	4	3	2	1

To calculate your score, add up all the points for the boxes you checked. The maximum score is seventy-five and the lowest is fifteen.

Scores: 60-75: **Shining Authentic Leader**—You have an exceptional ability to transform the chaos of disruption into valuable opportunities for exponential success. You lead with empathy to understand your own emotions and those of others, seeking growth in all experiences. You intentionally embrace change with passionate purpose and positive energy that guides you through uncertainty and lights your way forward. With your love of learning, you will enjoy discovering new maps, guidance and tools to maintain your balance as you level up on your hero's journey.

41-59: **Opportunistic Adapter**—You adapt well to change when opportunity knocks, successfully embracing the new situations you face, effectively expanding your brilliance from the outside-in. Building on your strong foundation of emotional intelligence and positive energy, you are perfectly poised to light yourself up even more from the inside out. You can accelerate authentic growth by intentionally leading change aligned with your unique purpose and intrinsic needs. Sparking your inner flame will fuel even greater motivation and resilience to thrive faster through any disruption.

22-40: **Tenacious Driver**—You are highly motivated and driven to overcome obstacles and fight for your goals, finding beams of light in the toughest situations. You've attained success, yet it's come at a high energetic cost. With greater self-awareness and compassion tools to quiet your left-brain critic, you can increase your wattage, productivity, and well-being. When you focus on changing yourself instead of pushing for an external change in all situations, you will reduce stress, beat burnout and build sustainable achievement—no matter what happens.

21 or under: **Burned Out Struggler**—You're stopped by disruption that feels wrong, weighed down by judgment of yourself, others, or circumstances. Start with acceptance, or you can't see new possibilities. Get unstuck with mindful practices such as focused breathing, meditation, or yoga to increase balance across your mind, heart, and body so you can shift at choice through disruption. Increase positivity to neutralize negativity bias and grow resilience. Also, remember you're not alone - enlist others to help you see more possibilities to move forward, one step at a time.

This chapter will help you navigate how to shine brighter through disruption from wherever you are. Importantly, try not to judge your score. Simply embrace what you're learning on your growth journey.

Responding to Waves of Change

During transitions, we are often thrown off balance and shocked at first, so it's hard to find the gift or opportunity immediately. Here's a personal story that exemplifies my typical reaction to change, which may raise awareness around yours.

In 2016, I attended a destination wedding weekend on Italy's Amalfi coast. One afternoon, I paddle-boarded in the Mediterranean on calm waters. I could feel the sun on my face and see my friends on the shore. I waved at them and smiled. All was perfect with the world.

Suddenly, I saw panic on my friends' faces and I looked around and realized why. A very large boat was coming fast towards me and bringing huge waves. They were screaming and gesturing at me, presumably telling me what to do. But I couldn't understand what they were saying.

So, I remained calm and thought, *OK, I'm just going to focus on being really positive.* I dug my feet into the board, closed my eyes, and concentrated on balancing. What do you think happened?

That large wave came at me, and not only did I fall off, but I flipped over headfirst into the water! I was literally underwater, which is exactly what happens when you fail to adapt to changing conditions.

Bouncing Ahead with Buoyancy

Later, I learned the secret to riding disruptive waves—simply pivot. If I'd chosen to shift my stance, I could have remained afloat and harnessed the wave's momentum.

Some say how you do *anything* is how you do *everything*. For me, pivoting through change was my critical lesson to learn because I liked to think I could control everything—even the waves. My inner beliefs dictated how I showed up whenever big waves came at me—I ignored them and focused instead on what I *wanted* to be true. Instead, I needed to become aware of what was really happening, so I could accept the situation and adapt well.

I now embrace Jon Kabat-Zinn's wise words, "You can't stop the waves, but you can learn to surf." (I even learned how to surf, but I likely set the record for the shortest time standing!)

When we keep adapting, we don't simply bounce back from challenges; we bounce forward buoyantly. That's the definition of *adaptive resilience*. It can be tough for those of us who crave control, but like anything, we get better with awareness and practice.

Number One Factor for Resilience

To persevere when we fall isn't easy, and our perseverance can become severely tested if we keep falling. We all have situations when nothing seems to go right, and it's at those times when we can become vulnerable to *learned helplessness*. After all, why endure further exhaustive efforts to change things when they've failed to make any difference so far? Based on decades of research, Dr. Martin Seligman found that all people face the same number of challenges in life, but those who developed learned helplessness lacked resilience. They were pessimistic about overcoming life's challenges. Pessimists go through life believing their karmic deck is stacked against them, whereas optimists expect a better future. The optimists' hope fuels their perseverance to prevail, overcoming the powerful negativity bias. Seligman discovered that although helplessness can be learned, so too can optimism.[69] Growing our resilience is key, and the number one factor for building it is *optimism*.

Optimism came naturally to me, probably baked into my DNA, as I come from optimistic parents. It served me well for every major disruption I've endured.

Optimism is so powerful because it can ignite mental, emotional, physical, and social resilience, all of which I experienced on my journey with cancer. It helped me mentally, to keep making progress on my marathon to recovery; emotionally, to overcome setbacks by finding positivity (remember, the 3:1 ratio to overcome negativity bias); physically, it spurred me to keep active, especially when I didn't feel up to it; and socially, it connected me to others, which increases the *cuddle* hormone oxytocin and strengthens our heart.

I also used my optimism to recover from smaller setbacks, not accepting failure as the end of my story. Optimism helped me still nail an interview for my dream job after I got lost and arrived an hour late. Instead of beating myself up, I told myself, "It can only get better from here." Optimism got me to stand up and learn how to ski, after falling into a frozen lake before my first lesson even began. I have a bracelet bearing an inscription that sums up my optimistic mindset: *She believed she could, so she did.*

And yet, while optimism served me well, with every superpower, there's a shadow side.

Toxic Optimism

When we're not paying attention to reality, *optimism* can turn into *toxic optimism*, which is dangerous. For example, when I returned to my advertising agency position after my second maternity leave, I knew organizational change was coming. My client was consolidating agencies, and I expected our team would be reassigned to other accounts. However, while many were fearful for their jobs and scrambling to find secure positions, I had a dream of an international assignment and was optimistic I'd land one—and relocate my two children under the age of three and my unemployed husband to an exciting new destination. So naturally, I was in shock and denial when my boss informed me that they were eliminating my job before my plan had come to fruition. It seemed inconceivable because it was so far from my perceived reality that *high performers don't get laid off.* Or that I could be laid off at the same time as my husband, who had lost his job a couple of months before. I was like Vizzini in the movie *The Princess Bride*, who so often says, "Inconceivable!" that he's told, "You keep using that word. I do not think it means what you think it means."

Kübler-Ross Model of Change

My typical reaction to abrupt change is *shock and denial*. It's not surprising, as these are the first two stages of the Kübler-Ross seven-stage model, a framework many organizations use to manage change.[70] Her stages aren't necessarily linear, but *shock and denial* are often followed by *frustration* and *depression*, reaching rock bottom. Then we rise when we start *experimenting, making decisions*, and *integrating the change*.

We are all unique in how we respond to change, but I find it comforting to know it's normal to have a *catabolic* stress response at first. We go below the line with *victim* feelings, followed by *anger*, which spurs us to change our situation. I've seen hundreds of profiles of executives in the assessments I do, and this is the most typical scenario. So if it sounds like you too, you're not alone.

Once we decide to take responsibility (level three) and accept the situation, we shift *above the line*. We can then make positive strides forward—experimenting with new tactics and integrating the new normal into our lives.

No matter how you respond, change makes us uncomfortable until we're comfortable again. We are no longer in our groove. The bigger problem is when we get stuck in overwhelm with our heads underwater. It's imperative we learn how to accept and adapt, so we recover faster.

Your Brains on Disruption

When we are stressed by a big transition, we are literally thrown off balance in our brains. Like a powerful wave, it forcefully shifts us to the right side of the brain. This can feel disabling, because our executive functioning goes offline, thinking we need all our resources to run or hide from a big bear (our bodies haven't adapted much since caveman times!).

When my client, Debra, entered a new company with a bigger role, she suffered from temporary brain freeze. It occurred in high-pressure meetings when she was taken off-guard by disarming questions.

It does feel like your brain is frozen, because the left brain shuts down, which controls language, how to speak, name things, compare them, understand how things interrelate, and communicate our experiences.

How we react to disruption varies based on what kind of disruption it is. But it's helpful to know we can always stop, pause, and breathe until our executive decision-making comes back online. Then, we can respond more effectively with our whole brain.

Pro Tip: I highly recommend having a go-to response in advance of getting disrupted in high-stakes situations (which I learned through experience!). It's perfectly okay to say, "I'll get back to you," or "What do others think?" so you can recover. Otherwise, our natural tendency is to dig in and defend our position, which is a clue that we're operating *below the line*.

Building Physical Resilience: Starfish Pose

We often underestimate the power of simply taking small physical actions to build resilience. I love the power pose of *Fearless Girl*, an icon of female empowerment on Wall Street, akin to Amy Cuddy's starfish pose. When we stand with our arms stretched outward, our body sends positive signals to our mind, and we feel empowered, more confident, ready, bold, and brave. As we know, thoughts, emotions, and actions are connected, so when we change one of the components, we create a domino effect that leads to new outcomes. Try the pose before a big meeting—you'll immediately feel more power. Over time, you'll improve your physical resilience.

Did You Know?

When game designer Jane McGonigal found herself bedridden and suicidal following a severe concussion, she had a fascinating idea for how to get better. She dove into the scientific research and created the healing game, SuperBetter. In her moving TED talk, McGonigal explains how a game can boost resilience—and promises to add seven and a half minutes to your life.[71]

Reclaiming Control through Disruption

We are all wired to want control, so we react in ways we believe will give us the control we need. When we perceive we have control, we operate at higher energy levels and can see more opportunities. But often, we grasp for control when it's just not possible, and everything turns to mud. With challenging situations that upend us, I find comfort in Viktor Frankl's insight: "When we are no longer able to change a situation, we are challenged to change ourselves."

The "I DO Disruption" Model

I created a new mental model for recognizing the types of disruption we face, so we better understand them and reap their benefits faster. With mastery, we can transform any challenge to our advantage. I DO stands for the three types of disruption, with I being Intentional (from *inside out*), and DO being Dramatic and Opportunist (from *outside in*):

- Intentional: proactively disrupting ourselves to achieve goals and gain mastery over our lives (e.g., coaching relationship, education, deep reflection, and mindfulness)
- Dramatic: the sudden, extreme disruption we typically didn't see coming, which powerfully changes our existence (e.g., global pandemic, financial crisis, 9/11, organizational change, health crisis, personal loss)
- Opportunistic: unanticipated disruption we want to embrace that opens new doors (e.g., relocating, a new position, getting married, having a child, even traveling)

Intentional disruption is the game-changer, for we can always disrupt ourselves and reclaim our control—based on our needs, goals, and timetable. We can bounce forward even without trauma or opportunistic circumstances, by starting from *inside out*.

We have the least control with disruption that comes at us from *outside in*: Dramatic and Opportunistic. However, what counts as Dramatic disruption for one person may be immediately seen as an opportunity for someone else. Disruption affects us in different ways, depending on what it is, how it happens, and who we are at this point in life. Even with similar situations, I've seen people react very differently. Some find gifts immediately, while others stop in their tracks.

For example, with a similar breast cancer diagnosis, three women leaders reacted in three different ways:

- I went quickly from fear to my typical achiever-mode, diving into an action plan for treatment and staying engaged in my career at the same time, trying to balance it all. I was well into months of treatment before I saw how taking a break would serve me, brought on by compassion from my leaders. This helped me realize the power of self-compassion to reshape my life and leadership for the better. (Dramatic—Opportunistic—Intentional).

- Taylor, a senior executive in financial services, went immediately from fear to overwhelm, which made her want to give up. Fortunately, she received external support to shift from victim to fighter mode, so she could recover and rise as a leader. (Dramatic—Opportunistic).

- With Kathy, cancer was like her get-out-of-jail-free card to stop trying to fit herself in a box that *felt acceptable* to others. Her diagnosis became a true turning point opportunity to embrace her authenticity, enjoy freedom and joy amidst her challenge, and define success on her terms. (Opportunistic—Intentional).

1. Dramatic (Outside In)

Dramatic disruption creates a seismic shift to crack us open to new possibilities. It will quickly change the fault lines in our bodies and souls. It blindsides us, obliterating the world as we know it. We're forced to see things differently, which gets us to act in ways we never imagined. While we have unique situations, everyone on the planet faced the upheaval of the Covid-19 global pandemic together, and none of us are the same.

I needed huge drama to wake me up to see myself and my life differently. Having the tendencies of a hyper-achiever/perfectionist/controller, I feared taking action unless I knew I had a strong game plan with a good assurance of success. Big disruption, like my cancer crisis, job elimination, acquisition, and the global pandemic, were the pushes I needed to catapult me unexpectedly out of my comfort zone. They forced me to build new muscles and new beliefs, so I could become more aligned with my authentic path.

2. Opportunistic (Outside In)

Sometimes we find new opportunities on the horizon or they find us, such as being recruited for a new position, rising to another level, or moving to a new location. These opportunities feel as if a wave came to our doorstep and transported us to a new place, sometimes desirable and exciting, sometimes scary and uncomfortable—or both. Fear and adventure live at the same energy frequency, yet feel very different based on the story we're telling ourselves.

Opportunistic disruption is a great way to try new things, learn, and grow. It's particularly useful when we don't know what we want, for we learn as much from what doesn't work as from what does. The danger is getting too comfortable or complacent—and not exploring what may light us up even more.

Post-pandemic, Anna embraced an opportunity to leap to a much higher level in a new company and was both excited and fearful of failing at the same time. She faced new colleagues, a new culture, and the added challenge of cultivating relationships while working remotely.

3. Intentional (Inside Out)

This disruption is rare and powerful. It's about how we move in the direction we really want and open up new possibilities around our specific goals when we desire them. This could include reaching for the next level in our career, improving a tough situation that seems to be a recurring pattern, or deciding we're ready for a meaningful career pivot.

Life is short, so intentionally disrupting ourselves helps us direct our own destiny. When we connect our inner fiery purpose and the power of our mindset, we make what we desire a reality. We see what we're meant to *do* and know how we want to *feel*.

Unfortunately, we're not taught *how*. When I was going through college and graduate school, the focus was definitely more on doing and achieving, starting with academics (IQ) to find the *right job* with strong earning potential and upward mobility. The focus was definitely not on aligning our minds, core desires, and feelings (EQ).

I love how a coaching relationship is all about intentional disruption work, helping clients remove blocks and blind spots that prevent them from reaching their desired outcomes. It's a game-changer for anyone committed to growing as an authentic leader to optimum potential. It yields an exceptional return on investment (ROI), leading to greater productivity, performance, and sustained well-being.

I've seen a remarkable shift in my identity and results from investing in becoming a coach and getting coached myself. I realize how disruption is critical to stretch, so we can step onto a bigger stage and play the game of life at a higher level (more on how to stretch in Chapter 8).

No matter how disruption occurs, it pushes us out of our comfort zone, which can be disarming. Thankfully, we can step back, sooner or later, and choose to transform adversity to our advantage.

Transforming through Disruption

All disruption opens us up to greater possibilities to think, see, feel, and act differently—which changes who we are. But it's up to us whether we embrace it. Post-traumatic growth means we don't simply return to normal, but we bounce forward. Our internal changes have ripple effects on our identity, relationships, and circumstances. They lead to new outcomes that change the trajectory of our lives in positive ways. Research shows people with post-traumatic growth have seven positive responses from adversity: greater appreciation for life, relationships, increased compassion, new possibilities or purpose in life, personal strength, spiritual development, and creative growth.[72]

Our Shining Transformation—Diamond Analogy

I love the analogy of a diamond to think about how we shine through disruption. The diamond starts as carbon rock deep in the earth's mantle and through both pressure and heat, its atomic structure transforms into the brilliant diamond, the strongest naturally occurring substance known to humankind.

Through the heat of disruption and the pressure of reflection, we transform from our rocky selves to shine with authentic fire and brilliance.

Through the heat of disruption and the pressure of reflection, we transform from our rocky selves to shine with authentic fire and brilliance.

With any type of disruption, the journey of transformation is the same. We begin with an experience, followed by reflection (what to change, what to keep), and then new action we're inspired to make. When we do it repeatedly, reflecting on our limiting beliefs and exchanging them for more empowering beliefs and actions, we transform in positive, intentional ways. With movement, we see the next best step—even if it's just learning what *not* to believe or do. Most executives get stuck thinking and planning way too long before taking action. With an experimentation mindset, we free ourselves from the *fear of failure* and *analysis paralysis*, favoring progress over perfection.

Experience → Reflection → Actionable Changes = Transformation

In 2020, when I joined my Book Creator's group, they nudged us to share stories and progress frequently to not only build support but also stretch into our new author identities. Still in my perfectionism zone, I found this really tough to do. How could I promote myself as an author before I was even published? But with pressure and heat, I got stronger. By September 2021, on my tenth cancer-free anniversary, I'd built the strength to quickly and spontaneously share from my heart. I posted *Ten Gifts I Got From Cancer* for my LinkedIn audience. I was blown away by the outpouring of support from that experience. I reflected and realized I could do more heartfelt posts in less time, which led me to take more action and share more frequently. Through repeated pressure and heat, I transformed into a more confident content creator with a much larger following before I launched my book.

We can also experience myriad types of disruption at the same time—across careers, personal relationships, and health—which apply more pressure and heat for transformation. It helps to build our muscles in advance, as Hailey did—and get outside support if needed.

Hailey moved internationally with her family due to her husband's career (opportunistic). She decided to disrupt herself and reinvent her career (Intentional), but needed to deal with the extra stress and uncertainty of the global pandemic at the same time (Dramatic)—and its impact on her three kids as well. Through coaching, she was able to see new opportunities for herself and her family, while better managing the continual stress, uncertainty, and change.

The Four Elements in Action
This model shows how to move from barely surviving to thriving through all disruptive experiences.

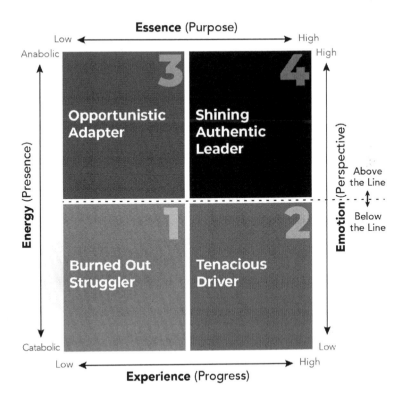

Leaders can shift through the four quadrants based on their mastery of the four elements of potential—their level of emotional awareness (perspective), anabolic/catabolic energy (presence), amount of agency/control around the experience (progress), and alignment with essence (purpose). Based on the assessment, you can see which box you tend to fall into and how to navigate to the top right quadrant of the Shining Authentic Leader.

The bottom x-axis represents the level of agency/control you feel after the disruptive experience. For example, if you decided to leave your job of your own volition, you would have higher agency/control and progress (quadrant two) than if you lost your job without warning, where you may feel powerless and stuck (quadrant one).

The top x-axis represents the amount of purpose you feel, which is grounded in your values and core essence, fueling resilience and momentum to catapult forward.

The y-axis represents the level of energy (left) and emotional awareness (right), which are positively correlated. For example, when you recognize your own emotions and those of others, you can choose your energetic response at will. Then, you can rise from victim and anger mode to the *above-the-line* positive anabolic energy levels.

Case Study: A Tale of Two Energetic Responses
Natalie was a senior marketing professional who had been working at a family-owned company for less than two years. She didn't particularly love her job, but felt like she performed well at it. When she was terminated suddenly without a severance package, she spent much of her time in lower catabolic level one energy. She felt like a victim, resentful and lethargic. She ruminated and replayed events in her mind, wishing she'd done things differently (quadrant one, Burned Out Struggler).

While she'd been working in marketing for many years, Natalie wanted to shift to a new career path in midlife that would make her happier. She expressed interest in real estate and had the financial resources to get her license. However, she assumed her high-achiever friends would negatively judge her for this profession, which made her angry. Additionally, she felt the financial pressure to get a job quickly, which created feelings of sadness, scarcity, and victimhood. Her catabolic energy kept her living in a dark cloud below the line, stuck in quadrant one. She didn't find a new job for nearly two years because her energy was focused on what was wrong and she was comparing herself to others (always a losing game). Without taking responsibility for her situation, or investing in professional support, she couldn't rise above the line to see new opportunities. She experienced high levels of constant stress, never pivoting to the new career she desired. Four years later, she told me she realized how much time she wasted and now wants to get that real estate license.

Will also lost his job unexpectedly, but had different reactions and outcomes. He was a senior marketing professional who worked for a sizable family-run business. He loved his job and shared with his employer his plan to retire in two years. Given his clear plan, passion, long tenure, and strong results, he was surprised when the owner terminated his role two years before he planned. Will felt a kick to his self-worth and identity, which led to sadness, followed by a bit of anger and resentment. His response was natural, given the disruption, and left him feeling victimized and stuck in quadrant one, but not for long.

Will quickly felt gratitude for his years at the company, and his positive emotion helped him appreciate his newfound freedom to choose his future path. When he took responsibility for his situation and forgave his former employer, he shifted *above the line*, where he explored new opportunities and decided to join former colleagues as a strategic consultant (quadrant three, Opportunistic Adapter).

Will loved the work and found a fulfilling balance between his passion for work and personal life, and shared, "I've never been happier." He elevated his energy levels, gained more awareness about what inspired him as a professional, and took positive control of his career. He shifted to quadrant four, Shining Authentic Leader, thriving through his disruption. Now, Will doesn't envision ever retiring in the traditional sense. He's found purpose, and balance, and lit his internal fire, which has changed his life's trajectory.

Summary: How We Shift through Change

We all have involuntary change thrust upon us from time to time, but Shining Authentic Leaders know they can adapt and become stronger. Like anything, the more we shift and rise through disruption, the better we get at it. We find that our limits are simply ledges we hang on to. When we let go, nothing stops us from rising to ever higher levels.

Pain Is Real, Suffering Is Optional

In the cases of Natalie and Will, they both suffered through the pain of losing a job. However, Natalie held onto the pain, like keeping her hand on a hot stove, while Will felt the heat and moved on. Natalie got burned and suffered in tangible ways, such as lost income, stress, anxiety, and not living with purpose. Will, on the other hand, rose higher in terms of his energy, awareness, and control. This led to even more engagement and happiness.

The irony is that we work so hard to avoid pain, only to prolong it. Neuroscience research shows we anticipate pain before it happens and hold on to it after the painful event ends, thus extending our suffering.[73] Have you ever refused to accept a situation and then relive the pain by complaining to others? How many people worry about losing their job or being tapped for early retirement? How many remain stressed out over organizational change instead of choosing to accept it or leave? The good news is we can learn to let go of the pain, as experienced meditators do, so we only feel what's really happening, which isn't nearly as bad as we think it will be.

Boiling in Toxic Status Quo

Sometimes we are stuck in pain, but we don't realize it because we've gotten used to it. A brilliant economist I worked with, Paul Kasriel, used the analogy of *the boiled frog* to explain why we don't leap from toxic status quo situations. The frog sits in a pot of water on the stove at room temperature and feels fine. Slowly, the water heats by one degree at a time, and the frog adjusts. Once the pot reaches boiling, it's too late. The frog never realized the danger.

Although scientists have experienced mixed results with this theory, when it comes to our work-life, it can be exactly like that. Most executives and senior professionals are very good at coping, tolerating, adapting, and making the most of every situation.

But often, our greatest strengths become our great weaknesses too. People who get used to the Toxic Status Quo don't realize when the situation has become intolerable and may be doing real harm to themselves. It often requires physical pain to wake us up to how our mental and emotional stress is taking its toll on our lives.

Reaching My Boiling Point

After our disruptive company acquisition, when the new president diminished my role and scope of authority as Chief

Marketing Officer, I coped by believing I could change his mind with data and success stories. When that didn't work, I slowly adjusted to the rising water temperatures, one degree at a time, trying to make it work before realizing that it wasn't.

In a matter of months, life was unrecognizable. I went from living on an empowered mountaintop to descending into a hole from which I couldn't see my way out. I felt isolated and alone, victimized and angry, and for the first time in decades, experienced debilitating back pain that I couldn't control. I was a **Burned Out Struggler** (quadrant one), until I realized I'd hit my boiling point and became highly motivated to leave, shifting to **Tenacious Driver** (quadrant two).

With outside advice and perspective, I saw the bigger picture and realized I could reclaim my power and leave on my own terms with a win-win exit package. I rose from catabolic *below-the-line* energy to anabolic *above-the-line* energy, landing in **Opportunistic Adapter** (quadrant three).

After my departure, I took time to recuperate and recharge. Then I used intentional disruption to help me envision and design a new future I couldn't even see yet, which led me to **Shining Authentic Leader** (quadrant four).

Intentional Disruption—Designing Your Life

Becoming a mindfulness practitioner, emotional intelligence trainer, and executive coach is a big leap from being a seasoned CMO. So how did I get here? I intentionally disrupted myself to my core by hitting the ESCAPE key.

In May 2018, I had just left my CMO role and was taking the summer to rest and reboot before seeking my next CMO position.

In June, I was invited to attend a three-hour *Designing Your Life* workshop at the Kellogg School of Management, inspired by the Stanford course and book of the same name.

For a mere ten minutes, they asked us to explore three different scenarios for taking our lives forward.

- Scenario 1: The first road was easy—a continuation of the life I'd already created, choosing the ideal scenario. For me, that was obtaining an empowering CMO position in a mission-driven company.

Then, I was disrupted big time. They said, "Now imagine that this job no longer exists. What would you do instead?"

After what seemed like a two-minute brain freeze for me to process this crazy new world with no marketing leadership positions, I spent the remaining eight minutes writing two alternative job titles and some next step experiments around how I could explore them.

- Scenario 2: Leadership coach and consultant
- Scenario 3: Published author and blogger who inspires creative experiences

What's fascinating to me is that simply voicing these disruptive new opportunities led me to new places, because it opened the portal to new possibilities. Just three months later, I took a two-day emotional intelligence workshop and dove headfirst into becoming a mindful leadership teacher, which led me to leadership coaching and consulting (Scenario 2). It was a huge turning point for me. I never interviewed for a CMO position again.

Within a year, I was certified to coach and teach, and writing a blog-type newsletter and this book to inspire more right-brain mindful emotional intelligence and creativity (Scenario 3). Within five years, I was living both of my alternative scenarios.

First, I needed to *disrupt* my mindset intentionally, escaping from my current reality. Then, I could envision my future differently and create a new pathway to achieve it.

Disruption's Power to Unlock New Paths of Perception

Since disruption interrupts our planned course of action, it's often judged to be *wrong*. However, there's always a *right side*. No matter how it shows up, disruption can be used to your advantage to unlock greater opportunity and innovation.

In business, we can see the same disruption as both good and bad, depending on our vantage point. For example, when I worked at a bank, disruption in the markets created uncertainty for our clients, so we wished it away. Yet, when I worked in the options industry, my innovative firm embraced disruptive volatility and created a way to trade it, so they were able to win whether the market was going up or down.

The Power of Escape

For Intentional disruption, I love the creative tool called *Escape*, used in the *Designing Your Life* workshop and in my *Mindful Leadership* course. It forces us to break free of a dominating idea that prevents us from thoroughly exploring alternatives. As a professional who had invested decades into creating a successful marketing career, how could I envision a completely new path? The Escape button was key; it provoked me to think beyond what I knew.

In your business and life, there are many things we take for granted. We took it for granted that we needed to work in the same location as our company, that substantive education couldn't be online, that private drivers were only for rich people, and that our brains were fully baked in early adulthood.

When we want to provoke using the Escape method, we remove whatever it is we take for granted, so we can think of alternatives. The pandemic forced escape under pressure. Here are just a couple of examples of how innovation blossomed.

- We take for granted that we need to work in an office.
  - o Escape: We cannot work in an office
  - o New idea: We meet via Zoom for business. Now, some people work from anywhere they please
- We take for granted that hotels are for travelers.
  - o Escape: Hotels are not for travelers
  - o New idea: Use empty hotel rooms for first responders during the pandemic

The Four Seasons Hotels empowered an expanded employee team to create a whole new system to deliver *quality housing for a high-risk population*. Instead of delicious breakfasts served to your door, they redefined quality as *feeling safe*.

Even if you don't desire a complete change in your life, I invite you to try hitting the Escape button and reap the benefits of seeing things differently, so you can overcome stress and allow new possibilities to unfold.

I've found escape helpful even in small ways. One day, I was about to run out of natural supplements that help me breathe better, but they were on back order online. I hit escape and said, "What if I can never order them again?" Immediately, I realized I could go to my local apothecary, and I found an alternative.

A New Mental Model: Embracing Whole Brain Disruption for Innovation

We are all familiar with how bad disruption can feel. Yet embracing disruption with your whole brain brings the opportunity to harness greater creativity and big-picture thinking for innovation. In Thich Nhat Hanh's beautiful words, *No Mud, No Lotus*, he showed that lotus flowers cannot blossom without mud, illustrating that there is no growth without challenges.[74]

If we're moving through life on autopilot, we are going to get the same outcomes we've gotten before. When disruption comes along—big or small—it gives us the opportunity to think differently, gain new perspectives, and create new paths forward. Disruption is called "the great unlock" because it's what's needed to unlock the doors to our imagination.

The Outsider Advantage

In the workplace, when we start new positions or enter new organizations, we have the outsider advantage—the opportunity to see things with a fresh beginner's mind. When I began as a CMO in my last firm, I reported to a long-tenured leader who wanted to capture my outsider advantage to find innovative ways to improve their standard practices. With a beginner's mindset and practice, we can cultivate greater innovation and success in our day-to-day lives. I like how Andrea Jung, President and CEO of Grameen America, suggests, "Fire yourself on a Friday night and come in Monday morning as if a search firm put you there as a turn-around leader."

How Our Brains Are Wired: Pattern-Forming Machines

Our brains are wired to perceive and make sense of the world around us, so we are rarely at a loss, but that means we rarely look at things in new ways. Many of us find it exhilarating to travel to new places since we are exposed to new experiences. When we are relaxed, *newness* feels like candy for our brains, which are typically saying, "Been there, done that," so we move efficiently through life. Creativity is the ability to discover new connections beyond the existing patterns.

Lateral thinking, coined by the brilliant Edward de Bono, is all about taking advantage of creative disruption to drive more ideas and opportunities for you and your team.[75]

When you disrupt your brain from its linear path, you can shift to new places and connections. It's not linear or sequential, which is why it's powerful, unexpected, and fun—like my 13 Crossings hike. This was a practice we used often in new product development. We'd find great products in different industries and think about how they could be laterally adapted for our industry.

Creating and Laughing through Disruption

Believe it or not, disruption from the path is the essence of both creativity and humor. We start off on a path where patterns and perceptions are forming in our brain, leading us to certain expectations. When we veer off the path unexpectedly and arrive back at our destination by surprise, we either feel a great *Aha!* of creative joy or a great *Ha! Ha!* of humor where we burst into laughter.

As Edward De Bono says, "It is precisely this phenomenon of asymmetry which gives rise to both humor and creativity."

Given our brains expect patterns, it makes sense that they light up with unexpected delight when they find the pattern disrupted and see a new path revealed.

One of my favorite games I found during the pandemic, the New York Times' *Spelling Bee*, allows us to hit the refresh button over and over, so we can see the game board with new eyes. I find immense creative satisfaction in disrupting my brain and finding new word patterns that were always there, but somehow eluded me until my perceptual view changed.

Humor and laughter work the same way. When we're being told a joke, we're led down the main track of a story. Suddenly, we're disrupted over to a new side track, without realizing we were being taken there. Once the punch line is revealed, we clearly see how it ties back to our original path. Our brains light up—we laugh. Time sequence matters, for the joke teller is laying down a pattern in our brain that we're latching onto. Leaving out a key piece of information can ruin the pattern and punch line, as those of us who botch up jokes know. When we get it just right, though, like the genius of Jerry Seinfeld, it seems like magic.

I love how Seinfeld masterfully disrupts us—veering us off the path and back again. Here's a great example in Seinfeld's *I'm Telling You For The Last Time* performance.[76]

"I saw a study, actually a study that said: speaking in front of a crowd is considered the number one fear of the average person. I found that amazing. Number two was death. Death is number two? This means, to the average person, if you have to be at a funeral, you would rather *be in the casket* than *doing the eulogy*."

Embracing Disruption Mindfully for New Products

So many of our advances have come from chance accidents that were noticed, embraced, and taken forward. The key to leveraging this kind of opportunistic disruption is mindful awareness, where we focus and pay attention to the present moment with an attitude of kindness and curiosity.

In the famous example of penicillin, Sir Alexander Fleming interrupted his experiment on the influenza virus with a two-week holiday. When he returned, he discovered the mold that contaminated his petri dish had killed off the bacteria. Instead of throwing it away, penicillin was born—one of the biggest breakthroughs in medical history, which treats everything from acne to pneumonia.[77] Now, if that's not a message to stop working until burnout, I don't know what is.

Disruption happens with regularity throughout our lives. How can you pay attention to what happens to embrace opportunity and growth in anything?

Chapter Mindset	From: Burned Out Leader	To: Shining Authentic Leader
5: Experience obstacles as opportunities to accelerate *progress*.	Gets stuck by *disruption as an interruption*—judging self, others, and circumstances.	Intentionally *dances with disruption*—exploring with curiosity through all situations.

The Four Elements of Potential

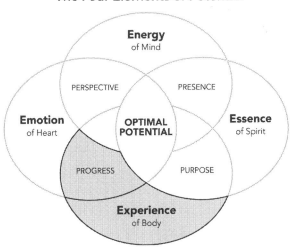

Exercises: You can do these exercises on your own, or go to www.ShiningThroughDisruption.com/resources to access the workbook and guided practices.

1. Powering your Light from Life's Disruption:
    o   Experience: Divide your life into five-year segments (e.g., If you're fifty-five, you have eleven segments, starting age 0-5). List key disruptive events that occurred in each portion of your life (e.g., crisis, loss, life transitions, etc.)
    o   Reflection: What did you learn from each disruption?
    o   Responsive Action: What changes were you inspired to make? What can you apply now?
2. Press the Escape Key:
    o   Choose a challenge you are facing, big or small.
    o   Now press the Escape key. Whatever you've done before, or have been trying so far, is no longer an option.
    o   What's a new path that opens for you?

PART II

Accelerating Authentic Success: The FAST Track

We've been on a journey to embrace the Four Elements of Potential—Emotion of Heart (Water), Energy of Mind (Air), Essence of Spirit (Fire), Experience of Body (Earth)—so we can dance with disruption and power the 4Ps to optimize potential: *Perspective, Presence, Purpose, and Progress.*

Now, in Part II, we'll take our powered-up potential on the road to navigate the ups and downs of life with our four-stage FAST Framework—Focus, Adapt, Stretch, and Thrive. We'll start by slowing down to accelerate, so we drive extraordinary success on our terms, fueled by the 4Is: *Intention, Innovation, Identity,* and *Interconnection.*

- Focus—with laser-sharp clarity, set *intention,* and let go of how it unfolds
- Adapt—accept what happens, begin again, and create possibilities for *innovation*
- Stretch—expand your *identity* to reshape your future with authentic confidence
- Thrive—embrace compassion to foster deeper *interconnection* and boundless co-creation potential

It's all doable and trainable, with dedication and practice. Are you ready?

FAST Framework

Chapter 6

Focus and Let Go

You cannot change your destination overnight.
You can change your direction.
—Jim Rohn

Moth Storytelling—Set Intention

In 2013, I went to a Moth (themoth.org) storytelling event and was enthralled. Ten individuals share their personal stories in front of a live audience, TED Talk-style, without notes. Stories must be no longer than five minutes, and an audience panel of judges picks one winner. Even though I was busy juggling my career and raising our two daughters with little time to spare, I felt a powerful pull to do it. I set an intention to perform at the next month's Moth on the theme of *Detours*. I planned to tell my story of taking a leave of absence from work, to return to Ohio and care for my ailing mother during her last three months of life.

With my strong intention set, I prepared in my usual perfectionist way. I spent hours writing the five-minute piece, tweaking, adjusting, and editing it, and then practiced it to perfection.

On the evening of *Detours*, I showed up and let them know I was ready to perform. Unfortunately, so did twenty other people—and they only choose ten, from a hat, one name at a time. During each performance, I felt my adrenaline surge, wondering if I'd be the next name called. Then, I'd wait with bated breath to be chosen. Each time I wasn't, I deflated and my stress skyrocketed again. And the cycle continued until nine people performed.

Being the eternal optimist, I was sure I would be the tenth name called. After all, I was born on the tenth day of the tenth month, and I had a strong intention and a powerful, heartfelt story to share. I could feel my love for my mother giving me strength as I waited for my last chance.

They called the tenth name. It wasn't mine. Even though I shouldn't have been surprised, I still felt deeply disappointed.

My husband whispered, "You can do it next time." But I closed the door in my mind, thinking I'd wasted my precious time, with no intention of repeating this ordeal. My limiting belief was that it took hard work and long hours to write a *perfect* five-minute story, with no guarantee of ever being able to deliver it. So I placed my Moth dream in a box, surrounded with heavy locks, and hid it away in a dark warehouse, just like the end of the Indiana Jones movie, *Raiders of the Lost Ark*.

What I later learned was that we can set intentions, but we have no control over how they unfold.

Amplifying Focus through Intention

An intention is part of us. It emanates from who we are now and focuses our energy on who we want to be. For the past twenty years, one of my big intentions has been plastered in black letters on my coffee mug: *Go confidently in the direction of your dreams*. Seeing Henry David Thoreau's inspirational words each day keeps me focused on my intention to live the life I envision, no matter what happens.

How Our Brain's Wiring Powers Intention and Outcomes
Where intention goes, energy flows. Our intention puts energy in motion. As an example, take a moment and look around you to find all the blue things you see. You may be surprised how quickly you now see blue items that blended into the background before.

> **Where intention goes, energy flows.**

The Reticular Activation System (RAS) is where all our senses come in (except for smell) to the emotional center of our brain.[78] The RAS connects that subconscious part of our brain with its conscious part, so it helps lead us towards our focused intention.

That's why when I was shopping for a red car, I saw them everywhere. Or when I found one heart-shaped seashell on the beach and wanted more, I couldn't stop finding them. The RAS brings to light that which we seek. Like magic, we have the power to hack into our RAS, so we get to our goals even faster.

RAS + Focused Intention = Outcome you Desire

Intention Leads to Outcomes: RAS Lights the Way
You can intend to find a cool car or take a pause in your day or your work. Or you can intend to reach the next level in your career, write a book, start a family, or just enjoy a quiet evening at home. Big or small, all intentions are valid.

Focus begins with the energy of intention, for it clarifies what we want and primes us for action. Always start with intention, for it's a very good place to start. When we set our focused intention and activate our RAS, we shine a light on what we want to unfold. But we can't steer a parked car, so we must take action for anything to happen.

Action: Tell Someone about Your Intention

Let people know what you want to do. We do this well when we network while job-seeking, because we have focus, urgency, and recognize the value in connections. However, it's also a great strategy to tell people about your future intentions that you don't urgently need. Why? First, when we speak them out loud or write them down, we create clarity. Second, people help connect us to opportunities and ideas. Third, action is an antidote to fear, which can bury our true desires to protect us. Lastly, we have no control over the timing of when intentions unfold, so get the ball rolling!

When I voiced my desire to write a book, I heard from an acquaintance about joining a book creators' group that got me moving towards making it a reality. Aligning with like-minded people is a powerful way to keep us motivated, for they face the same challenges and can help support us through the inevitable ups and downs.

Cara was looking to expand her business into a new niche opportunity at mid-life for which she had a lot of excitement and little knowledge. As she shared her thoughts out loud with her network, she was connected quickly to people to help her make her vision a reality.

Sarah told me she was ready to get serious and get married, so I introduced her to my only bachelor friend. They've been married for twenty-five years.

Fueling Our Intention

To fire up an intention, it helps to bring the power of both our left and right brains together. We state what we want (left/verbal) and why it's important to us (right/heart).

Let's build on our empowering belief that we can create a more integrated work/life balance from Chapter 2. If we want to create more work/life balance, what focused intentions would serve us?

Maybe one intention is to start embracing "No" as a complete sentence. Or to set clear priorities and boundaries and communicate them to others. Of course, it's not easy to shift old, ingrained habits and patterns, especially when others expect us to show up as we always have. So how can we put more emotional energy behind these intentions to make them real? We can bring in our right brain to connect to why this is meaningful for us. We often forget this step, and it's why so many New Year's intentions fall by the wayside.

For example, I can think about why I want balance (e.g., to improve my health, spend time with family, become a better leader, enjoy my life more), how I will feel when I get it (e.g., energized, happy, proud, satisfied), and who else will benefit from me being in balance (my family, my team, my clients, my friends, myself!). I can even draw a picture on paper, or visualize it in my mind. All of this creates more power than just thinking about balance in an abstract or rational sense. When we fire up our intentions with our whole brain, we create more energy to achieve it.

Whole Brain Intention Setting: Balance

Left Brain/Rational Intention (What I Want)	Right Brain/Emotional Intention (Why it's Important to Me)
Say "No" more and set boundaries; block off time for exercise five times a week; prioritize daily meditation practice.	I want to take care of myself and experience holistic well-being, living my life to the fullest.
Increase quality time with myself, family, and personal relationships.	I desire meaningful connections that foster joy, growth, and love.
Delegate, collaborate, and garner support, so I'm more productive.	I can be more creative— empowering and inspiring greater potential and impact.

To keep my intentions lit each day, I play a game with Angel Numbers, which is when numbers are repeated in sequence, such as 11:11, 1:11, 2:22, 3:33, 4:44, or 5:55. Whenever I catch one on the clock, I create a mindful moment. I stop, close my eyes, and think about my intention for that moment. It's fun and powerful. PS: just as I finished this chapter, the clock struck 11:11, and I set an intention for this to resonate and inspire your intentions.

Did You Know?

In many cultures across centuries, new moon rituals are performed to unlock the powerful energy of the moon to bring our intentions to fruition. Since our bodies are mostly composed of water, like the earth's surface, we are affected by the moon's gravitational pull. The science reveals an intricate relationship between the lunar cycle and human behavior, suggesting that we may experience heightened emotional and intuitive energy, with lower physical energy. So try setting an intention at the new moon and see what happens.

Clarifying and Aligning Intentions

When our intentions involve others, whether co-workers or family, it's good to engage them and ensure we're aligned. This may seem more obvious in the workplace. However, it had never occurred to me to align intentions with my children.

Instead, like many women in my company's *Women in Leadership* Affinity Group, I set unrealistic standards for what *the perfect mother would do* and always felt I was falling short of my expectations at work and home.

During one of our women's group sessions, I asked our senior mentor leader for advice on balancing it all. I was stunned by her simple answer: "Prioritize by asking your kids what's important to them." When I asked my daughters what school events and sports games they wanted me to attend, it was shockingly very little! At times, I overrode their answers and showed up, anyway. But it enabled me to set clear intentions that led to the outcome I desired (connection). And I let go of the stress and guilt I didn't need to carry anymore.

Intentions versus Goals: Deep versus Shallow Wins

Dr. Pippa Grange talks about the danger of *Winning Shallow*, which is "winning to avoid not being good enough, winning to beat the other guy, winning to be seen as good enough."[79] When we are below the line, and motivated by negative feelings, that's shallow. *Winning Deep* is about achieving real fulfillment versus avoiding loss.

The deep wins come from tapping into a stronger intention that's grounded in the values you hold dear. Deep satisfaction comes from showing up each day in ways that matter. We win some; we lose some. But when we are playing the long game, we know it's worth it, because it's what we really need to fill ourselves up inside. It's not about getting approval from others, although that's certainly nice. It's about getting approval from ourselves, which is infinitely more important.

Balance Intention and Letting Go

Leaders want control, so letting go is not easy, but it's critical to balance this tension of opposites. Just as we can experience joy and sadness at the same time, we can hold on and let go simultaneously. Rarely do our intentions unfold the way we want, like my Moth storytelling event. How they come to fruition may look very different from what we expect. All we can do is focus our energy towards what we want and then surrender to what actually happens.

Moth Part 2—Letting Go of How Intention Unfolds

In 2016, several years after I'd *not* been selected as one of the ten people to perform at the Moth *Detours* storytelling event, we took our daughters to their first Moth event at a new venue on the south side of Chicago. To my great surprise, we faced the opposite problem. They announced, "We only have five storytellers and need ten for the show to go on."

My first reaction was simply, "Wow! How lucky that everyone who prepared a story can deliver it." Then I realized that would not happen unless five more people stepped up. Now I was assured of a spot if I wanted it, but my big problem was that I had absolutely *nothing* prepared.

That evening's theme was *Ambition,* a topic I knew a lot about as a CMO in financial services, yet I couldn't think of a specific story that would be entertaining. I also couldn't fathom delivering a five-minute impromptu story, with no preparation, after the number of hours I'd spent writing and memorizing my first one.

Clearly, I was facing an Opportunistic disruption that aligned with my strong earlier intention, but I felt too scared and caught off guard to dive in.

Thankfully, though, I'd never been quiet about my intention to do this. So my family knew about my strong desire and keen disappointment when it never came to fruition. They shouted, "You have to do it!"

I needed that nudge because fear was popping up to protect me from making a fool of myself. Yet, the pull from my heart and gut was strong too, so I responded with a mixture of excitement and nervousness, saying, "What would I even talk about?"

My youngest daughter, Olivia, immediately came up with an idea. "Mom, talk about the time you won the tequila drinking contest in Mexico!"

I smiled and realized that was a pretty good idea. I'd beaten every woman with my masterful ability to gargle tequila while singing *La Cucaracha* at the same time. With absolutely no preparation, could I make that into a solid five-minute story with a beginning, middle, and end?

I barely thought about it before jumping to my feet and declaring, "I'll do it!" In the next minute, I was registered.

Adrenaline started flowing, my face was flushed, and I got butterflies galore. I couldn't believe this was finally happening! I wasn't sure how it would all flow, but I thought of my first line: "I'd always wanted to be a diva, but my lack of natural talent got in the way."

I wanted to convey why winning this funny, seemingly low-stakes singing contest felt meaningful to me and worthy of my ambition. I loved singing and performing with all my heart and soul in high school. But I also loved achievement and winning, and I realized I would never be a good enough singer to really excel at it.

When they called my name, I told my story with the same amount of ambition I'd mustered to beat out all my competitors in Puerto Vallarta, Mexico, and win that tequila-gargling singing competition. Of course, I wasn't *perfect,* but I had a blast! I even got third place, right behind the two guys who do the Moth circuit regularly and had *amazing* stories, clearly well-prepared ahead of time.

I learned a big lesson that night. Magic happens when we set a powerful intention and let go of how it unfolds. The universe has our back, even if we don't know how.

Magic happens when we set a powerful intention and let go of how it unfolds. The universe has our back, even if we don't know how.

Who really knows when the right timing is? We just need to keep leaping towards what we want and laughing with the universe when it goes sideways, knowing we can't see the full path forward.

To see my impromptu Moth *Ambition* performance, watch youtube.com/watch?v=BJCE5_-QhaY or access here:

Gifts of My Moth Opportunistic Disruption

Later, I realized how opportunistic disruption can shatter our limiting beliefs and false assumptions our left brain believes are true. Before that evening, nobody could have convinced me that it wouldn't take me hours upon hours to prepare for a Moth. Now, in five minutes, I'd broken through my limiting perspective by simply doing it—empowered by my heart and soul.

But it went even deeper than just facing my fear with action. I was able to change my story.

The essence of My Moth *Ambition* story was that I believed I didn't have enough talent to sing on a big stage. Yet my impromptu Moth experience showed me I *could* use my voice, just differently than I envisioned: by telling stories that entertain and inspire.

With no preparation, I'd connected to the audience in the moment with a story that lit me up and energized them. I felt alive, happy, and proud. Fear disappeared. The best gift I hadn't seen coming was I unlocked a gateway for more of my authentic self to emerge.

Everything we do opens the door to the next thing. In March 2020, I was paid to be a keynote speaker at the first University of Chicago Women's Business Group, International Women's Day Event, just as I launched my coaching consultancy, Mindfire Mastery. I felt privileged and energized to use my voice to inspire other women professionals. By March 2023, my rate had tripled, as I used my voice more and more.

Life creates opportunities for us all the time. When we take action, we are able to see more clearly how we can reshape our lives for the better, breaking down the invisible barriers that bind us—the gremlins of doubt, assumptions, interpretations, and limiting beliefs.

Flow with Your Whole Brain

How did I prepare for my first Moth? I got in touch with my heart to fuel the content. But I spent much more time in my left brain—writing, editing, and memorizing the story to make it perfect.

In my second Moth, I had a good balance of my left and right brains working interdependently, and I was completely in flow. My right brain was in touch with the experience I was retelling. I could remember the setting, and how I felt watching the other women struggle to gargle and sing. I was able to laugh, smile, and physically show how I was able to dig into my diaphragm and bring that song home! With my tone of voice, positive energy, and body language, I could communicate with much more than my words. I experienced what athletes call being *in the zone*.

You can experience the joy of balance between your right and left brain by simply getting into flow. As children, we do this naturally, feeling pure joy and freedom in the now, whenever we are engaged in an activity where time flies. We all have the ability to do this well when young. However, we learn to be self-conscious and judge ourselves as we grow up, so our left brain interrupts our natural ability to flow with effortless ease. Meaning and flow are two key characteristics of work aligned with our core values and purpose.

Ask yourself: "Where does time flow without my noticing?" When you're completely involved in an activity—

focused, happy, and absorbed, with *just enough challenge*—you are being propelled by intrinsic motivators. This state of flow was discovered by Mihaly Csikszentmihalyi, a Hungarian-American psychologist, who spent more than two decades studying it in individuals. We get out of flow when we're overwhelmed and need to cultivate new skills—or when we're bored and need to increase the challenge.

I experience flow when writing or creating—with time flying by without me needing to eat, drink, or move one inch. Simply going for a walk in nature or taking a bike ride gets me in flow too, creating clarity and new ideas. It can be experienced in any field: when a finance executive is diving into numbers, when musicians are fired up by the music they play, or when surgeons perform operations.

The key is that our mind and body are connected—our right and left brains are balanced. Once that occurs, our typical default state of distracted *monkey mind* goes away, and our critical mind goes with it. Sheer brilliance and joy happen in flow. It's blissful!

As discussed in Chapter 4, flow feels easy, effortless, energizing, and so it's easy to discount it as being valuable. When we are in flow, we are in the zone of our superpowers. The myth is that great work comes from working harder. The truth is that the greatest work comes from being in flow. Realizing where we tap into flow naturally, like delivering my impromptu Moth story, is a great clue to what we may want to do more of in our lives.

Mindfulness helps us ease into flow faster, since we get better at blocking the normal distractions of life, such as the judging chatter of our left brains. Like ice cream, there are so many flavors of mindfulness to try. Meditation and yoga are two ways that I recommend, but it's important to choose which *flavor* works best for you.

Balance of Eustress versus Distress

When both the left and right brain work in flow together—we are in the *good* stress of flow called *eustress,* and we are balanced. We go into *distress,* the *bad* stress, when we become overwhelmed and shift into exhaustion, burnout, and breakdown.

I face eustress when I'm facilitating a workshop or developing a presentation, where I can be visionary and creative. I have just the right amount of adrenaline which keeps my energy and motivation high.

For me, distress kicks in when I'm under a critical deadline, time is running out, and I don't feel I have enough resources to get the job done perfectly. As a recovering perfectionist, I now tell myself "Progress over perfection," so I can stop myself before burning out. Perhaps you can relate to this? I also keep my bad stress on the back burner by starting important projects earlier. When I'm feeling the abundance of time, I enjoy spaciousness for creativity, ease, and flow. To mitigate stress, I reach out to others for external perspective and force myself to take breaks for walks and exercise, which never fails to create room for more innovation and productivity.

As leaders, we have the power to increase flow and eustress with stronger right brain muscles and whole brain power. When we're able to quiet our left brain's inner critic that causes distress, we can flow, flow, flow. In our competitive Western society, we've been continually incented and rewarded to strengthen our left-brain thinking and work harder to achieve. Counterbalancing this requires intentional focus and practice.

That's why mindfulness is so critical for leaders now, so we can wake up to better ways of living and leading at the same time. You knew this when you were a kid, and you lived in the moment, climbing trees and jumping in the lake with friends during the summer. Or when you were kicking a soccer ball into the goal, drawing pictures, writing, and telling creative tales. Just look at a toddler playing on the beach and you remember the joy of being in the present moment. But it's been beaten out of us, and it's time to rekindle the right-brain fire so we can live and lead with more happiness, creativity, and well-being.[80]

The Power of Intention in Action

Focus with the Power Pause

In Chapter 2, we saw the power of pausing in stressful situations. This is particularly useful when we're in a catabolic mode where we have narrowed thinking and can cause damage we'll regret.

We also have the power to pause in anabolic mode—and use focus to drive creative solutions. Wherever we pause, we put focus. For example, if I pause as I'm writing a story or creating a presentation and take a walk, my brain keeps working in the background to fill in the gaps and make connections. This is because I've turned on my RAS and my intention. If we are stuck in a certain place, the Power Pause can be like dousing it with water, to get whatever may be stuck flowing again.

Wicked, complex problems certainly exist that seem to require a high degree of creative technique or skill, but sometimes the tool of focus is the easiest place to start solving them. It's simple and effective.

Remember how the three breaths exercise helps you reduce stress and create a focused path forward when you ask, *What is really important right now?* Well, we can bring this clear level of focus to any topic with powerful results. Just creating the space to focus will unlock more opportunities for new ideas and intentions to unfold.

Once you've created the intention, asking powerful questions frames the focus for our brains to answer them:

- Maybe you want to focus your intention on making something specific even better, like how you spend your meeting time more productively. You can ask: *how can I reduce the number of hours I spend in meetings?*
- Or focus your intention on something general, e.g., Ask: *how to improve meetings?*
- Or simply noticing what is working well on a project, so you can provide encouragement and support to yourself or team members who value meaningful progress. Ask: *what went well?*

> **Pro Tip:** If you are telling yourself, "*I don't know.*" Ask: "*What if I did know?*" You may be surprised by what wisdom you'll unlock.

Intentionally Feel Positive Emotion

Positive emotions are a key aspect of flourishing, so be intentional about feeling them. Gratitude is critical, along with compassion, pride, joy, hope, love, and amusement. When we practice invoking them, we cultivate well-being, reverse the harmful effects of lingering negative emotions, and promote resilience.

As an example, about ten years ago, I began to write *Five Things I'm Grateful For* in my journal each day to become happier. I'd noticed a strong thread of negativity in my journals also seeping into my life, and I wanted to override it. While we all have a negativity bias that naturally seeks out and remembers what went wrong, recall that we can neutralize and override this bias with three-to-five times more positivity. It helps to be specific when expressing gratitude, like saying "I'm grateful for being strong in my high-intensity workout today," instead of "grateful for my health." It worked! I felt increasingly more positive (and still do this practice quite often).

The more we look for anything, the more likely we are to find it. And even better, it's contagious! The more you express gratitude to others, the more they will do so too. It becomes a happy, virtuous circle. In one of my newsletters, I asked my readers to "Take a small action to show someone your gratitude today." Within fifteen minutes, a leader reached out to say he was inspired to share his gratitude with a specific person in his office that day. Two weeks later, he sent me a TED Radio Hour where A. J. Jacobs pulled together a series of TED Talks he was grateful for and why. We both amplified our gratitude, positively influencing each other with ripple effects.

More powerful people tend to express less gratitude at work, so giving the gift of gratitude will make a big impact.[81] You'll likely attract more happiness and influence higher retention with your company.

Discover the Gift and Opportunity

A powerful way to focus on positivity is to ask yourself this question: For every outcome or circumstance that seems *wrong*, what is the opportunity that can be *right*? Essentially, we're asking, "What's the gift?" because, I promise you, there always is one.

Just imagine how many more inventions and opportunities for growth would arise if more people could tap into the power of their whole brain to find a gift in any situation.

In a walk in the woods in 1943, George de Mestral got the idea for Velcro from cockleburs that got caught on his clothes and dog's fur. On closer inspection through a microscope, he realized the burr's hooks would stick to anything loop-shaped. So he created a hook-and-loop fastener of his own. It took eight years to experiment, develop, and perfect the invention that is now used ubiquitously, based on finding the gift.[82]

Importantly, positivity can be toxic if we ignore reality. However, if we accept the situation, we can convert anything into a gift or opportunity.

As we know from the power of neuroplasticity, our brain can be trained to take a new path if we keep diverting it from the old one. So asking for gifts will get new neurons firing together and wiring together to innovate faster.

In my own life, I do this activity often, and I've become better at converting my challenges and mistakes in positive ways.

My Challenging Obstacles	Upside Gift or Opportunity
Getting breast cancer and needing to fight for my life.	Learning to let go of control and empower others, while giving and receiving compassion.
Reporting to a new boss who didn't value my role or contribution as a CMO in our post-acquisition world.	Realizing my power to say, "No," and create an exit package to open the door to a more meaningful next act.
Losing my job when my husband was unemployed, with two kids under the age of three, a full-time nanny, and a big mortgage.	Creating a better balance between work and family while reclaiming control of my weight (lost forty-two pounds in six months).

My Challenging Obstacles	Upside Gift or Opportunity
Getting feedback on how I could improve as a facilitator.	Strengthening my facilitation for multiple clients on bigger stages.
Every time I come into conflict with someone.	Explore my blind spots for growth.

Intentional Focus On Purpose

When we create a laser-sharp focus, we get results. It's why Japanese noodle shops excel — they focus on udon or ramen, not both. It's how elite athletes excel — they put their 10,000+ hours into their sport of choice: basketball, or baseball, not both.

My mother loved to remind me, "You can't dance at every wedding," even though I desperately wanted to! She wisely recommended we focus on what truly matters to soar to new heights — instead of spreading ourselves too thin and falling flat on the ground.

When we combine purpose with intention, we create more power to achieve greatly. Each of us is here for a great purpose, and yet we can get confused, sidetracked, and distracted. Then, we don't make progress on what we are here to do. This is the issue many of us faced at a four-day Transformation Retreat, which was all about progressing with your purpose. Together, we coined the phrase, "Follow the Thread", which I've found to be a motivating mantra to stay on track with my biggest intentions.

Attaining My First C-Suite Role

Here's an example of how I leveraged the power of intention and purpose to clarify and achieve a big, audacious goal. Sharing my intention amplified its power and accelerated my results.

In early May 2008, I served as a Marketing Director for a financial services firm and felt ready for a change to a new marketing role. While I had a general intention, I lacked clarity on what my move should be, so I started working with a coach.

I began by sharing the inner work I'd already done to define my purpose: to inspire others to grow their businesses. With her disruptive questions, she challenged me to dig deep and discover more of my inner fire. I realized I ignited growth by being both a creator and a connector, which helped me envision my greater leadership potential.

Based on our work, I set a clear, more specific intention — to lead a growing global marketing team as a Chief Marketing Officer. What's more, I started communicating this intention with others in my company, including our firm-wide Chief Marketing Officer. She hadn't realized I was ready for a change and shared her plan to create a new CMO position to do exactly what I wanted — lead a global marketing team across our two institutional businesses. Even though I hadn't worked in either area before, I had the conviction of being rock-solidly aligned with my intention and purpose — so I put my hat in the ring, prepared well, and interviewed.

By July 2008, just two months later, my intention came to fruition; I became the new global CMO across our institutional businesses! It was a dream come true — until the financial crisis struck two months later. Even though the crisis was challenging, demanding, and stressful, I was able to keep my fire burning with abundant resilience, since I was so aligned with my purpose.

**Intention (mind's energy) + Purpose (inner fire) =
Authentic Success**

Amplifying Intentions

There is huge power in knowing our essence, values, and purpose. They're like seeds we've planted that grow with the water of our heart-driven intention. Connecting to others through our experiences is like bringing sunlight to our soil, helping us to flourish even faster.

After two decades at the same law firm, Mike intended to find a new firm to maximize his earning potential on his own terms. Within several months, his clear intention, purpose, and communications had resulted in multiple great offers from which to choose.

Cindy intended to sell her business and create a meaningful second act. She tapped into the power of coaching to help her clarify her purpose so she could see new possibilities.

Setting your intention is the closest thing to magic I've experienced in life. It's like planting a magic beanstalk that reaches up to the sky, extending toward any star we desire. What's frustrating is that we can't see its path as it grows.

This doesn't mean we don't set plans or take action. But it does mean we need to be able to let go of our tight reins of control and trust that the universe is working on our behalf. Embracing this duality is key: focus your energy on your desires while relinquishing control of how they manifest. Then we can adapt with agility (the focus of our next chapter).

Chapter Mindset:	From: Burned Out Leader	To: Shining Authentic Leader
6: Focus with strong *intentions* and let go of how they unfold.	Holds tightly to reins of control which impedes flow—harming productivity and resilience.	Creates whole-brain intentions that feed flow—fueling productivity and perseverance.

FAST Framework

Exercises: You can do these exercises on your own, or go to www.ShiningThroughDisruption.com/resources to access the workbook and guided practices.

1. Journal for three minutes on each of these prompts:
    o What's a powerful intention you want to set in motion to drive new outcomes?
    o Why is it important and meaningful for you?
    o What must you let go of now?
2. For each meeting and activity you do this week, ask: "What is my intention for being here?" See how your intention shapes your experience more powerfully.
3. Focused Breath Micro-practice: For two minutes, bring attention to your breath, breathing in and out. If your mind wanders (and it will), no problem; just gently bring your attention back to focusing on your breath.

Chapter 7

Adapt with Agility

Act as if it were impossible to fail.
—Dorothea Brande

Accept and Begin Again—Lin-Manuel Miranda Story

In 2015, I almost met Lin-Manuel Miranda, but I blew it. He's on my list of top humans I would most want to meet, and I regretted it ever since.

Lin walked out of the Shubert Theatre in New York City just as I was walking in. I recognized him immediately, but I was too stunned to move. *He wasn't supposed to be here—Hamilton was playing in another theater!* In the few moments it took me to regain my senses, he was already walking quickly down the street, far enough away that I would need to run like a mad stalker to catch him.

Even so, I thought, *Should I run after him?* I'd say what an absolute genius and inspiration he is, and how much I enjoyed seeing him in *Hamilton* the night before, on my fiftieth birthday, and how I'd been blown away by *In the Heights* seven years before. But I decided to be civilized and let Lin go. I held onto this failure, telling myself a chance to meet Lin (or fill in your own star) comes along once in a lifetime.

Fast forward to Thursday, April 25, 2019. I received a cryptic text from my husband, Peter, at 6 p.m., which simply said, "He's here. Go find him."

Lin had tweeted a poem about Chicago, the Cubs, and hot dogs—it was clear he was in our town. But where? I began sleuthing, and I found only one article, but it was enough. *Hamilton: The Exhibition* was to open that weekend.

I was excited to learn that the first visitors to arrive on Saturday would get to meet Lin, but unfortunately also discovered no tickets were still available. (Many people had apparently been more on the ball than I.) Thankfully, I had one other option: he was speaking at the press conference on Friday. My plan was to crash it.

The problem was, I didn't know where it was or when it would happen. However, as a marketer, I made two reasonable assumptions:

1. It would occur at the exhibition venue on Northerly Island.
2. It would be held at cocktail hour.

I planned to be *in the room where it happened.*

On Friday, I biked to my exercise class at lunchtime and then biked the eight miles south to Northerly Island along the lakefront. I was still in my exercise clothes with no makeup, which somehow lowered the stakes.

Instead of setting up a win/lose scenario, where I'd only win if I met Lin and lose if I didn't, I told myself the encouraging story that I would win by simply giving it a shot. That way, I wouldn't chicken out and live to regret what may have happened. No matter what, I'd enjoy a great bike ride on the lakefront. I had a strong intention of finding Lin, but I let go of the outcome and embraced a spirit of play and adventure.

As I neared the *Hamilton* exhibition, I heard the song *Meant To Be* surface on my playlist and got chills.

Boldly, I passed the guard station and headed right up to the building, a former airplane hangar. After locking my bike, I bravely walked up to let myself in. Unfortunately, I discovered the first door was locked, as were the second and the third. I tried to keep my cool, and nonchalantly tried the fourth and final door—thankfully, it opened!

Once I stepped inside, I realized my timing couldn't have been more perfect. They were announcing Lin and the designer, David Korins, to go on stage for the press conference to begin. I found an unobtrusive spot with a perfect view of Lin and took a selfie with him in the background to prove I'd made it. Then I focused on every word they said about their audacious vision— to make history fun, engaging, immersive, and educational. I didn't think I could love Lin even more, but now I did.

After the press conference ended, Lin exited the stage, and I excitedly moved closer to meet him. But alas, he was whisked away before I could introduce myself. Was I disappointed? Yes, but I was grateful I'd seen him and enjoyed myself, so I let go of any further expectations.

Yet, something kept me hanging around. Maybe it was the waiter who offered me hors d'oeuvres. Cocktail hour was beginning, followed by a ribbon-cutting ceremony and there was excitement bubbling in the air. I thought, *Why not stay and see what else unfolds?* I was having fun! I ran into a friend in the media (who probably could have gotten me a legit ticket), and then I wandered into the gift shop to look for souvenirs. To my amazement, I saw Lin, standing in the corner, talking to a friend.

Suddenly, I realized, *I am not throwing away my shot to meet Lin!* I took a deep breath and walked towards him with a big smile that I hoped looked friendly versus crazy. I remember the moment his eyes locked on mine, and I could see an openness and willingness to engage, even though he didn't know who the heck I was. I introduced myself and told him our story of almost meeting in NYC on that fateful day in 2015.

As the words poured out of me, he listened with such mindful attention. I didn't think I could like him even more, and there I was, my awe redoubled. With his presence and kindness, he inspires me now as a leader and role model beyond his brilliance at his craft.

What's more, I realized the liberating power of setting a strong intention and letting go of how it unfolds. By leaning into agility, I can create new possibilities.

Success and Failure

Whenever we succeed or fail, we have a tendency to latch onto that moment as if it's permanent. But it's not. In the next moment, we always have the option to *accept, let go* and *begin again*. When we don't, we're a prisoner, like the royals in *Game of Thrones* who lived in fear of losing the throne, or those who judged themselves failures for never achieving it. When we realize nothing lasts, life is freeing! It's like waking up from a bad dream and realizing it's just not real. Who knows when something begins and something ends? They are two sides of the same coin, as are joy and suffering, dark and light. Keep showing up and magic will happen when we least expect it.

Survey: Craving Control versus Letting Go

In 2019, I surveyed hundreds of executives to learn what got in the way of bouncing forward from big disruption. Based on the results, the number one challenge was, "Letting go of the outcome." Interestingly, there was a subgroup of people who were better at letting go: those who had experienced disruptive, existential crises.

This makes perfect sense. High-achieving professionals want more *control* to drive successful outcomes. They get rewarded for creating order from chaos, so they double down on control as uncertainty increases. But those who undergo a huge disruption begin to realize that control is often an illusion. They discern what's truly controllable and what isn't. Then, they can let go of the disruptive stress that's simply not controllable.

Learning to Let Go from Pandemic Chaos

If there was any doubt before, the Covid-19 global pandemic showed how little control we have over what happens in life. At every conference I've attended since the pandemic, each speaker's narrative has a *before* and *after* story, because everyone needed to suddenly adapt.

I'm sure each of you has a unique story about how life changed dramatically in ways you didn't expect during that chaotic, uncertain time.

For me, when the pandemic struck, I'd just become certified to teach mindful emotional intelligence in a two-day, high-touch, in-person transformative experience. Suddenly, this was no longer an option. Along with my fellow global teachers at Search Inside Yourself (SIY), we pivoted as quickly as possible, but it was tough.

I'm thankful SIY built new tools and techniques so we could deliver the experience online without sacrificing quality. But I still faced two issues. First, I couldn't find people who wanted to spend two days online while the world was falling down around them—and second, I wasn't confident with technology. So, I needed to adapt again, creating and delivering shorter-length workshops online and building new skills, including *technological confidence and equanimity*, so I could roll with whatever happened.

In the fall of 2020, I was delivering a ninety-minute live online workshop, *Four Keys to Resilience*, to all six hundred incoming MBA students at the University of Chicago Booth School of Business, as they began business school virtually. Despite all our prep beforehand, my technology froze briefly—but felt like an eternity. I took three breaths and kept my calm, but I was not as self-compassionate as I would be today. After the session, though, I learned from my client that during the technology glitch, the chat room blew up with how terrific the training was! This insight helped me release my judgment and adapt to the new normal.

Change the Formula, Change the Results

When we try something new, and we fall down literally or figuratively, it can feel painful in the moment. But our bigger problem is when we pile on how horrific it was, which makes it feel exponentially worse. When we resist reality, or judge what's happened as *bad*, we pile on and create more suffering.

Judgment + Resistance = Suffering

To shift to *our greater energetic potential*, we need to let go of resistance and accept what has happened to make space for what can really emerge now.

The more empowering formula is:

Acceptance + Choice = New Opportunity

How to Practice? Learn your ABCs

Instead of the binary *Yes* or *No*, *Success* or *Failure*, remember what it was like being a kindergartner when you were simply in the moment. My ABC model unleashes the inner child in each of us so we can adapt and thrive no matter what happens. (It also jives with what I learned as a mindfulness teacher, executive coach, facilitator, and improvisation graduate.)

A = Accept What's Happening

Acceptance is the essential first step, which means being aware of what's happening and letting go of judgment. If we have one foot still embedded in the past, it is very difficult to step into the future. We get stuck wishing for what was or grasping for an ideal state that isn't possible now. But if we accept what's unfolding and embrace it, we can move past rumination, regret, disappointment, and sadness. This is a stoic philosophy concept, known as *Armor Fati*. It doesn't mean that we're stuck with the situation, only that we're releasing judgment of what's really unfolding.

B = Begin Again (And Breathe!)

Sometimes we fall down and it feels like the end of the world because the world we know is irrevocably changed. While it is the end of something, it's the beginning of something else. We often need time and the support of others to help us gain perspective. But in the moment, we can always take a mindful breath to calm ourselves. Then, choose to begin again and wipe the slate clean. As Shunryu Suzuki said, "In the beginner's mind there are many possibilities, but in the expert's mind there are few."[83]

It helps to embrace a growth mindset, believing that we can learn and reshape whatever happens.[84] If we think we have all the answers, what growth is possible? Intentional disruption is a great way to begin again, helping us see things afresh and create new neural pathways. With the pandemic, we were forced to rethink and begin again at work and home, well beyond our comfort zones. Yet, we have the ability to embrace change and create anew each day with an adventurous mindset.

C = Create Opportunity

In the last chapter, we found the gift from whatever happens by focusing on this powerful question: "What's the opportunity?" This query opens the portal for our brain to create new possibilities even faster and faster. If the gift eludes us, we can dive into positive action and discover what happens.

As leaders, the sooner we accept and adapt to what's happening, the faster we create new opportunities for success. Entrepreneurs and smaller businesses often have an edge over corporations in being more agile in finding the cracks and maneuvering through them.

Outstanding at Change

I am in awe of how the organization Outstanding in the Field (OITF) has cracked the code of adapting to change, beginning again, and finding new opportunities. Their unique business model embraces the most volatile of all things—our unpredictable weather. A great part of their magic is accepting whatever happens and improvising.

OITF is essentially a roving restaurant that travels the world to create unique, unrepeatable alfresco dining experiences. Each dinner celebrates ingredients harvested from the setting (farm, vineyard, or seashore), created by different local chefs. Their guests gather for one magical night, convening at one long, iconic outdoor table that seats up to two hundred diners. Part of the adventure is embracing the wildcard of the weather, which is out of everyone's control. But OITF is masterful at planning and adapting, so they deliver an outstanding experience, whatever the meteorological conditions. They have been to our orchard dozens of times and really shine through disruption. One year, a downpour arrived just before dinner, and we all ran into the cider barn, which had been magically transformed into a lovely restaurant with flickering candles. Through the open barn doors, we watched the rainstorm during our meal. Then, along with dessert, we were treated to a beautiful double rainbow (I'm still marveling how they pulled that off!).

Lessons from Improvisation

In 1997, I worked for a leading advertising agency that understood improvisation was a great tool to help us become more creative, collaborative, and agile leaders—a big advantage in our idea-driven business. They offered us the opportunity to take improvisation classes at the Players Workshop of the Second City, and I jumped at the chance. This is where I realized the importance of our ABCs for success in business and life.

As the first class began, I was very nervous. *Am I going to be any good at this?* But they immediately got us out of our heads by encouraging us to run around the room like kindergarten children at recess. We screamed with unbridled joy and exuberance. It was pure playfulness without fear of judgment, and I can still feel that exhilaration and freedom in my body when I recall that experience. We all knew how it felt as children—to be utterly alive in the present moment with wide-eyed wonder and curiosity.

Once we felt safe, we could dive in and play. We soon learned that some improv games flowed well and others completely flopped. The key was simply to be present in the moment, so we could accept, begin again, and create anew.

When you improvise, you gain confidence that you can handle anything that arises, which helps you let go of fear and become a better leader across life.[85] Working interdependently forces you to listen and pay close attention. Together, it's possible to create something magical, beyond what anyone could have imagined on their own. This entails really noticing what's happening. For example, picking up cues from body language allows you to work with *anything* your partner gives you, even if it's subconscious.

A nifty trick I learned was that if you couldn't think of anything to say, you just started moving your body. With movement, your mind relaxes and thoughts naturally form, so words will follow. And frankly, just moving your body can be funny and entertaining all on its own. Plus, you can spark your scene partners' creativity, without knowing how.

Moving helps you get out of your critical left-brain, which gets stuck thinking about the past or future, overanalyzes what went well or didn't, and causes you to freeze with fear. Being grounded in your body and right brain keeps you floating *above the line* where you can co-create with openness and joy.

Innovating with the Power of Yes

One of my favorite improv tools for creating new possibilities was *The Power of Yes*. We simply learned to say, "Yes, and..." instead of, "No." Nothing closes down creativity faster than pessimism, so you surrender to "Yes," which opens the doorway to new ideas. "No" is another way of saying, "I don't accept this," while "Yes" lets things flow. Nothing is too crazy either. For example, if your partner says, "Let's build a tower to the sky!" you can respond, "Sure, let's use my magic rope to the clouds!"

Brainstorming: Diverge Then Converge

In business, "Yes" leads to more possibilities too. In brainstorming sessions, our fundamental rule is, "No idea is a bad idea." This is a great way to create positive energy that attracts and builds, leading to innovation (candy also helps!). We begin with *divergence*, generating many ideas. Later, we use *convergence*, relying on the strengths of our left-brain rational mind to organize and explore which ideas to shape, drop, or pursue. The key is to quiet our critical minds upfront, so they don't interfere with letting our creativity run wild to create more possibilities.

I saw the potential damage of "No" when I tried to control an improv scene. Whenever I had an idea about where a scene should go and tried to push it that way, it felt harder, because people had minds of their own. The best scenes were truly about releasing expectations and co-creating in the moment. We responded with agility in ways that surprised and delighted us. And when things didn't work, we laughed. We all suffered failures, so we had compassion and the knowledge and perspective that we weren't alone.

In business meetings, especially when we are in the midst of uncertainty—whether it's a crisis or creating something new—we need to release our strong need for control. More important than having a tight agenda or plan, uncertainty calls for strong intention and agility. And remembering your ABCs, so you Accept, Begin Again, and Create Opportunity—together.

How Psychological Safety Impacts Teams and Creativity

Google did robust research on what makes the best teams by analyzing nearly 200 internal high-performing teams, so they could reverse engineer what drove success.[86] What they discovered surprised them.

They expected team success might be driven by the experience of the leader, how well the team got along, or how complementary their skills were. But above all else, the top factor predicting team success was *psychological safety*, just like my improv class. When we trust those we work with, our work just keeps getting better, as more of our holistic brilliance (mind, heart, and gut) is safe to shine through.

I've noticed this in myself and maybe you do too. When I'm my best self, where I'm articulate and most creative, I feel completely safe to be me. At other times, when I've been in environments where I don't feel safe to voice what I feel, I pre-judge myself. I hold myself back from speaking or overthink what I'll say. I feel like a different person. And I would kick myself when someone else would voice what was on my mind.

Creating *trusted environments*, showing up grounded and present in our bodies, and leaning into "Yes and..." are ways we can respond with agility to anything. And we get immediate feedback to learn what's working, and what isn't, so we can adjust in real time. In my improv group, I grew to feel so safe that I accessed more creativity and kept surprising myself with what I could do. I'll never forget the day I improvised a song with a cool melody and perfectly rhymed lyrics. They simply flowed out of me as if I did it every day (which I absolutely don't).

I was thirty-one years old and hadn't felt this kind of safety in the workplace. I realized it was extremely special and didn't want to let it go. Even though I became pregnant with my first child a couple of months into classes, I kept attending sessions. I didn't even pause during my maternity leave, so I could participate in our improv graduation show at the year's end. My baby daughter, Mikaela, waved at us (with help) from the audience. My engagement was off the charts, and it started with feeling safe, so my authentic self could shine through. Research overwhelmingly shows that when people believe they can speak up at work, their organizations experience greater learning, innovation, and performance.[87]

Embracing *Perfectly Imperfect* for Greater Agility

As someone with hyper-achiever and perfectionist tendencies, I've always placed enormous pressure on myself to reach the next milestone beyond reproach, which has slowed me down when I'm facing big new challenges or disruptions. My *it's-not-good-enough-yet* mindset is very typical of high-achieving professionals who crave control and typically accumulate more as they rise to higher levels. This makes volatile, uncertain times that much harder to swallow.

At work, my tendency was to not share my ideas until I felt they were ready for prime time, which often led to disappointment if they weren't accepted. As an entrepreneur, this kept me from progressing, testing, and learning.

While I've worked to weaken my sabotaging tendencies for years, they really flared up during my book-writing journey, since it's such a big-stakes project that opened me up to greater vulnerability. Instead of my limiting belief, *It's not perfect yet,* I adopted the more empowering belief of *progress over perfection.* This perspective allowed me to share my work in progress sooner and learn how to improve it for readers and clients.

I also realized that perfection wasn't truly possible. In a master class led by bestselling author Malcolm Gladwell, he helped me realize that no book can ever be truly perfect, even his own. Books stop evolving at our fixed publish date, while we never do.

These powerful reframes allowed me to share my ideas earlier with collaborators, such as The University of Chicago Booth School of Business, which led me to launch my *Mindful Leadership* course for their Executive Education curriculum two years before I published this book on which it's based! Ironically, if I'd waited to get it all *perfect,* I'd have lost the opportunity to keep improving and continuously learning from the hundreds of leaders who have now taken my course. It's a virtuous cycle that begins with a whole-brain mindset that *all is perfectly imperfect now.* What's amazing to me is that during dark times when I felt the book wasn't *good enough,* I reminded myself of the great impact I was already seeing from leaders who took my course, which fueled my confidence to persevere and finish it.

It's liberating to embrace the Japanese life view of Wabi Sabi which views *everything or every situation as perfectly imperfect.*[88] In the artistic realm, this philosophy is expressed in Kintsugi, the Japanese art of repairing broken pottery. While the artist can't restore the piece to its original perfection, they fill the gaps with gold, silver, or platinum, which

It's liberating to embrace the Japanese life view of Wabi Sabi which views everything or every situation as perfectly imperfect.

makes the imperfections vital in transforming the piece into a new state of imperfectly perfect beauty. Like pottery, our human vessels evolve with wrinkles and scars that can deepen our beauty if we accept and embrace them with care, allowing our next phase to emerge as gracefully as a butterfly from its chrysalis.

Randy's Story

My friend Randy's story shows the power we have to reframe failure, begin again, and thrive with new possibilities. In 2011, Randy, an architect, found himself newly unemployed for the first time in twenty-five years and aspired to reinvent himself as a speaker and author. He secured a huge speaking opportunity at his industry's Knowledge Management conference and knew it could launch him on a successful new trajectory as a thought leader. To differentiate himself, he painstakingly crafted his talk, determined to deliver it TED Talk-style, from memory, to give his audience the perfect experience.

For months, he diligently prepared. He got the content just right, memorized each word, and practiced it to perfection. He visualized how successful he'd feel walking off that stage after delivering his stellar performance. As the day loomed closer, Randy felt confident that he was going to *hit the ball out of the ballpark.*

Finally, the day of the big conference arrived. Randy walked out on the stage to an audience of 350 people, intending to dazzle them.

But that isn't what happened, not by a long shot.

Randy couldn't remember a single word. With all eyes on him, and a cameraman videoing the entire debacle, he fumbled around searching for notes on his phone. After several awkward minutes, he simply walked off the stage, never uttering a word.

Despite months of preparation, practice, perseverance, and his passion to be perfect, he *had failed epically.* If his talk was meant to be the perfect vase, Randy had just smashed it to the floor and broken it into pieces.

After Randy's talk-that-never-was, there was a panel discussion where the five preceding speakers returned to the stage. To everyone's shock and surprise, Randy joined them, just minutes after exiting the stage in silence. Randy said, "Not only did I participate, I knocked it out of the park!"

Afterward, the event organizer took Randy aside and said, "Holy cow! You just blew up on stage and then you're able to perform like that. I would have gone into hiding!"

Randy excelled at his ABCs: Accepting, Beginning Again, and Creating Opportunity. He could have held onto his vision of what *should have been* and not let it go. Instead, he accepted the situation and dove into action, choosing not to beat himself up by ruminating over the past. Just like Kintsugi pottery, Randy filled in the hole he'd created with gold—creating a perfect outcome for an imperfect situation.

What that 350-person audience saw was not a broken man, but a brave one—shining with brilliant ideas through the cracks he'd recently revealed. And this created real magic for years to come. Randy said, "What's remarkable is that all these people who I didn't know in the audience would go on and be so helpful to me in my life. Twenty or more incredible things happened from people in the room that I didn't even know before that event."

Randy is now a prolific author who speaks around the globe and also teaches as a university professor who continues to adapt with creativity. He has since collaborated with many in the audience that day, including a Harvard instructor and an audience member who buys all Randy's books as client gifts (after she sends them to Randy to autograph each one).

Negative events are going to happen. Some of them will be within our control and some won't. Yet, the real power comes from realizing that we can always choose our response. Anyone who aspires to pivot or grow is going to find themselves in new and scary situations. They may get hijacked and feel the sting of failure, as Randy did. Failing only turns to failure if we refuse to move beyond our current limits. When we go down the negative shame spiral of intense disappointment and judgment, we don't take action. When we let go and move forward, even if it's just one step at a time, we rise even higher.

Don't be afraid to start over again. You may like your new story even better.

The Power of 3:1 Positivity to Negativity Ratio

Positivity helps us stay in the game and prevail. But as you know, given our strong negativity bias, we need at least three positive thoughts to override each negative one. When Randy acted quickly, he built positives to neutralize the negative keynote experience. This helped him adapt, recover faster, and find new possibilities beyond what he originally envisioned.

Negative Thoughts:	Positive Thoughts:
1. *I failed to deliver my keynote speech and left the stage without saying a word.*	1. *I have another opportunity to speak—on the upcoming panel!* 2. *Wow! They liked that answer. I can do this!* 3. *I knocked that panel out of the park!* 4. *That applause from the audience feels so good.* 5. *The conference organizer is really influential, and he's blown away by my comeback.*

By the time the panel was over, Randy had neutralized the negative experience with at least five positives, which was possible because he accepted his situation, began again, and created new outcomes.

Whether we choose positivity or negativity, we will get what we choose. Which outcome would you prefer?

Superpower of Optimism: Adapt Faster

What separates star performers from the rest, whether they're athletes, professionals in business, medicine, or law, or an architect turned thought leader is this: they're able to adapt with the right balance of optimism and realism, faster and faster, under disruptive pressure. Optimism doesn't mean we aren't seeing what's really happening. It means we're not succumbing to pessimism to process it.

> **Optimism doesn't mean we aren't seeing what's really happening. It means we're not succumbing to pessimism to process it.**

What We Can Learn from Elite Athletes

Athletes are like improvisers because they are literally playing a game (albeit with high stakes), as part of an interconnected team and never knowing how it will go. All they can do is prepare, show up with the best intentions, and be present in each moment. Working with their teammates, they respond to opportunities and challenges throughout the game—and keep rebalancing their mindset. It's challenging, but it's also an exciting adventure. And the elite know it requires mental fitness as well as physical.

Story—Mindful Mike

In 1997, I got to see one of the best elite athletes in action, when my boss asked me to attend a Bulls game with clients one evening. When I called my husband to let him know why I'd be working late, he screamed, "You get to see Michael Jordan in the playoffs!"

I had no idea how lucky I was at the beginning of the night, but I certainly did by the end! Seeing Michael Jordan play basketball was a life-changing experience for me. I saw beauty, bravery, boldness, and artistry in motion. I saw a passionate, masterful leader at the top of his game, who inspired everyone around him to achieve higher potential. I felt like time stopped as he soared through the air to make his breathtaking dunk shots. How did he do these superhuman feats, especially when the pressure and stakes were so high?

Michael was coached by Zen master, Phil Jackson, whose philosophy may have been part of the inspiration for one of my favorite shows, Ted Lasso (Jason Sudeikis plays a soccer coach who exudes mindful positivity and garners the love and respect of his team). Phil and Michael won six NBA Finals together, including the year I attended in 1997. In a 1998 interview, Jordan credits Jackson with teaching him to calm his body and emotions during pressure-filled situations. He explained, "What I do is I challenge myself in big games. I try to find a quiet center within me because there's so much hype out there and I don't want to fall into it."[89]

Jordan knew how to prevent getting hijacked by the pressure through the discipline of mindfulness. While a fierce competitor, he also knew how to stay grounded with the perspective of *It's a game*, and not fall into the negativity spiral when it didn't go his way. He mastered being completely aware in the present moment, so he could strategically choose how to deploy his energy to win. Thankfully, our positive energy is contagious too, so it helps lift everyone around us. But it starts with us.

For a big infusion of positive energy with Jordan's winning smile, I recommend checking out the classic "I want to be like Mike" Gatorade commercial. I dare you not to smile!

The Bullet Time Effect

In the film *The Matrix*, Keanu Reeves played Neo, who seemed able to stop time just as Michael Jordan did, with the Bullet Time Effect. In an amazing scene, bullets shoot fast and furiously at Neo, and he expertly weaves around each one to save himself. His superpower is to be so fully present that he can respond with such agility, almost as if he is slowing down time.

With expanded mindfulness, we can slow down in each moment to choose our response versus reacting compulsively. Knowing we have the power to handle anything that flies at us brings incredible confidence. We realize we can create the lives we choose, and begin again, no matter what the circumstances.

Anyone who has been in an accident (or narrowly avoided one) has experienced this time effect to some degree. I once skidded on black ice on the highway and felt my car do a 180-degree turn, moving as if I were in slow motion. Time appeared to slow down, because my right brain and body took over with a heightened awareness of all my senses, enabling me to face the threat at hand. As I spun around on the highway, that moment was embedded in my body's memory forever. Super agility comes from the ability to stop and take a pause consciously, without a life-threatening incident.

Implications for Leaders—Innovation + EQ

Building adaptive agility is key for creativity and design thinking—the process used to build innovative products, design a better future, and solve *wicked problems* (where we're dealing with constantly changing issues that need to be addressed iteratively, in an interconnected way).

I find it fascinating how all the steps of design thinking parallel the building blocks of emotional intelligence. Essentially, becoming a better leader sets you up for greater success in innovation as well.

With design thinking, there are six stages that aren't linear, but a good place to start is *Accept*. As we learned in this chapter, acceptance allows us to begin again and create anew with a compassionate growth mindset. The other stages are *Empathize*, understanding what's important to stakeholders and digging to learn more; *Define*, focusing with awareness on what's most important; *Ideate,* innovating new ideas; *Prototype,* envisioning and stretching into new areas of possibility; and *Test,* making choices, failing fast, reflecting and learning—all of which motivates true transformation.

In a workshop I designed for Indonesian leaders who wanted to build EQ and Innovation skills, our concluding breakout addressed this big question: *How might we drive greater innovation with emotional intelligence?* They brainstormed, crowdsourced, and converged on principles, which overwhelmingly featured empathy as the star. Empathy is critical to forge deep connections and insights, which is why we practice exercises such as Mindful and Empathetic Listening (Chapter 3). We cannot build anything effectively—from a new product to a relationship—if we don't deeply understand *what* or *who* we're dealing with. They also arrived at this human insight: *A big smile is where connection begins.* They intuitively realized the power that comes from positive energy to create a safe space for innovation to flourish.

For companies and their leaders, it can seem overwhelming to dive into messy, non-linear *wicked problems* that are changing constantly, just as we do. That's why values, purpose, and vision are paramount to adapting well. With *values,* we're grounded in what's most important, which anchors us amid swirling change. With *purpose,* we can make choices that feel right amid myriad options. And with *vision,* we can move forward, even if we don't have a clear roadmap on how. We learn and redefine along the way to build a future beyond what we can even imagine.

In our own way, human beings are *wicked problems* to solve. Empathy helps us better understand ourselves so we can adapt and stretch into evolved identities. Through testing, learning, and iterating, we change who we are and how we relate to our interconnected world. (More on stretching in Chapter 8, and thriving connections in Chapters 9 and 10).

Chapter Mindset	From: Burned Out Leader	To: Shining Authentic Leader
7: Adapt with ABCs: Accept, Begin Again, and Create *innovation*.	Latches onto success and failure as permanent— adopting a win/lose fixed mindset.	Knows success and failure are temporary— adopting a win/ learn growth mindset.

FAST Framework

FOCUS | ADAPT | STRETCH | THRIVE

Intention   Innovation   Identity   Interconnection

Exercises: You can do these exercises on your own, or go to www.ShiningThroughDisruption.com/resources to access the workbook and guided practices.

1. Three good things and why: Each day this week, think of three positive things about your day and write them down. Be specific about why they are good (e.g., instead of *good health*, maybe *that thirty-minute workout I did today because I'm building strength at my age*; or instead of *family*, try *speaking with my father and cheering him up*). Include how it made you feel at the time, and how you feel now. Tap into what caused this event and your part in it. Many studies show when people do this regularly, they report feeling more optimistic and better about their lives overall, which is key for resiliency.

2. Try the "Yes, and..." improv game with one or more people around this topic: *How can we increase mindfulness practice at work or home?*
   - First person: What I like about that idea is... (focus on the 20 percent you like), and... (Add another idea that's triggered by what you liked).
   - Then rotate around the others until you feel complete.

3. Open Awareness Practice: Take a few breaths in and intentionally longer exhales. Then let your breath settle into its natural rhythm. For the next two minutes, expand your awareness to include whatever is arising, with an attitude of curiosity and spaciousness. Let thoughts, sensations, feelings, and sounds come and go. Watching them arise and pass away, like clouds in the sky.

Chapter 8

Stretch Your Identity

If you change the way you look at things,
the things you look at change.
—Wayne Dyer

The Power of Envisioning—My Best-Case Eulogy Story

It was summer 2018, and I'd just left my CMO position to take time to relax and figure out my next move. Another CMO in transition recommended reading Burton and Wedemeyer's *In Transition: From the Harvard Business School Club of New York's Career Management Seminar*.[90] One of its recommended exercises was to write my Best-Case Eulogy. This is where I had to summarize my life so far—and write about my future life in any way I chose. Yet, I could only see a continuation of my current life as a CMO, followed by the classic retirement dream of walking off into the sunset. It didn't light me up, and I didn't believe it would lead to the true impact I desired to make in the world.

So, I threw out my first draft and began again.

I'd spent my life chasing accomplishments, and I'd racked up some good ones in my career. I'd supported causes I cared about with my time and money. But my biggest meaning came from raising my two daughters, who were now ready to launch lives of their own. While they would always be a part of my life, one thought kept nagging me: What would give meaning to my next chapter of life?

I couldn't help feeling as if my best days were behind me, yet I knew I could have decades more to live. So I pushed myself to be brutally honest and tap into my heart and soul's desires, even if it scared me.

I started to envision a new future—where I reinvented my career and never wanted to retire because I was having too much fun. Excitement coursed through me. I even boldly stated I'd written a book in my fifties to inspire others to step into their greater potential.

"The best part of the book is that Stephanie admitted she didn't know exactly where it would lead, but like the improv she took as a young adult, she just needed to start doing it and see what unfolded."

With my eulogy, I felt my life's purpose and vision to be a published author emerge—not eventually, but in this decade. I was already fifty-three, so the clock was ticking.

Nearly a year later, as I was moving forward to become a leadership coach and instructor, I discovered my life's mission workbook that I'd completed in July 1996, twenty-three years before. I was surprised to find I was following my long-held dream, expressed but forgotten within those 155 pages: "to write a book and teach seminars on how to live and lead a better, happier, more fulfilling life, helping people look at things in creative, different ways." Immediately, I understood what had gotten in my way. I'd placed my dream on a shelf with my limiting beliefs, convinced that I couldn't be successful enough.

Envisioning the end of my life created the urgency to live it more fully now. When we envision the future we desire, we put energy towards making it a reality. We get closer to doing what we're meant to do.

In my eulogy, I planted a seed to write my book, but this time I didn't put it on a shelf. *I sprinkled it* with water by making it part of my core identity. And I gave it sunlight by sharing my vision with my network, family, and friends. With these actions, my dream started to take root, and I was inspired to do more. I interviewed a couple of writers to learn about their process. I wrote in my journals and captured thoughts as they came to me while biking or walking. I interviewed people about the topic of disruption and learned how they reshaped their lives. I looked for patterns in those that grew in positive ways. I was motivated, even though I had no structured game plan or guarantee of success.

In March 2019, six months after writing my eulogy, one of the people with whom I'd shared my intention connected me to a Book Creators Group. I joined the supportive community and began learning skills to become an author. My most

> **Nobody can stretch into a new life that exceeds their identity. And nobody can stretch into a life they can't envision.**

important lesson was how to get out of my way and act in the face of fear. And eventually, my vision to publish a book in my fifties became a reality.

Like so many things, it's simple, but not easy. Two limitations bind us:

1. Not dreaming big enough—can't see what's possible
2. Fear of change—not believing in our new identity

These guardrails hold us back, tethered to the status quo—not stretching into our optimal potential. Nobody can stretch into a new life that exceeds their identity. And nobody can stretch into a life they can't envision.

Stretching into New Territory

Part of why we don't dream big enough is the biology of our three-pound brain. Our brain processes about 70,000 thoughts each day; yet ninety-five percent of them are repeated daily.[91] This means we're running a program, and only five percent of our thoughts are new. Without hacking into our minds, we have a very limited chance of innovating because we're doing the same thing over and over again—without realizing it. So, paying very close attention to what you're thinking is critical. Your thoughts become your beliefs, which, in turn, become your mindset. Your mindset fuels your feelings and actions, which create your reality.

Predicting Brain versus Envisioning Brain

In *The Predicting Brain*, Psychiatrist Regina Pally says, "In a sense, we learn from the past what to predict for the future and then live the future we expect."[92] We are constantly telling ourselves stories, and the brain is acting them out to dictate our future. This is going on at an unconscious level, whether or not we realize it. In Chapter 2, we explored how our stories developed from childhood form our unconscious limiting beliefs. Yet we always have the ability to hack into our brains and consciously choose a new story about how our future will play out, even if we don't completely believe it yet. As Natasha Bedingfield sings, the future is *Unwritten*.

The stories we tell ourselves really do matter. Fortunately, our sapiens superpower is our ability to see what's not yet manifested and to coalesce around making it real.[93]

The Importance of Firsts

What about when we don't see someone just like us? We can learn from the *firsts* how they did it—and believe more is possible for us too. When we don't see *firsts* in our field, we need to look further out.

Anyone trying to achieve a *first* must believe that something they've never seen can actually happen. They need to envision big—and without guardrails, knowing who they are and what they really want. *Firsts* give us permission to dream beyond our current reality and create a desired new one.

That's how Kamala Harris became the first female, the first Black American, and the first Asian American Vice President of the United States.

That's how Katie Sowers became the first female football coach in Super Bowl history. Katie said, "When you ignore the barriers that come along with 'gender norms', you will find that the love of football knows no gender."[94]

That's how Ruth Bader Ginsburg became the first Jewish woman, and the second woman, voted onto the Supreme Court.

Your Role Models Inspire

While each of us walks our own journey, role models help us see more of what's possible. Who are the role models that inspire you? What do they say? How do they look at the world? What do they do that you aspire to do? How do they make people feel? Analyze everything you can about them. Even think about how they dress. Actors often say that wearing a certain costume helps get them into that role. When I speak on stage, I put on a power jacket and a statement necklace, which helps me feel the part.

My Envisioning in Action

Aspirational Role Models

I have always been a huge fan of how Ruth Bader Ginsburg drove meaningful change and resiliently persevered through adversity. When Ruth graduated from Harvard Law School, she didn't even have the opportunity to join a law firm due to gender discrimination. So, she traveled to Sweden, where she saw a seven-month pregnant judge presiding over a trial. She could then envision something different for herself and our country.

She inspires me on multiple levels to live my true purpose as she lived hers:

- As a woman who balanced career and family, passionately pursuing her dreams
- As a cancer survivor, supporting her husband's battle and her own
- As a leader who exposed patriarchal injustices in our laws and drove gender equity, paving the way for a better balance beyond the status quo

While I'm no RBG, I'm inspired to make progress in my own way, balancing career and family, surviving and thriving through cancer, and driving more balanced, emotionally intelligent leadership, which includes more opportunities for women to rise to the top.

Leadership for a New Generation

We'll envision a better future when we realize what got us here will not get us to the next level—or best serve the next generation. As we rise in awareness, we can grasp the significant toll our traditional approaches have taken on the collective health of ourselves and our planet. Then, we can create a more sustainable path forward.

I'm passionate about exchanging the patriarchal command-control leadership model for a new paradigm of holistic leadership that celebrates our diversity as authentic human beings.

The traditional model is very competitive, rational, and data-driven, and doesn't embrace the full spectrum of holistic intelligence. It's more critically focused on comparisons that play the short game of win-lose, quarter by quarter. We have the opportunity to power up our whole brains, see the big picture, and creatively solve the most complex problems, so we prevail long term. As Shining Authentic Leaders, we can play the bigger, collaborative *everyone-wins* game.

When we ignite our optimal potential, balancing our left brain (IQ) and right brain (EQ), we can lead with more empathy, compassion, and inclusion. There is plenty of evidence to show how we'll all benefit

Authentic Leadership isn't about copying a model. It's about confidently living with integrity across your mind-heart-body-spirit.

from positive results, such as higher engagement, retention, innovation, impact, and well-being.

Authentic Leadership isn't about copying a model. It's about confidently living with integrity across your mind-heart-body-spirit. You're lit up from inside, fueled by purpose. You know your value, inspire others and accelerate success for your teams, organizations, families, and communities.

Dialing up Aspirational Qualities

In 2019, as I started to become an emotional intelligence teacher, I wanted to become more like the teachers and coaches who were training and inspiring me—with qualities such as a calm presence and vulnerability. I learned that my tendency from my corporate career was to convey confidence as an expert. However, as a coach and facilitator, being an expert could distance me from others instead of deepening relationships. I needed to stretch and practice sharing from my heart, so I could balance my confidence with vulnerability and become the mindful, authentic leader I aspired to be.

Vulnerability helped me remove blind spots and unlearn what I thought I knew. It allowed me to build a high-resolution awareness of what I needed to grow into my best self. Embracing it opened a doorway to more trust and connection, so I could help my clients and students feel safer to step into their own vulnerability and grow. I knew I was at a new level when I agreed to sit on a coaches' panel with three other former C-suite executives and was thanked for sharing so vulnerably.

What do you want to cultivate in your next phase as a leader? Who do you want to emulate?

Stretching with Vulnerability for Trust

Many leaders think vulnerability is soft and will undermine their authority, yet vulnerability is brave, bold, and necessary for us to grow as trusted emotionally intelligent leaders.

According to Charles Feltman, author of *The Thin Book of Trust: An Essential Primer for Building Trust at Work*, "Trust is defined as choosing to risk making something you value vulnerable to another person's actions."[95] By sharing fears, missteps, and challenges, vulnerability creates trust while releasing us from our restrictive pedestal of perfection.

But vulnerability is uncomfortable because it's about facing the messiness of our true emotions. I think Brené Brown nails why that's so scary: "The courage to be vulnerable is not about winning or losing, it's about the courage to show up when you can't predict or control the outcome."[96] Since leaders want control, no wonder we avoid it like the plague.

I didn't realize how vulnerability is critical for authentic leadership until I experienced its power for myself. Now I encourage leaders to lean into this superpower by modeling it and asking them to reflect on how it makes them feel. Overwhelmingly, they tell me their trust in me increases and I witness their *Aha!* moment of clarity.

I worked with a senior leader who took my Mindful Leadership class and asked me to bring its benefits to his larger team at their annual retreat. Realizing he needed to enroll them in its value, he asked me: "How do I share why I'm bringing it to them?" He knew the answer before I said it: vulnerability. Yet, it was difficult for him to embrace because he worried that sharing why he took a leadership class could convey he wasn't 100 percent confident in his abilities. I encouraged him to tap into his bigger why—how he wanted to keep growing and learning to be the best for the team. And he did. His opening remarks were authentic and appropriately vulnerable, which created space for greater trust and connection.

Envision your Future Identity and Life

Navigation is the power we have to see into the future. We must first see it, to become it. Once we stretch our identity and expand our energetic potential, we can successfully leap into the bigger life we're creating.

Camille's Story—Reinventing What's Possible

Camille was an artist with a superpower for creative envisioning. She had already reinvented herself as a very successful real estate managing partner when we began working together in 2020, achieving a higher level of financial success than she'd ever imagined. However, she realized she'd reached the limits of her envisioning and wanted to see what the next five years could look and feel like for her, with work/family balance on her own terms.

We envisioned bigger by looking at models of successful women she admired. They were building more high-vibe businesses in her industry that felt unique and authentic, while also living rich personal lives. As Camille defined her big vision, she realized her current business partner didn't align with it. Bravely, she parted ways and began again, rebuilding her own group from scratch.

Fast forward to 2022. Camille had moved passionately toward making her vision a reality. She created a new, thriving team who she says, "I'm proud to call my work family," and planned to expand her Chicago office footprint. Personally, she's also delighted by the expansion of her family with the birth of her third child in March 2023.

Camille told me, "I recall visualizing, with your help, being pregnant, standing in my new home at the kitchen island, and it's exactly as I had pictured it would be. The whole family is so happy, and I'm working on visualizing what the next one-to-two years will bring."

Camille is living her desired, authentic life because she embraces disruption and keeps stretching out of her comfort zone. By visualizing what she truly wants, she successfully evolves on purpose.

Why Visualization Works

Visualization is an often-taught mental rehearsal technique in sports because it's extremely effective. It's frequently used by elite athletes to improve performance.

In a University of Chicago study, they found that people who *visualized* making basketball free throw shots for thirty days enjoyed similar improvement to those who actually practiced throwing free throws for that same time period (23 percent versus 24 percent).[97] My friend, who was a competitive gymnast, said visualization was key to her training. Our minds are incredibly powerful when we focus their energy with intention. They create the same new neural pathways, whether we visualize or actualize new behaviors.

Tips on Successful Visualization

To experience the full benefits of visualization, you need to involve your right-brain senses: sight, sound, and touch, to create stronger, deeper connections in your mind and body.

For example, if you just picture yourself shooting basketball free throws in the third person as if it were happening to someone else in a movie, you probably won't improve as much as you could. You need to visualize everything through your eyes (in the first person). You have to be there at the free throw line, feeling the basketball, seeing the goal, and hearing the noise.

As you shoot, you should *feel* the ball roll off your fingers. You should *see* the ball traveling through the air with a perfect backspin. You should *see* your hands out in front of you with the perfect follow-through. You should *hear* and *see* the ball swish through the net. Once you do this, you're guaranteed to realize results.

Real Life Visualization—Medicine

My father practiced the power of visualization as an orthopedic surgeon to get better at surgery. Early in his career, he told me about a hernia surgery he'd botched up with the attending surgeon. "It was technically correct, but it was clumsy." He kept thinking about that surgery and replaying how to do it better in his mind. He could see himself doing it technically, feeling his hands, and seeing the results. The next time he performed the hernia surgery with the same surgeon, it was flawless. The surgeon was shocked because he knew my father hadn't physically practiced another hernia surgery in between.

Visualizing Do-Overs

How often do you wish you could go back in time and recreate a past event that didn't go well? Maybe we said something in the moment that triggered a spiral of negative feelings and ruined our day. Believe it or not, we can visualize a *do-over and create* new neural pathways, so we're more likely to respond that way in the future. Simply picture the situation and how you would respond differently next time.

Visualizing: The Mind-Body Connection

Managing Pain

While I was a student at Duke University in the eighties, I learned biofeedback techniques for my temporomandibular joint (TMJ) syndrome. TMJ creates terrible pain in the jaw joint, causing headaches and difficulty chewing. Biofeedback therapy teaches patients to control their body's involuntary processes without medication. I wore electrodes during each session to monitor how well I was relaxing my jaw muscles. Over time, I learned how to relieve pain just by thinking, with no further monitoring.

Cleaning up Cancer

In 2011, during my cancer recovery journey, I visualized eradicating cancer from my body. After each chemotherapy treatment, I pictured my ringleader inside my body, magically sweeping away the malignant cells while protecting the healthy ones. I felt peace from knowing I could trust this strong force within. I even drew an image of this mighty leader that we put on a T-shirt for my cancer-free celebration party. I now realize the figure was in a starfish pose — in control and powerful.

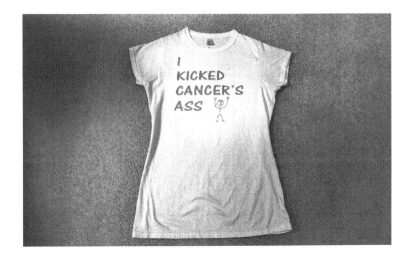

Pro Tip: It's helpful to envision what you *do want* versus what you *don't want,* given the energetic power of positivity.

Pivoting to New Paths—Addressing Fear

It was March 8, 2020, several days before the pandemic lockdown. I had just delivered the keynote speech at the University of Chicago Booth School of Business—for their first International Women's Day conference. Afterward, I was mingling and talking to attendees, and one of the student organizers congratulated me, saying: "I don't know if you remember me, but we met two years ago at Booth's Management conference. You had just left your CMO role and were planning to become a leadership coach and instructor."

I recalled meeting her, and how fired up I was about my new stretch vision.

"I can honestly say I thought you were nuts," she continued, "but I'm so glad it's all worked out for you."

I laughed inside, very grateful for what I achieved and knowing that my journey was far from over. Yet, I'd always had a clear vision and strong passion to work with Chicago Booth to bring a new wave of leadership forward, so I kept stretching on the very bumpy ride. Several days later, we went into pandemic lockdown, so I was in for much more turbulence than I ever realized.

Stretching is tough, and it's damn uncomfortable. I don't think comfort and courage go together. I'd certainly taken a big risk in leaving a lucrative career path and felt great pressure when the pandemic hit and my plans needed to adapt dramatically. The environment was a perfect storm for my fearful sabotaging critical voices to rise up again.

Pandemic Pivot—Outside My Comfort Zone

During the summer of 2021, I pushed myself to re-envision my coaching consultancy as a global online community—given I could no longer deliver workshops or speaking engagements in person. I invested in an expensive eight-week coaching program to help me market myself globally and envision what success could look like. My coach painted a picture for me: collaborating with other coaches and teachers around the world, seeing the impact of the leaders who worked with me in private coaching or taking my online course, and taking a break to walk along the beach or exercise. I could start to see and feel the impact of the new life I was creating, which connected me more strongly to making it a reality.

Even with a strong vision, stretching was still uncomfortable. I felt compelled to extract the maximum value and succeed at all costs. I went from being optimistic that I would find my ideal clients and grow my business quickly, to feeling like a complete failure and ragged mess. And that was only week two.

My Stress Reaction

While I'd come so far with my mindfulness emotional intelligence practice, I realized I still had this incredible cocktail of hyper-achiever, controller, and perfectionist sabotaging reactions that kicked into high gear with big stakes and time pressure. I refused to accept failure as an option, and yet I was judging myself as failing all the time. As I felt deadlines encroaching, I became even more overwhelmed and stressed, which made me even less productive.

By week three, I was near burnout. I showed up for meetings with my mindful emotional intelligence teachers, who were alarmed, and told me to *sleep* and *slow down*. I was turning back into a workaholic with no boundaries.

I didn't have enough skills yet for the new challenges I faced, so I was never in a flow state. I was operating in unfamiliar territory with a team that was only available on certain days and at certain times for calls and support. After being a successful CMO, I felt I should be better at marketing myself and judged myself harshly for not moving faster. I felt alone, frustrated, impatient, and powerless.

Stretching through Chaos and Uncertainty

When we change our mindset, we change the outcome. I had gotten myself as stressed as the highly stressed executives I was trying to reach and coach.

Thankfully, I was vulnerable with our mindset coach, Lisa, who wisely said, "Nobody wants a fried coach." It was a lightbulb moment for me and others. How was I going to help fried leaders struggling with constant stress and uncertainty if I didn't learn how to manage my own stress responses effectively?

Like me, leaders were dealing with the chaos of ongoing uncertainty of the pandemic. Like me, they also needed to do things they'd never done before. I realized in my soul I needed to go through this experience so I could coach with even greater empathy and understanding. Of course, I rationally knew we always had the power to slow down and choose our responses. But when we're in the middle of a hurricane, we can't see clearly; we need others to help us light the way out. We also need lots of practice to rewire our brains—preferably before the crisis happens, since our old habits are ingrained!

While I desperately wanted to control the outcome, I realized I could only control how I showed up each day. I practiced patience when I didn't get a quick response and reframed success as making progress.

We think we're running in a sprint, like my eight-week program; but we're really in a marathon, so pacing is key. I reframed my mindset from *This is so hard*, to *What if it were easier?* It helped me step away and get sleep, instead of staying up late on something that frustrated me. It helped me reach out to others sooner, celebrate the interim milestones, and stay in the race.

I'd always worked myself to the bone, revising work to make it *perfect*. I began to realize that believing *perfection* was the end state kept me from making real progress now. Slowly, I learned to let go sooner, so I could test, learn, and iterate. I got some amazing new coaching clients and realized the impact I could make. I created new models that became the basis for my course, even though it never launched in that eight-week timeframe.

We have the power to reframe our mindset, which is like flipping a switch. Whenever something feels hard for me now, I ask, "How can I lower the stakes to decrease my stress?" I remind myself, this is not life or death. I realize I'm never alone—if I let others in to help me.

The pandemic forced more pressure and heat to become stronger and even more resilient through change. With deep coaching and diligent practice, I rewired my brain. I learned how to recognize and shift from my sabotaging activities that pushed me into overdrive, so I could adapt faster and support leaders at an even higher level in the real world.

Power of Community
If I'd surrounded myself with traditional thinkers and naysayers, I would have found the new climb much scarier. I may have been tempted to jump back onto my last mountain, returning to my life as a corporate executive.

Instead, I surrounded myself with supportive communities through both my pivots—before and during the pandemic. They helped me see and believe in what was possible and embrace my fears to grow to the next level. I found inspiring, relevant role models to show me the kind of life I could have—as a speaker, author, coach, educator, and facilitator.

I was stretching into an identity that I could see, feel, taste, and believe—as if it were real. And eventually, it was. It only takes one person to show us what's possible. We then need to keep our vision alive and believe we'll succeed.

Deciding to Succeed

We will succeed when we *decide* we will. When we haven't explicitly decided, we take failure as final. We may believe it's a sign that it *wasn't meant to be.* But when we really decide, we will do whatever it takes to make it happen. When one way doesn't work, we'll find another. We change the question from *"Can* we succeed?" to *"How* will we succeed?"

My client, Paul, Dean of the College at Colgate University, made a strong decision to bring students back to campus in the fall of 2020 because he knew it could lead to a better outcome for them and the community that relies on Colgate economically. He and his team created a safe bubble by isolating students in their rooms for two weeks to ensure no Covid outbreaks before they opened up the campus again. This required painstaking planning and a myriad of things they'd never done, such as delivering meals one-on-one to each student. But at the end of the two weeks, Paul and his team succeeded because they decided they would.

Early in 2022, I decided I was finally ready to succeed in launching a coaching course and started with a small pilot group. Two months later, the University of Chicago Booth School of Business asked me to create my Mindful Leadership course for their Executive Education online curriculum. Now I was ready to say, "Hell, yes!" I possessed the confidence and mental muscle to keep stretching with more balance.

Implications for Leadership and Life

High Stakes Situations

In leadership and life, envisioning ourselves doing well on a big presentation or a big event goes a long way toward making it happen. When I work with new leaders taking on new roles in an organization, I ask them to envision their first ninety days. I give them a plan with structure and guidance for how to approach the new role, but that's only part of success.

The bigger opportunity is to envision yourself in the role—how you'll feel, how you'll act, what you'll wear, how you'll respond, and what you'll say. Envision yourself being who you want to be, and eventually, you will be.

When I was leading the company-wide rebrand of our firm, I needed to share our final research and recommendations with the board. I visualized myself in the boardroom, in my dove-gray suit, feeling energized and confident, seeing my colleagues' friendly faces and our CEO smiling at me with his nod of approval. And that's exactly what happened (and it felt even better than I'd envisioned).

Growing as Ambidextrous Leaders

It also helps to strengthen our positive qualities, well in advance of needing them, overriding our inner critics. In 2021, I took an alumni course at the University of Chicago Booth School of Business with my leadership mentor, Harry Davis, called *Ambidextrous Leadership*. The premise of the course was to get out of our comfort zones and become more ambidextrous by stretching and practicing new skills. Thinking of ourselves as multifaceted beings, we were encouraged to peel back our layers to expose more positive qualities, such as showing empathy, agility, or being innovative.

If our lives are like a stage performance, we tend to bring out the tried-and-true characters into the limelight instead of the secondary characters who live more in the shadows. For example, most C-level executives (and I'm no exception) have a strong achiever *action* character. They show up as confident, persistent, accomplished, always moving towards the next goal, and capturing results. What they don't practice nearly as often is empathy. To rise as leaders and human beings across our lives, we need to connect and understand people's needs, so empathy is critical. Not surprisingly, nearly all of us wanted to strengthen our empathizer character.

We designed experiments to test out our new character more, starting in places where we felt comfortable. For example, maybe we try showing more empathy with a family member, or at a trusted team meeting before trotting it out at a board meeting. Empathetic listening is a great way to do this, giving the gift of attentive listening at the invisible feeling level to the person who is speaking.

Stretching Far—into Uncharted Territory

Where identity stretching gets tough is when you're going into territory where you've never gone before. What do you envision then? How do you know how you'll feel? How do you stretch into *being* someone new?

Reinventing Next Chapter

For leaders ready for their next chapter, envisioning something new can be difficult because they only know the life they've created for themselves or what they've seen before.

I'm part of a new generation of people over fifty who are realizing that a conventional retirement like that of our grandparents is not our ideal scenario. We are likely to live a great deal longer than prior generations and have the opportunity to evolve our careers and personal lives. My vision of an ideal future is to love what I do so much that I never want to stop. I want to have meaning and purpose until the day I die. Without many role models showing us how, envisioning can be tough. I've heard this refrain quite a bit: *I want a change, but I've invested too many years to do something new now. Or, I've achieved the success I wanted, but how do I create more meaning and joy?*

So it's helpful to seek out people who are reinventing their lives in their fifties, sixties, seventies, and beyond—so we know we aren't alone and see more of what's possible.

The Power of Learning Communities

For high achievers and generous givers who want to reinvent what's possible within a connected learning community, they can. Top universities, such as Harvard, Stanford, and the University of Chicago, are offering up to year-long residencies to align with purpose and bring social impact to the world.[98]

One of my former clients, and a fellow Booth alum, attended both Harvard and Stanford's year-long residency programs to explore what he wanted to do and how to best honor his time and values. He became an adviser to help create the University of Chicago's new program, *Leadership and Society Initiative*. I was honored to attend the preview, along with CEOs and leaders from around the globe. We all benefited from hearing how people pivoted with purpose and created a great impact, opening up new pathways for envisioning ourselves. I smiled when the first speaker said he benefited most from writing his own eulogy!

Personal Envisioning: It's My Turn Now

In my coaching practice, I love working with leaders who are ready to reimagine and reinvent the next phase of their purposeful life. They have been successful in their careers, but typically don't have the mental space to figure out what's next until they retire or commit to setting new boundaries.

One of my clients, Alexandra, was a very successful entrepreneur and board member, but she had let her huge aspirations take a back seat to her husband's since he was the bigger breadwinner. While she kept working as her children grew to adulthood, they were always her first priority. Now, in her fifties, she said, "It's my turn," although she wasn't sure what that meant. To give herself space to envision something new, big, and audacious, she began setting new boundaries, such as only accepting ideal clients and saying, "No" to the rest. She created spaciousness to explore what lit her up and learn new skills, such as how to create clarity and dream bigger.

Dream big! The world needs you to stretch and take up all the space reserved for you!

As we experience disruption over time, reflect and envision differently, we stretch our potential. We are always connected to who we are at our core—our unchanging essence—and yet we keep growing and evolving. With awareness, intention, and support, the sky is truly the limit.

Chapter Mindset	From: Burned Out Leader	To: Shining Authentic Leader
8: Stretch your *identity*, and live the future you envision.	Plans based on the past and gets a *future by default*—limiting possibilities.	Dreams and disrupts self to create a *future by design*—breaking through guardrails.

FAST Framework

| Intention | Innovation | Identity | Interconnection |

Exercises: You can do these exercises on your own, or go to www.ShiningThroughDisruption.com/resources to access the workbook and guided practices.

1. Write your Best-Case Eulogy: How I Want to Be Remembered. Write as detailed an essay as possible. No one needs to see this exercise. Don't limit yourself to what you've done before or even to your current realities. Remember, this is your *best case*. Write with the awareness that change is possible and your future is ahead of you. Strive to get at what is most important to you.

2. Reflection: What strength do you most need to grow to step into your desired future? Empathizer? Innovator? Activator? How can you test and learn in a safe environment?

3. Friends Game: Stretch with reframing glasses to see a challenging situation you're facing from different points of view:
    o   Joey: What would your inner child do?
    o   Monica: What possibilities unfold if you let go?
    o   Chandler: How can you laugh at your inner critic to take away its power?
    o   Ross: What if you let go of being right (e.g., "We were on a break!") and focused on the relationship instead?
    o   Rachel: What magic could happen if you listened to your heart?
    o   Phoebe: What if you trusted the universe had your back?
    o   Your best friend: What would they say?

Chapter 9

Thrive with Compassion

We're all just walking each other home.
—Ram Dass

From Surviving to Thriving on Purpose

It was June 2022. I awoke and looked out my hotel window at Chicago's beautiful skyline as the sun shone through. Soon, I would head downstairs to support fifty professionals on the brink of burnout to help them reboot, recharge, and reconnect. It was a huge mission, and I was nervous, excited, honored, and grateful.

After meditating, I left my room and connected with my co-teacher, Barbara, who had traveled from Connecticut to deliver the eight-hour session with me. Together, we practiced the Three Breaths exercise. Then we created positive intentions for the day and walked into the light-filled room with greater calm, focus, and positive energy.

Six months earlier, I'd met the leaders of this mission-driven team who were dealing with post-pandemic burnout, while being severely understaffed. Their group had lived and worked remotely for nearly two years through the stress, anxiety, and uncertainty of the pandemic. Now, they all realized its toll on their personal lives, the organization, and culture.

People were overwhelmed and wanted to return to how things used to be. While the leaders couldn't reverse all that pain, they wanted to help their overworked and disconnected team to pause, rejuvenate, and navigate towards a better future. They were hopeful our mindful emotional intelligence workshop would be the solution they sorely needed.

When we communicated the purpose of our workshop to the team, we acknowledged that this current pace was unsustainable. Everyone was sprinting at full speed in a marathon that required resilience for the long run. To encourage people to take the pause and attend, we shared what happens in every Grand Prix. Even Formula 1 drivers, who are racing to finish as fast as possible, know how important it is to take an intentional break. While every second counts, they still stop to change tires and refuel, knowing that these pit stops are necessary to make it safely to the finish line.

At 8:30 a.m., I kicked off the day with a vulnerable story on my journey—about how the biggest disruptions in my life helped me find my purpose, so I could help them now. I wanted to convey from my heart that I understood their pain—and set the stage for trust and deep connection.

At the first break, our head client stopped by and exclaimed, "Wow! This is even better than I imagined," which made me even happier than I'd imagined. Throughout the day, I felt alive, energized, and *in the zone*. During the afternoon breakout sessions, I listened to the buzz in the room—and savored how the sun illuminated everyone's smiling faces while they animatedly shared their values. Given the picture-perfect weather, we finished the session outdoors, where we embraced the sun's warmth and captured the group's takeaways. I was thrilled to see how they planned to apply these accessible practices to beat burnout and build greater productivity and deeper connection.

At 5 p.m., I felt that sense of pride and accomplishment from having made it through to the other side of this big day. I was so happy that I'd organized a dinner with our client, so we could celebrate with flickering candles and delicious cocktails and dinner. I took in the delighted faces across from me and soaked in the moment. *This is why I do what I do, so I can collaborate with incredible people like this, and feel such joy from the impact.*

Just like my client, I'd experienced the isolation and chaos of the pandemic, and now I felt what it meant to flourish in the company of people again. We transformed our pain into purpose.

I felt in balance, with all my senses alive. I knew I was having a peak experience, where my profound joy comes from knowing profound pain and making meaning from it. I love Kahlil Gibran's phrasing, "Your pain is the breaking of the shell that encloses your understanding."[99] Facing our pain elevates our awareness and helps us see everything more clearly, with greater perspective and capacity for joy. I used to think my life's journey was about *getting past* the pain. Now I realize that persevering through pain is what makes my best stories, and connects me to my messy, authentic self—and to others with vulnerability and compassion. Through reflection and action, I dance with disruption to shine even brighter.

And while flourishing starts with us, positive relationships fuel us energetically, so we thrive faster together.

Biology of Human Connection

When life is most difficult, we are biologically primed to surround ourselves with people who care about us, so we get the support we sorely need. Relationships can be a lifeline for compassion when we need it most. We intuitively feel this because our bodies pump out the hormone oxytocin, nicknamed the cuddle hormone, which makes us want to bond and hug someone when times are tough. We experience the power of hugs as transformative, for they provide a visceral human connection to let us know that we are not alone. They even strengthen our heart, while also reducing stress, fear, pain, and severity of illnesses.

The power of touch is immense, and we can even give comfort to ourselves by placing a hand on our heart, placing our chin in our hand, and hugging our own bodies.

In my mother's journal, she spoke about her primal need for hugs and kisses as she neared the end of her life.

> Assuage my fears
> Hug my body and soul
> Sing me a lullaby
> Kiss my brow and rock my being
> Let me cry on your chest
> And tell me all will be well.

Compassion Eases Suffering

Immediately after my mother's funeral, we experienced a four-day period of mourning called Shiva, where family and friends came to our home to grieve with us. I felt the profound wisdom in this Jewish ritual to surround us with compassion when we needed it most and ease our suffering. I learned the value of being present through pain, which is why I've flown overseas and driven all day to be with others during their times of loss. During my fifty-fourth birthday party, I looked at my dear friend

Kathryn with fresh tears in my eyes. I thanked her for flying in for my mother's funeral, twenty-four years before.

Laughter Lifts

While grieving, I found laughter was an unexpected gift. At my mother's funeral, we told funny stories about her that connected us and helped bring me out of my darkness. I was surprised that laughter flowed so easily. Now I realize it's a powerful way to get us through a stress cycle, as it triggers the release of endorphins, our *feel-good* hormones, and bonds us to each other.[100]

The Yin and Yang Duality of Compassion—for Leaders

Dr. Kristin Neff and Dr. Christopher K. Germer pioneered the *Mindful Self-Compassion* program, and I'm one of the hundreds of thousands of people globally who took their course. I learned how compassion is a positive quality with the power to transform suffering through high-level, loving energy. Compassion is *when love meets suffering.*

We often perceive compassion as soft, nurturing, and warm, like a friend supporting us in grief. Yet, Neff's research shows its dual nature as a fierce, powerful force too. For leaders, it's critical to cultivate both the yin and yang sides of compassion, because they can protect *and* serve, which are both necessary in different situations.

For example, the yang (fierce) compassion looks like a firefighter going into a burning building to protect the people inside, or fighting to save my life during my cancer recovery. Or a leader fighting to protect their team from layoffs, or dealing firmly with a toxic colleague.

Yin (soft) compassion may be needed for the person who is working hard and not performing well, or to comfort someone who is laid off. Or it could be to support an employee dealing with a tough personal issue, such as a health crisis or the loss of a loved one.

Busting Myth: Self-Compassion Is Being Soft on Ourselves

Many high achievers believe that self-compassion is being soft on ourselves. They believe it's like taking your foot off the gas pedal, which will put an end to achievement. But that's a myth. In fact, self-compassion is critical for resilience. It motivates us to work harder and face reality, instead of beating ourselves up, pushing ourselves harder, and succumbing to burnout.

Without it, we're unable to handle the growing weight that we accumulate in our roles as leaders, parents, and members of our families, firms, and communities.

Self-compassion essentially means "to take a perspective towards yourself as you would a friend or colleague who is facing a setback or challenge."[101] Research shows 75-85 percent of us treat *others* better than *ourselves*. So, we have an immense opportunity to treat ourselves as we would a friend, for radical improvement. Self-kindness is one of the three key elements of compassion, along with common humanity (*I'm not alone*) and mindfulness.

Ground to Grow

I like to think of self-compassion as the essential nourishment we need to grow from the ground up, like a flourishing tree. When a tree takes sufficient nourishment through its roots, it has the strength and resilience to support an entire canopy of branches and leaves.

In Lahaina, Hawaii, I visited a banyan tree that was planted in 1873. At over 150 years old, it was given the space it needed to grow and covers an entire city block—towering over sixty feet high with more than forty major trunks. When I sat under this majestic tree, no matter how hot the temperature felt outside, it provided me with ample shade, as well as a resting place for other people, birds, and animals. This tree is a symbol of the interconnectivity we have with each other and the greater planet that we share.

Sadly, the banyan tree was scorched by the devastating wildfires in August 2023 and traumatized into a coma-like condition. But like the people in Maui, it's shown strong resilience. While it had nourished itself for years, its suffering has brought compassion from the community who call it their "giving tree" and rallied around to save it. With water, nutrients, blessings, and hope, they are giving it the daily nourishment it needs to help it thrive again.

Compassion Is a Necessity

His Holiness The Dalai Lama XIV says in his book, *A Handbook for Living: The Art of Happiness*, "Love and compassion are necessities, not luxuries. Without them, humanity cannot survive."[102]

In Eastern contemplative wisdom, there is no distinction between self-compassion and compassion. However, in the West, we think of compassion as being outwardly focused because we are biologically wired to help others through suffering. We have a bias that self-compassion is *selfish*. In reality, self-compassion is brave and bold, and utterly necessary to survive.

> **We have a bias that self-compassion is selfish. In reality, self-compassion is brave and bold, and utterly necessary to survive.**

Self-Compassion for Survival

Since 2019, I have served as a mentor for Imerman Angels, a non-profit whose mission is to ensure that nobody goes through cancer alone. Over the years, I've been matched with eight mentees with my former triple negative diagnosis, so I can relate to their situation and give them the compassion and support they need. Even with the same diagnosis, each person is different—so I always start by listening. In December 2020, Donna unleashed a torrent of strife she'd endured during the pandemic—nine painful deaths, including her sister, who died of cancer and could be a cautionary tale because nobody knew her cancer was dire until she lay on her deathbed. When Donna paused for a breath at the fifty-minute mark, I asked if I could share an observation, and she replied, "YES!"

I said, "You are clearly a hugely compassionate person who has made your family your number one priority your whole life, despite your hardships, which now include a life-threatening cancer that keeps recurring and getting worse. Your first thought is always, 'How do I help others?' Instead, what if now is the time to give to yourself, to get better—and share *that miracle* with the world?"

She got very quiet and said, "Oh, my God. I'd never seen it that way before, but I think I always knew deep in my heart that this is true."

Balancing Purpose and Self-Compassion

Just before the pandemic, Kathy expanded her business by launching her new spiritual community space, Altar, for lifting up women. Like many, she adapted virtually for many months, going into overdrive post-pandemic when we could finally convene again. In early 2023, I attended one of her special events. Here, she confided in me how her own self-care had slipped off her priority list as she passionately worked to serve others. Knowing her tendency to go into overdrive—both as an over-giver and hyper-achiever, like me—I hugged her and sent her a note of compassion the next day. I reminded her how precious she was and to fill her own cup. Even when we are living aligned with our passion and purpose, we can give too much and work too much, which can lead to burnout. So self-compassion is critical for any high-achieving leader's toolkit with a big heart and a big purpose.

Self-Care to Stop Harm

Nourishing compassion is like watering your roots, so you flourish like the healthy tree, with the ability to support others. Without it, we dry out, burn out—or worse. We know what burnout feels like—exhaustion, cynical detachment, or feeling a lack of control or efficacy. Yet, we often don't realize what to do to stop it.

Most high achievers work harder during stressful times, often shouldering more work and stress for their teams so they don't fail. While they hope their Herculean efforts will do the trick, they dig deeper holes of mental, emotional, and physical exhaustion.

Sometimes it's hard to see the harm being done to ourselves when we're in the eye of the never-ending storm. We're used to adapting to pressure, so much so that it becomes our new normal. That's why it's important to check in with our emotions mindfully. If we're feeling fear, anxiety, and stress—on an ongoing basis—we're doing harm. We're meant to complete the stress cycle and move on. Otherwise, we need to ask: *What can we do about it?* We always have a choice. I've started a new rule that if something consistently bothers me each day, I address it. Small things add up over time, so I try to tip the scale to feel more positivity. As James Clear says, "If you get one percent better each day for one year, you'll end up thirty-seven times better by the time you're done."[103]

As shared in Chapter 2, the most effective burnout recovery tools are re-energizing acts of self-care. Self-care is a big bucket and can include things like a ten-minute meditation session, cooking a nice meal, walking in nature, or even a nap. Post-pandemic, I treated myself to a handmade coffee mug that feels so good to cradle each morning and makes me smile at its beauty, reminding me of the essence of the talented artist who created it. (Interestingly, everyone who visits me gravitates to my special mug too!) Most people neglect to include compassion in their self-care, and it's a game changer.

Did You Know?

Compassion can be simple acts of kindness for yourself or others, such as encouraging words, smiles, or hugs. Just a little compassion goes a long way and correlates strongly with lower levels of reported burnout the following day.

Building Boundaries with Compassion

Boundaries are critical to give us the space to grow, like the banyan tree. We know that work, people, and life will take up as much time as we let it. So be intentional with your time and prioritize boundaries.

Over-givers often neglect boundary-setting, which drains their energy. Interestingly, Givers live at the *top* and *bottom* of the leadership hierarchy. The difference is that Givers at the *top* know how to set boundaries and protect them. The ones at the *bottom*? Well, they don't—and experience burnout.

Before my cancer diagnosis, I was a workaholic who lived close to burnout without firm boundaries. My workday was long and filled with meetings, and I'd always make time for my team. So I stayed late many nights to get my thinking or creative work done, often missing dinner with my family. While I tried to see my kids before bedtime, I didn't find time for exercise, for there didn't seem to be enough hours in the day. One day I saw a Nike ad: "Someone who is busier than you is running right now." It got me thinking, but not acting.

In January 2012, just after my cancer recovery, I knew it was time to commit to new actions to protect and nurture my health. So, I prioritized workouts three days a week. If something important came up, I would switch days, but I stuck to my three-day-a-week commitment. Exercise became non-negotiable, along with work and family, and I enjoyed a better balance with this three-legged stool. Today, my commitment to exercise is a rock-solid boundary and has expanded to a daily activity. I don't feel right without it. I've also added a morning routine of meditation, which began as a ten-minute action and has expanded to thirty.

I've learned the first key to succeeding with boundaries is making sure they are aligned with what I truly value. The second is building success slowly over time. High achievers hate failure and avoid it at all costs, but we value achievement! So, to create a new habit successfully, create an achievement you are guaranteed to win. You'll get the dopamine rush you crave, and gain the confidence to raise the bar, one step at a time. Before you know it, you're addicted to your new habit, because it makes you feel better—and your momentum builds.

Importantly, when life inevitably gets really crazy, be kind and compassionate, not judgmental, so you don't fall down the rabbit hole of shame. Realize you can simply begin again. When I let my exercise and/or meditation slip for a day or two, I feel the difference. I'm foggier, more reactive, and less calm and centered. I know it's a tangible warning signal that my self-care is in jeopardy and I take action with compassion, as I'd advise a friend to do. I remind myself *I'm worth prioritizing across my mind, heart, body, and spirit.*

Compassion Builds Healthy Resilience

Compassion builds resilience, for it cultivates a motivation to improve and fosters a growth mindset. Conversely, harsh criticism can yield short-term results but comes at a high cost of stress and burnout. Self-compassion can feel uncomfortable at first. But like any quality we want to grow, it strengthens with practice.

Compassion can have a positive ripple effect on one's local environment too. When we see others acting with compassion and empathy, we are motivated to act in the same way. It's essential to reaching your potential and thriving as individuals, teams, and a society.

Did You Know?

Compassion also makes us healthier. If one practices compassion with intention, it has as many physiological and well-being benefits as exercise or even being at your ideal body weight.

My Self-Compassion Letter

One of the most valuable exercises I learned during my mindful emotional intelligence training was writing a self-compassion letter. I wrote a letter to my future self when I felt under pressure—but from the perspective of a mentor or friend who knows me well and would want the best for me. I asked these powerful questions:

- What would my inner mentor say about the challenges I'm facing?
- What words of encouragement would be valuable to keep me going?

In the freewriting journaling style (introduced in Chapter 1), I invested about seven minutes. I imagined myself in hyper-achiever mode, stressed about meeting my urgent timeline—or facing unforeseen challenges that slowed down my achievement. Here's a snippet of my message, which never fails to be what I need to hear:

11/17/20
Dear Stephanie,

I can only imagine what you're going through now. I want you to know that you are so incredibly strong and open and will be able to handle anything that life is throwing at you now or in the future. Whenever you feel impatient, as if you can't wait to achieve the next milestone, remember that each stage is helping carve out the person you need to be to get where you are going.

Building Compassion Beats Burnout

Self-awareness and empathy are building blocks for compassion. Empathy's first component, feeling what others feel, is necessary for connection. But empathy's second component, maintaining a clear discernment about your own and the other person's feelings and perspectives, is also critical. Without discernment, we can succumb to empathetic distress, which activates the pain centers in our brain and drains our batteries.[104] That's why growing our compassion is so valuable, because it allows us to be of service while lighting up the pro-social network in our brain—which promotes optimal well-being instead of burnout.

In his lab at the University of Wisconsin, Richard Davidson has done extensive functional MRI brain scans during compassion meditations for experienced meditators and novices. Both show increased activity in brain regions responsible for monitoring emotions and generating positive emotions, such as happiness. The regions that tracked *self* and *other* became quieter, showing subjects opened their minds and hearts.[105]

I think of compassion as the magic elixir you can pour everywhere to alleviate suffering. And it never runs out! When you pour it on your body, you heal. When you pour it into your mind, you become more resilient. When you pour it into your heart, you trust more in yourself, in others, and in humanity.

Compassionate Leaders in Action

Overwhelming research points to compassion as critical for the best leaders, because they are aware of suffering and know how to transform it for themselves and others. Compassion enables leaders to take action in service of colleagues and teams, without succumbing to empathic distress or burnout.

A former client and fellow Booth alum, Ann Mukherjee, was Chairman and CEO of Pernod Ricard North America, a premium spirits company. Ann was the keynote speaker at our University of Chicago Booth annual marketing summit where she shared her vulnerable personal story of abuse from alcohol consumption. She transformed her pain into purpose as she stewarded her firm's growth responsibly.[106]

Former LinkedIn CEO, Jeff Weiner, was the highest-rated CEO on Glassdoor in 2020 when he was interviewed at the annual Wisdom 2.0 Conference about his compassionate leadership.[107] He shared a personal example of how he used fierce compassion to speak truthfully and with kindness to a colleague, guiding him to change his problematic behavior.

How do you feel when you get feedback? It's not unusual to feel uncomfortable when it comes across with judgment (*below-the-line* energy), for we may feel blame, like we've done something wrong. In contrast, compassionate feedback (*above-the-line* energy) comes from a place of openness and service, where we feel the intention to support our highest growth. When we receive compassion, we don't feel the need to defend ourselves. We can listen, accept, and grow with a healthy perspective.

Accelerating Teams of Trust

Trust is like a valuable currency—it grows over time with deposits or erodes with withdrawals. However, trust can also accumulate faster if we agree to put it on the table, like a bunch of poker chips.

> **Trust is like a valuable currency—it grows over time with deposits or erodes with withdrawals.**

During the Covid-19 global pandemic, people were forced suddenly to work remotely from home instead of at the office. Before this, many companies were concerned that their employees couldn't be trusted to be as productive out of the office unless they had a proven track record. However, in the throes of crisis, putting trust on the table paid off. Research conducted during the pandemic showed productivity didn't suffer with remote working across a wide range of businesses and often improved.[108]

As a leader, how can you increase the currency of trust in your life with the underused superpower of vulnerability? Many leaders are still figuring out how to operate in the post-pandemic remote/hybrid working world. Sharing your own personal struggles and limitations can open the doors for more candid discussions with your team. Why should you expect your staff to be honest with you if you aren't with them? Open dialogue, baby steps, and positive examples of what's working will create positive, collaborative change.

Dangers When Psychological Safety Is Lacking

To rise to the C-level in the financial industry, where I spent the last half of my corporate career, I learned the norms and behaviors of my companies, so I knew which parts of me to show and which to hide. Despite working for companies and leaders whom I respected, I was often in the minority as one of the few women at the executive table, while also being more right-brain/creative in a left-brain/rational, male-dominated world. I learned which emotions were acceptable: the positive ones. When I was unsure, I did what we all do—I held my tongue. The impact of a lack of psychological safety is silence.

Whenever we're not part of the dominant group, we perceive ourselves to be *other* and tread more carefully. Everyone is sometimes part of an *in-group* and sometimes part of an *out-group*. For example, Tom is a CEO who just joined a new advisory board where he wants to push for more compassionate leadership, but he is staying quiet and listening first since he feels he's in the *out-group*.

Psychological safety is something that all leaders can get better at cultivating and modeling from the top down. When people don't feel safe to speak their truth, we're squandering natural gifts and sub-optimizing team performance. Studies also suggest that burnout is higher. It's lose-lose versus win-win. Remembering what it feels like to be in the *out-group* can help us cultivate more belonging when we have the privilege of being in the dominant *in-group*. Belonging is critical to creating diverse and inclusive environments, which are able to encourage greater creativity, engagement, and loyalty.[109]

Pro Tip: Leaders are often in isolation in a lonely bubble, not hearing the truth or assuming silence is agreement. When there's negative energy, we know it. To realize more potential, create safe spaces, so everyone can bring their diverse views forward. Ask powerful questions and really listen.

Unconscious Bias

Becoming aware of our blind spots and unconscious biases is critical to finding further growth as emotionally intelligent leaders. Relationships can feel easier when we are similar, but more challenging and disruptive when we come from different backgrounds and can't understand each other's stories. People tend to underestimate how valuable reaching out will be, in good times or challenging ones. Whether or not we know people well, research shows we'll be pleasantly surprised at the impact we can make by connecting in conversation and offering support.[110] Through connections, we gain perspective. Just like with disruption, the biggest relationship challenges enable our greatest growth to emerge.

I love how Martin Luther King Jr. said, "…I am convinced that men hate each other because they fear each other. They fear each other because they don't know each other…"

Healthy Conflict: Getting It Right versus Being Right

We often think of conflict as a bad thing. Yet healthy conflict is unavoidable. How many of you have managed to avoid conflict in your relationships with your team, colleagues, boss, children, or even your spouse or partner, who presumably loves you and knows you best? My guess is *zero*. You know why? You're human! It's impossible for two or more people to come together and not have a conflict at some point. None of us sees or experiences the world in the same way. In fact, Daniel Pink's research shows an inverse relationship between power and perspective-taking; in other words, we find it more difficult to see another person's point of view as we rise in the hierarchy unless we intentionally reduce our perception of power.[111]

When we sit, metaphorically or physically, on the same side of the table, with a mindset of *we're here to solve this challenge together,* we can collaborate to find the bigger picture solution. Since we're operating less from ego and more from service to a common goal, we dial up trust, psychological safety, and the best teams.

In a senior leaders' workshop, I told my personal story of leaving my CMO role when my new boss diminished my scope. A participant later asked, "What if your boss was right, and you were wrong?"

"We were both probably a bit right and a bit wrong," I responded, "but that's not the point. The real point is getting it right versus being right." Then, we benefit from *intellectual friction* without *social friction* getting in our way.

Interestingly, earlier in that workshop, this same leader (who was a physician) had criticized the *Above/Below the Line* video I'd shown, questioning the research and deeming it "marketing propaganda." As a high achiever and former marketer, I was definitely a bit triggered and needed to breathe deeply. Then, I calmly defended the scientific validity of the video. I also benefitted from his physician peers sharing their opinions on why they liked the video. Minutes later, during our break, I realized my need to defend anything is because I want to be right, which keeps me from exploring the other person's viewpoint. I learned a valuable lesson that I can grow and learn from friction—even getting hijacked on stage!

In my career, I've had to do many things I disagreed with, such as layoffs and budget cuts. However, when I received empathy, compassion, and psychological safety from my leadership, I was able to step up and do what was needed—hoping life would get better, eventually. Without those fundamentals, we don't feel heard and validated, so nothing works. Unhealthy conflict ensues.

While it takes two people to create conflict, I do think it's the senior leaders' responsibility to learn how to cultivate more empathy and compassion for their team members. Sadly, many leaders just aren't taught how, so they don't probe when employees are unhappy, even when they intuitively feel something is wrong.

Disgruntled employees often go into protection mode and stay silent. Without probing, emotions fester, the team and organization suffer, and people don't do their best work. They may eventually explode, sabotage, and/or leave.

A Leaky Boat of Trust—My Leadership Story

When I was a CMO, I didn't realize how critical psychological safety was for opening productive dialogue, and this blind spot led to my biggest failure as a leader.

I'd promoted a high-achieving employee, Patricia, with every expectation she'd succeed. To my surprise, she stopped communicating well, failed to meet deliverables, and got angry and agitated when I probed for more information, asking, "Why don't you trust me?"

Unfortunately, I didn't see that she felt less competent in her new role and was too scared to let me know. What I saw was someone to whom I'd given greater trust, responsibility, and compensation without receiving commensurate results.

My trust was spiraling south, but I didn't realize this important truth. Trust is not a binary all-or-nothing equation. As we discussed in Chapter 4, trust (T) is built on the factors of *credibility* (C), *reliability* (R), and *intimate connection* (I) and is diminished by *self-interest* (S).

Trust Equation

$$T = \frac{C + R + I}{S}$$

I could have acknowledged that our trust was decreasing, like a leaky boat, based on the loss of *reliability* (i.e., not meeting deadlines or communicating), even if I still believed in her *competence*. With a candid, vulnerable discussion, we could have connected more deeply and increased our *intimacy*. Additionally, I could have decreased my *self-interest* to explore what she needed from me as her leader. All of that would have improved our *trust equation*.

As her leader, I needed to create more psychological safety by asking *open-ended* questions, modeling curiosity, and listening deeply to what was said—and not said—using questions like:

- How are you doing…really?
- How can I support your success?
- What's going on? (And keep probing …)
- What do I have to learn here?

I like how Susan Scott says in the final step of her book, *Fierce Conversations,* "Let silence do the heavy lifting."[112]

Although I did my best at the time, it was a personal failure for me as a leader. By the time I started really probing, Patricia exploded in rage and blamed me for promoting her too high so I could watch her fail and leave. Knowing my intentions were good, I had the unearned confidence that I was *right*, which didn't serve either of us. I've transformed my pain into a greater purpose by growing my awareness and emotional intelligence, which allowed me to apologize to her eventually. I'm now motivated to teach other leaders how to strengthen their compassion and embrace healthy conflict, so they retain and grow their talent and build more trusted relationships.

When you are feeling uneasy about trust, take a moment to ask yourself: *How can I inspire more trust in this moment?* Maybe it inspires you to listen mindfully, be vulnerable, or assume the best possible intent.

Transparency Elevates Trust

During the financial crisis, I believe our team's transparent, consistent communication was the key to us successfully retaining so many of our global clients in the midst of ongoing volatile change and uncertainty. Transparency can ignite all aspects of trust when we communicate authentically. *Credibility* comes from displaying competence with our words. *Reliability* arises from doing what we said we'd do, such as creating expectations and consistently meeting them—critical for creating more control during chaotic times. *Intimacy* grows from being vulnerable and honest about the challenges we face. *Self-interest* decreases when we focus on others' needs, showing our agenda isn't the only agenda.

Golden versus Platinum Rule: Intention versus Impact

Much of our external conflicts come from operating on the Golden Rule: to treat people as *we* would like to be treated. Yet, we're being judged on the higher standard of the Platinum Rule: to treat people as *they* want to be treated.

That's because we judge ourselves based on intention, but others judge us based on impact. With empathy and compassion, we can reduce interpersonal conflict for the better. While it's always helpful to see someone else's perspective, the simple truth is that we don't know their story. There is no substitute for asking and exploring with kindness and curiosity.

Steve is a CEO who sends emails to his team over the weekend, with the intention of getting thoughts off his mind rather than expecting an immediate response. However, Bridget reports to Steve and becomes resentful, because she prides herself on responsiveness and feels compelled to address each email as she gets it, working over the weekend. While it wasn't Steve's intention, Bridget was suffering.

Think about the implications in the workplace when you act with the best of intentions but create a negative impact. To complicate matters, each person reacts differently, so we need to modulate behavior based on specific people and situations. One of my biggest wins was listening and adapting to one of my direct reports' feedback to be more transparent and vulnerable with the team during our disruptive acquisition instead of putting on an overly positive face. It not only created more trust and safety, but I was eventually honored to hear her say, "I will follow you wherever you go."

Chapter Mindset	From: Burned Out Leader	To: Shining Authentic Leader
9: Self-compassion is necessary for thriving with *interconnection*.	Perceives self-compassion as *selfish* and *soft* — achieving at a high cost.	Knows self-compassion yields resilient growth — achieving sustainable success.

FAST Framework

FOCUS > ADAPT > STRETCH > THRIVE

Intention   Innovation   Identity   Interconnection

Exercises: You can do these exercises on your own, or go to www.ShiningThroughDisruption.com/resources to access the workbook and guided practices.

1. Do your own Self-Compassion Letter: Journal for between five and eight minutes using the freewriting tool where you don't stop writing, using these instructions:
    o Imagine writing a letter to yourself from the perspective of a close friend or mentor.
    o They know you well, understand you, and want the best for you.
    o Journal prompt: What would they say to you about the challenges and opportunities you are facing?

2. Micro-practice: when you feel trust is wobbly, think about the *trust equation* — and ask: How can I inspire more trust in this moment? For example, dialing up credibility, reliability, or intimacy? Or decreasing self-interest?

Chapter 10

The Shining Authentic Leader

What lies behind us and what lies before us are tiny matters
compared to what lies within us.
—Henry Stanley Haskins

Getting off the Train

It was September 2017, and I was taking the train downtown to my office like I did every day. But this day was very different. My CEO and I were about to unveil our company's new brand identity to all our employees. I felt like this represented the pinnacle of my marketing career that I'd been preparing for over the past three decades.

We had acquired another firm earlier that year, catapulting us into the S&P 500. As the Chief Marketing Officer, I'd led the charge to unify our companies under a singular brand purpose, identity, and core values—and bring it to life with a new company name and visual identity. I'd never been prouder of what our team pulled off under such a tight timeline, or been in charge of a project of this sweeping magnitude. Fueled by passion and purpose, I'd worked tirelessly, in flow, largely in my zone of genius. It was finally the big day. I was excited, nervous, and pumping with adrenaline.

I looked at my watch. It was 8:00 a.m., one hour until the company-wide town hall. I'd left just enough time to oversee the final preparations—like the light show and music—to stimulate the senses and create a unique and memorable event. Our team had planned every last detail, wanting our employees to feel the thrill of excitement in their bones.

Suddenly, my phone rang, and I saw it was my daughter, Olivia. She was a seventeen-year-old senior at Walter Payton Prep High School, old enough to come and go independently. She was the kind of kid I never worried about—smart, responsible, compassionate, and kind. Since her school day had already started, I was surprised to hear from her. My heart skipped a beat as I answered her call. I could feel a tightening in my gut that something was not right. But I prayed with optimism that it was nothing, as I greeting her. "Hi, Olivia. What's going on?"

"Mom, I'm feeling really sick and I need to go home. But since I'm not yet eighteen, I can't check myself out of school."

Now I felt sick to my stomach. On this day of all days, in the hour before our town hall meeting—the most important project of my career—my daughter needed me. Had it been any other day, I would have hopped off the train in an instant. Had it been any other day, my husband wouldn't have been traveling and would have jumped to the rescue. But it wasn't any other day—it was this day. One hour until our big brand launch.

I felt my heart pounding, my pulse racing, and a tightness in my throat. I didn't say, "I love you more than anything in the world, and you are most important to me," because I was literally frozen and couldn't think straight. I was feeling hijacked, going *below the line,* where we can't see all our options. Instead, I started explaining that I had this big brand relaunch meeting—so it was the *one* day I needed to be there to oversee and deliver for all our employees.

Olivia listened and softly said, "I understand. I'll just stay in the office until your meeting is done and you can come and get me." That's my Olivia. So sweet, kind, and empathetic.

I felt grateful the situation wasn't more dire, appreciative of her compassion, and relieved that I could proceed as planned. "Thanks, honey," I replied. "I'll be at your school in a couple of hours," and I hung up the phone.

Then I took a few deep breaths. Within a couple of minutes, my nervous system calmed down. And that's when I realized something didn't sit well with me. During my entire working career, I'd done my best to balance competing priorities at work and home. But I'd always known in my soul that my family came first. My values of courage, freedom, and family were strong—and they tugged at me now. I realized that actions speak louder than words. *Would my daughter realize she was more important to me than my work, while she sat suffering in that office for the next two hours? Was this the best I could do for her right now?*

The sun shone into the train, and I looked up and realized we were coincidentally nearing her high school within minutes, which I passed each day en route to my office. My right brain's creativity kicked into high gear, and my left brain joined in with its rational superpowers.

What if I hopped off the train at the next stop? I quickly calculated the time it would take me to check her out of school and get an Uber or taxi instead. I knew I could communicate with my team and trusted they'd manage all the final details. The best preparation I could do for myself was to ensure my daughter was well cared for.

With no time to spare, I jumped off the train. Checking her out of school took longer than expected, but we did it. I hugged her, told her to get plenty of rest, put her into a taxi, and hailed another one for me. Then I continued downtown and looked at my watch. It was 8:30 a.m.

I knew my father would never have gotten that call from me before doing the surgery of his life, because my mother was on point for anything we needed. I knew my mother would have picked me up at school, procured whatever I needed, and sat by my side. But I also knew my best that day was good enough. It was more than good enough.

At 9:00 a.m., the meeting began with our light show. Soon, I stood next to my CEO, feeling nothing could dim my light. I shared how our new brand would power our potential forward. It was authentic to the core—built on what mattered most—to *our employees, customers, and key stakeholders*. That day, fueled by my strong sense of purpose and values, I showed up as a Shining Authentic Leader across my life—as a leader, a mother, and a whole human being. I'm thankful I accessed my whole brain's intelligence—from my head, heart, and gut—so I could shine through disruption.

The next day, the new president to whom I now reported called me into his office. I expected him to congratulate me on our successful launch the day before. Instead, he said, "Branding no longer matters." Disrupted yet again, I felt a punch to my gut. But that disruption led me to where I am today, so who's to say *what is good and what is bad*?

The real world we live in is a roller-coaster that never stops. Disruption is going to call for us when we least expect it, at the worst possible times (who could make this stuff up?). We can try to control everything and suffer. Or, powered by our Four Elements and 4Ps, we can *focus, adapt, stretch,* and *thrive* together. *Do we stay on the train—or get off the train?* I don't think there's one right answer. The answers lie in your awareness—the starting point for this journey.

I've aspired my entire life to *have it all*—the big career, the loving family, the balance between both worlds. Now I realize that *having it all* doesn't mean our lives are perfectly balanced each moment or we're moving up to the next rung on the ladder. It means we know we're progressing in the *right* direction, fueled by our meaningful purpose, living with integrity.

The answers lie in your awareness—the starting point for this journey.

Then, we can flourish faster in this messy, imperfect, beautiful world and create our extraordinary lives—one moment, and one train ride, at a time.

Your Transformational Journey

Congratulations on taking this bold adventure with me. Let's look at how far you've traveled and the roadmap for what's to come.

In Part I, we explored how to achieve your authentic, optimal potential by dancing with disruption across the Four Elements—Emotion, Energy, Essence, and Experience—and igniting the 4Ps: Perspective, Presence, Purpose, and Progress. To build mastery, we expanded our capacity across all elements, transmuting fear into love to optimize potential. We flowed with our emotions (water) to gain a deeper perspective, elevated our energy (air) to enhance presence, ignited our essence (fire) for a clearer purpose, and turned obstacles into opportunities across all our experiences (earth) for continuous progress.

In Part II, we followed our FAST framework—Focus, Adapt, Stretch, and Thrive—to accelerate extraordinary success on our own terms. To focus, we increased awareness to energize intention and achieve our goals. To adapt, we turned obstacles into opportunities by accepting situations, beginning anew, and creating innovation. To stretch, we transcended our default future to design the future we envision, expanding our identity to step successfully into it. To thrive, we shifted from being critical to compassionate leaders, inspiring strong interconnection and enabling us to travel faster and farther together.

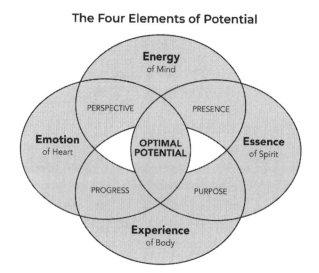

The Four Elements of Potential

FAST Framework

Building on these foundations, The Shining Authentic Leadership Roadmap synthesizes our journey through the Four Elements and the FAST framework, providing nine actionable mindsets to embrace change, ignite potential, and accelerate extraordinary life-changing success. The Nine Mindsets can transform our approach to life and leadership from wherever we are now.

In this chart below, you'll see the biggest shift from the default mode of Burned Out Leader to becoming the Shining Authentic Leader you're destined to be.

The Shining Authentic Leader Roadmap

The Nine Mindsets	From: Burned Out Leader	To: Shining Authentic Leader
1: Transmute fear into love, and power up *optimal potential.*	Remains *below the line* in 'fight, flight, or freeze' mode with blinders on.	Chooses to rise *above the line* with self-awareness to see exponential possibilities.
2: Dive into emotions and find treasure in *perspective.*	Relies on their harsh inner critic who limits and drains—riding the *stress-success cycle.*	Replaces limiting beliefs with empowering, energizing ones—accessing *deeper wisdom.*
3: Shift and lift energy, elevate your *presence.*	Gets stuck in *catabolic* energy that repels and destroys—harming self and relationships.	Rises with *anabolic* energy that attracts and builds—inspiring creativity and collaboration.
4: Ignite your TRUE essence, fuel your unique *purpose.*	Leans on the left brain which hides the whole story—*dimming their light.*	Reveals the hidden pieces of their story—*illuminating authenticity and meaning.*

The Nine Mindsets	From: Burned Out Leader	To: Shining Authentic Leader
5: Experience obstacles as opportunities to accelerate *progress.*	Gets stuck by *disruption as an interruption*—judging self, others, and circumstances.	Intentionally *dances with disruption*—exploring with curiosity through all situations.
6: Focus with strong *intentions* and let go of how they unfold.	Holds tightly to reins of control which *impedes flow*—harming productivity and resilience.	Creates whole-brain intentions that *feed flow*—fueling productivity and perseverance.
7: Adapt with ABCs: Accept, Begin Again, and Create *innovation.*	Latches onto *success and failure as permanent*—adopting a win/lose fixed mindset.	Knows *success and failure are temporary*—adopting a win/learn growth mindset.
8: Stretch your *identity,* and live the future you envision.	Plans based on the past and gets a *future by default*—limiting possibilities.	Dreams and disrupts self to create a *future by design*—breaking through guardrails.
9: Self-compassion is necessary for thriving with *interconnection.*	Perceives self-compassion as *selfish* and *soft*—achieving at a high cost.	Knows self-compassion yields *resilient growth*—achieving sustainable success.

THE SHINING AUTHENTIC LEADER

With the Nine Mindsets, you now have the firepower to trailblaze through any disruption you face instead of succumbing to overwhelming stress and burnout. You can see more clearly through the cracks and doorways of disruption to create new opportunities.

Practice these mindsets, and you will change your story, living and leading at the next level—with greater productivity, relationships, and wellbeing.

The Movement: Conscious, Collective Intelligence

Let's start a movement where leaders model compassion from the top, where psychological safety is the norm, and where people feel respected, trusted, and heard. Companies such as LinkedIn, Google, SAP, and Patagonia demonstrate how doing good and doing well are not mutually exclusive.

Instead of the old left-brained command-control paradigm, which stifles inclusion and sub-optimizes growth, this new, winning whole-brain paradigm creates leaders who are more conscious and compassionate. Their emotional intelligence harnesses collective intelligence.[113] They embrace their team's diversity of thought and experience to thrive faster and farther. I love this saying, often cited as an African proverb: *If you want to go fast, go alone. If you want to go far, go together.*

Did You Know?

When people show up as their authentic selves with belonging, inclusion, trust, and safety, we realize myriad tangible benefits on the bottom line, such as improvement in financial performance, productivity, collaboration, and innovation.

Boundless Interconnected Potential

As we unveil our brilliance as Shining Authentic Leaders, we become the stars we truly are. Our ignited flame illuminates and amplifies the fire in others. We expand beyond protecting and supporting each other to co-creating with collective intelligence and inspiring boundless potential—that outlives our lifetimes.

The Story of W. S. Merwin's Forest of Dreams

In 2023, there were eight of us who had the privilege of touring the Merwin Palm Forest Conservancy with Sarah. More than a guide, she was one of the stewards of the land, carrying on the legacy of its creator, William Merwin, the US Poet Laureate and Pulitzer Prize winner. He fell in love with Maui, purchased a property, and created a big dream: to restore the land that pineapple growers had destroyed. It was an uphill climb, for the public record stated: "Nothing will grow here."[114]

Before we entered the forest, the wind picked up, and I felt rain on my face as Sarah asked our intentions, "Why are you here?"

Six people said they loved plants and wanted to see the collection of palms, unparalleled on the planet. My husband said he loved Merwin's poetry.

While I love plants and Merwin's poetry, I replied, "I'm inspired to see how one person with a big dream can create such an incredible impact."

I'd been to the forest before and been blown away by William's story—his vision, patience, and resilience. For the first ten years, he consulted with experts, but it didn't help; he still planted trees that seemed "happy to die."[115] Yet, William never gave up. He continued with his daily ritual of meditation and writing each morning, followed by planting one tree each afternoon. He watched carefully, in the way artists do, with exquisite attention. He noticed that *palms* seemed to grow here, so he began to plant only palms—and started to succeed. When more land became available, fortune smiled on him and his wife. They inherited just enough to purchase more. And William kept planting one tree a day. Experts from around the world heard of his dedication and sent endangered palm species to thrive here.

When he died in 2019, William had planted one tree every day for forty years. His labor of love resulted in more than 3,000 trees, representing over 400 species of endemic, indigenous, and endangered palms. What transformation he achieved on a human scale by simply showing up each day! His legacy now lives on in perpetuity with the conservancy he and his wife created.

As we left the Merwin palm forest, and overlooked the ridge where we started, the sun now shone through the trees and revealed the ocean peeking through. Sarah read one of William's poems, *Place*, which brought tears to my eyes with its core message—that even on his last day in the world,

William would want to plant a tree. Of course, he'd never see it grow to its potential, but he would enjoy *his place* in bringing the tree to *its place*. It's about the joy of doing and being in this moment.

He'd revel in knowing this tree is becoming part of the soil that's filled with what's come before and what's here now. William had a huge intention and let go of how it unfolded by trusting his partnership with nature. He never knew how large his ripple effect would be—with his words and actions—in the years to come. We never know who will enjoy the fruit of our labors from what we are planting today. But if we show up with purpose and trust, such miraculous wonders are possible.

What would you want to do on your last day in the world?

We are Unique and Universal

My connection with many incredible people in this universe began after their death. However, their effect on me has nevertheless been real and powerful. Their energy lives on, which keeps raising our level of consciousness. That's the power of human connection and collective intelligence. We are never really done, even when we die. Especially if we truly live.

How lucky we are to be part of a common humanity that is interconnected and boundless, building on the shoulders of those who've come before. We are one—and yet each of us plays a unique role in this ever-evolving story. We can learn about the human experience through different eyes, voices, and expressions—including those we've known, those we've encountered, and those we've experienced through the legacy they leave behind. In the musical Hamilton, one of the songs that never fails to move me to tears is *Who Lives,*

Who Dies, Who Tells Your Story. I used to fear that I would run out of time, like Hamilton and my mother. Her life had a beautiful ripple effect on me and everyone who knew her, and it still has the power to touch people in different ways beyond her lifetime. Now, I feel fortunate for each day my story keeps unfolding. I know my mother's story is inextricably interwoven with mine, and I will continue writing my own story too. I am grateful for how my path crosses with others and changes each of us for good.

Our lives are precious and short, in my humble opinion. We are never done, but I no longer believe the point is to finish. I believe it's about discovering what lights up our souls, so we live a story worth telling and make the most of our time.

> **We are never done, but I no longer believe the point is to finish.**

Imagine what the future would be like if we embraced our full authentic, messy selves—and our *whole-brain's* boundless brilliance. We would shine even brighter as stars who light up the world.

Exercises: You can do these exercises on your own, or go to www.ShiningThroughDisruption.com/resources to access the workbook and guided practices.

1. Reflect: What would you do on your last day in the world?

2. Expressive Journaling: Using the freewriting tool where you don't stop writing, journal between five and eight minutes on this prompt:
   o *In one year from now, if we were celebrating how your life/work has evolved and grown beyond what you could have ever imagined possible, what are all the things we are celebrating?*

3. Take action: To reach your one-year vision, what goal would you like to achieve in the next three months?
   o Why is it meaningful to you?
   o What does success look and feel like?
   o What's an object, a song, or an image that represents this goal for you?
   o What specific actions (up to three) will you commit to?
   o What limiting belief might get in the way?
   o What empowering belief will enable you to power forward?
   o How will your unique essence, purpose, and values support you?

Invitation to What's Next

Congratulations on your progress as a Shining Authentic Leader! You are exactly where you are meant to be right now, and you've already opened the door to greater potential. Keep showing up and rewiring your brain based on *your choices,* so you transform and shine through disruption.

If you wish to continue your growth journey, I invite you to take the next small step to download and complete your personalized roadmap in the workbook. Like a GPS, we need to follow the right map that guides us to our desired destination, meeting you exactly where you are. You'll also find extra valuable tools and resources to ignite your ongoing momentum at ShiningThroughDisruption.com/resources.

Thank you for being on this journey with me, and I hope we continue on this extraordinary path forward together. To join our free monthly newsletter or schedule a consultation to explore more personalized support, go to mindfiremastery. com/contact.

Acknowledgments

Publishing a book has been a lifelong dream, and I'm so grateful for the people who've been part of my long journey to birth it.

First, thanks to Eric Koester's Book Creators Group, who got me started on my book-writing quest and showed me the power of diving in and sharing work before it's perfect. I'm thankful for Christine Kloser's wisdom and her heart-centered Capucia publishing team, who helped me bring this book to the finish line.

Thanks to everyone who agreed to be interviewed and share their stories, even those who I couldn't fit into this book. I'm particularly grateful to my coaching clients who enabled me to learn and grow through our co-created sessions and witness your transformations. You inspire me, and I know your stories will be inspiring to many others. Special thanks to Camille for being my first book interview and coaching client, showing me what is possible when we set a big intention, envision, and let go. Thanks to my dear friend and brilliant mentor, Beth Cassiday, for always believing in me and championing me forward, even when I couldn't see the way clearly myself.

I am so grateful to my beta readers who helped me breathe fresh air into my manuscript with their insights and compassionate feedback. Thanks to my book *naming angels* for your time and talent in helping me select a new name when Amy Edmondson's book, *Right Kind of Wrong*, disrupted me.

Thank you, Amy, for being my catalyst to dig deeply into my book's essence and find a title that resonated even more than *Waking Up on the Right Side of Wrong* for me and my readers.

I am honored to be part of the Positive Intelligence (PQ) coaching community and inspired by its leaders, Shirzad Chamine and Bill Carmody, as well as my wise, collaborative, and compassionate pod-mates who open me up to new perspectives on applying the power of positivity in our lives. For introducing me to the Search Inside Yourself Global community, which led me on my journey into mindful emotional intelligence, I wish to thank Ashley Nelson. You and our launch pod have shown me the power of true psychological safety and helped me trust my voice, for which I'm eternally grateful.

Huge thanks to the Executive Education team at my alma mater, The University of Chicago Booth School of Business—particularly Randy Kroszner, Meena Wehrs and Maggie Quijada—who believed in my vision and empowered me to create my *Mindful Leadership* course. It's incredible to partner together and reach hundreds of leaders, even before finishing this book.

I thank my family with all my heart: Peter, who supports me in being unapologetically me, even as I keep evolving what that means; and to my incredible daughters, Mikaela and Olivia—you are my proudest accomplishments and have shown me what loving and letting go really feels like, which is the lifelong lesson I needed to learn. Dad, thanks for being a role model who inspires me to follow my dreams with passion and perseverance, no matter what gets in the way.

I am so grateful for the encouragement, wisdom, and trust that you all placed in me. This book wouldn't be what it is without you. Thank you all.

About the Author

Stephanie Klein, MBA, CPC, ACC, ELI-MP, is a speaker, author, certified executive coach, leadership trainer, mentor, and educator. She helps high-performing leaders and organizations build mental resilience and peak performance, so they can optimize impact, relationships, and well-being. She teaches her course Mindful Leadership (now translated into Spanish and Portuguese) to executives worldwide through the University of Chicago's Booth School of Business to increase emotional intelligence and maximize potential. In 2022, she was a contributing author to the bestselling anthology, *Turning Point Moments,* which has been featured on NBC, MarketWatch FOX, and CBS.

For three decades, Stephanie ignited authentic growth for businesses, serving as a three-time Chief Marketing Officer (CMO), where she navigated the challenges and stress of leading through uncertainty, crisis, and organizational change. In 2020, she founded Mindfire® Mastery to combine her branding expertise with mindful emotional intelligence, backed by neuroscience and research. She now ignites authentic growth for leaders from the inside out, with powerful ripple effects across teams, organizations, families, and communities. Drawing on her experience as a mindfulness practitioner, senior executive, entrepreneur, mother, partner, and cancer survivor, she empowers leaders to shift from burnout to balance, so they can transform across their lives.

Stephanie is a sought-after keynote speaker and has trained thousands of courageous executives and entrepreneurs worldwide through workshops and coaching. She is passionate about helping them unleash 'whole brain intelligence' to embrace change and ignite greater potential, so they can accelerate extraordinary success. She's had the privilege of working with many leading organizations, including Hallmark, United Airlines, Kraft, Coca-Cola, Alberto-Culver, Cboe Global Markets, Northern Trust, Colgate University, and Northwestern's Kellogg School of Management.

She is a Certified Professional Coach through the Institute for Professional Excellence in Coaching (iPEC), Positive Intelligence® Coach, and SIY (Search Inside Yourself) Global leadership instructor. She earned her MBA from the University of Chicago Booth School of Business and a BA in Psychology from Duke University. She's also a graduate of the Players Workshop of The Second City. Stephanie is grateful to be a cancer survivor since 2011 and a mentor with Imerman Angels, who helps ensure no one faces cancer alone.

Stephanie can be reached at:

Website:
www.shiningthroughdisruption.com

Linked In:
www.linkedin.com/in/stephaniekklein

Instagram:
www.instagram.com/stephkklein

References

1 Nietzsche, Friedrich. 1889. *Twilight of the Idols.*
2 Kurzweil, Ray. 2001, "The Law of Accelerating Returns." *The Kurzweil Library.* 7 March. https://longnow.org/seminars/02005/sep/23/kurzweils-law/#:~:text=Ray%20Kurzweil%20*%20Ray%20Kurzweil's%20 Homepage.%20*%20Ray%20Kurzweil's%20Wikipedia%20page
3 Parke, Matte. 2017. "Thomas Friedman: Technology is accelerating faster than our ability to adapt. We can catch up." *Working Nation.* 2 August. www.workingnation.com/thomas-friedman-technology-accelerating-faster-ability-adapt-can-catch/
4 Fisher, Jen. 2018. "Workplace Burnout Survey: Burnout without Borders." *Deloitte.* www2.deloitte.com/us/en/pages/about-deloitte/articles/burnout-survey.html
5 Cooks-Campbell, Allaya. 2021. "What is learned helplessness, and how do you unlearn it?" 3 November. *Betterup.com.* www.betterup.com/blog/learned-helplessness
6 Kaufman, Scott Barry. 2020. "Post-Traumatic Growth: Finding Meaning and Creativity in Adversity." 20 April. www.scottbarrykaufman.com/post-traumatic-growth-finding-meaning-and-creativity-in-adversity/
7 Feiler, Bruce. 2020. *Life is in the Transitions: Mastering Change at Any Age.* New York. Penguin Random House.
8 Rogers, Fred. 2019. *The World According to Mister Rogers.* Hachette Books.
9 Gilbert, Elizabeth. 2016. *Big Magic: Creative Living Beyond Fear.* New York. Riverhead Books.
10 Van der Kolk, Bessel. 2015. *The Body Keeps the Score: Brain, Mind, and Body in the Healing of Trauma.* New York. Penguin.
11 Eurich, Tash. 2018. "What Self-Awareness Really Is (and How to Cultivate It)." *Harvard Business Review.* 4 January. www.hbr.org/2018/01/what-self-awareness-really-is-and-how-to-cultivate-it
12 Landry, Lauren.2019. "Why Emotional Intelligence Is Important In Leadership". *Harvard Business School Online.* 3 April. https://online.hbs.edu/blog/post/emotional-intelligence-in-leadership
13 Goleman, Daniel. 2004. "What Makes a Leader?" *Harvard Business Review.* 1 January. www.hbr.org/2004/01/what-makes-a-leader
14 The Conscious Leadership Group. 2021. "Locating Yourself – A Key to Conscious Leadership." 17 February. *Facebook.* https://www.facebook.com/consciousleadershipgroup/videos/1433064413801994
15 Cherry, Kendra. 2022. "What Is the Negativity Bias?" *Verywell Mind.* 14 November. www.verywellmind.com/negative-boas-4589618

16   Robinson, Bryan. 2020. "The 3-to-1 Positivity Ratio and 10 Ways It Advances Your Career." *Forbes*. 16 October. https://www.forbes.com/sites/bryanrobinson/2020/10/16/10-ways-the-3-to-1-positivity-ratio-can-advance-your-career/

17   Amabile, Teresa M, and Steven J Kramer. 2011. "The Power of Small Wins." *Harvard Business Review*. www.hbr.org/2011/05/the-power-of-small-wins

18   Bhandari, Smitha. 2021. "How Does Stress Affect Health?" *Web MD*. 8 December. https://www.webmd.com/balance/stress-management/effects-of-stress-on-your-body

19   The Culture Conference. 2018. "James R. Doty, M.D.: Compassion as a Leadership Skill". *YouTube*. 18 June. www.youtube.com/watch?v=i-zlCU5-O2w

20   McGonigal, Kelly. 2013. "How To Make Stress Your Friend." *TED Global*. 4 September. www.ted.com/talks/kelly_mcgonigal_how_to_make_stress_your_friend/c

21   Nin, Anaïs, 1969. *The Diary of Anaïs Nin 1939-1944*. New York. Harvest/HBJ.

22   Dalai Lama, His Holiness The, and Howard C Cutler. 1998. *A Handbook for Living: The Art of Happiness*. New York. Riverhead Books.

23   *Red Mage's Ballads*. 2020. Blog Post. *Tumbler*. 21 March. https://autumnslance.tumblr.com/post/613208057421414400

24   Gelles, David. 2020. "Are Companies More Productive in a Pandemic?" *New York Times*. 23 June. www.nytimes.com/2020/06/23/business/working-from-home-productivity.html

25   Frankl, Viktor E. 2006. *Man's Search For Meaning*. Boston. Beacon Press.

26   Pattakos, Alex. 2010. *Prisoners of Our Thoughts: Viktor Frankl's Principles for Discovering Meaning in Life and Work*. Oakland. Berrett-Koehler Publishers Inc.

27   Spera, Stephanie P., Eric D. Buhrfeind, and James W. Pennebaker. 1994. "Expressive Writing and Coping with Job Loss." *Academy of Management Journal*. Vol 37, No3.

28   Burton, Chad, and Laura King. 2008. "Effects of (very) Brief Writing on Health: The Two-Minute Miracle." *British Journal of Health Psychology*. https://wholebeinginstitute.com/wp-content/uploads/Burton_King_Effects-Brief-Writing-Healthpdf.pdf

29   Lieber, Emma. 2021. *The Writing Cure*. New York. Bloomsbury Academic.

30   Shmerling, Robert H. 2022. "Right brain/left brain, right?" *Harvard Health*. 24 March. www.health.harvard.edu/blog/right-brainleft-brain-right-2017082512222

31   Taylor, Jill Bolte. 2009. *My Stroke of Insight*. London. Hodder & Stoughton.

32   Taylor, Jill Bolte. 2008. "My Stroke of Insight." *YouTube*. 13 March. https://www.youtube.com/watch?v=UyyjU8fzEYU

33   ASU Research. 2021. "Children do not understand concept of others having false beliefs until age 6 or 7." *Arizona State University News*. 28 September. https://news.asu.edu/20210928-children-do-not-understand-concept-others-having-false-beliefs-until-age-6-or-7

34   Chamine, Shirzad. 2012. Positive Intelligence: Why Only 20% of Teams and Individuals Achieve Their True Potential and HOW YOU CAN ACHIEVE YOURS. Austin. Greenleaf Book Group Press.

35   Goldsmith, Marshall. 2007. *What Got You Here, Won't Get You There*. New York. Hachette.

36   Wind, Y., C Crook and R.E. Gunther. 2006. *The Power of Impossible Thinking: Transform the Business of Your Life and the Life of Your Business*. Upper Saddle River. Wharton School Publishing.

37 Orbé-Austin, Lisa and Richard. 2020. *Own your Greatness: Overcome Imposter Syndrome, Beat Self-Doubt, and Succeed in Life*. New York. Ulysses Press.

38 Sharma, Natasha. 2017. "What We Feel Matters More Than What We Think." *TEDx Talk*. https://www.youtube.com/watch?v=DsDVCQnqcy4

39 LeanIn.Org and McKinsey & Company. "Women in the Workplace 2022." *LeanIn.Org*. www.leanin.org/women-in-the-workplace/2022#!

40 Grant, Adam. 2014. *Give and Take: Why Helping Others Drives Our Success*. Penguin.

41 Heng, Yu Tse, and Kira Schabram. 2022. "How Other- and Self-Compassion Reduce Burnout through Resource Replenishment." *Academy of Management*. 14 April. https://journals.aom.org/doi/10.5465/amj.2019.0493

42 Eagleman, David. 2021. *Livewired: The Inside Story of The Ever-Changing Brain*. New York. First Vintage Books.

43 McGreevy, Sue. 2011. "Eight Weeks to a Better Brain." *Harvard Gazette*. 21 January. https://news.harvard.edu/gazette/story/2011/01/eight-weeks-to-a-better-brain/

44 Sollisch, J. 2016. "The Cure for Decision Fatigue." *Wall Street Journal*. 10 June. https://www.wsj.com/articles/the-cure-for-decision-fatigue-1465596928

45 Jha, Amishi. 2021. *Peak Mind: Find Your Focus, Own Your Attention, Invest 12 Minutes A Day*. New York. HarperOne.

46 Stanford University (@Stanford). 2012. "According to Prof. Luskin, we have over 60,000 thoughts a day with 90% being repetitive – how to change and find peace". *Twitter*. April 5, 2012 11.15pm. https://twitter.com/Stanford/status/188027203383066624

47 Williams, Margery. 1922. *The Velveteen Rabbit*. New York. George H. Doran Company.

48 Ekman, Paul. 2016. "An Interactive Map of Emotions." *Paul Ekman Group*. 6 May. www.paulekman.com/atlas-of-emotions/

49 Brown, Brené. 2021. *Atlas of the Heart*. New York. Penguin Random House.

50 Molinsky, Andy. 2015. "Emotional Intelligence Doesn't Translate Across Borders." *Harvard Business Review*. 20 April. www.hbr.org/2015/04/emotional-intelligence-doesnt-translate-across-borders

51 Schneider, Bruce D. 2022. *Energy Leadership: The 7 Level Framework for Mastery in Life and Business*. New Jersey. John Wiley & Sons, Inc. and 7 Levels of Energy. Energy Leadership. Institute for Professional Excellence in Coaching.

52 iPEC. "Study Validates That People with Higher Energy Accrue a Greater Sense of Life Satisfaction" *Institute for Professional Excellence in Coaching*. https://www.ipeccoaching.com/blog/study-validates-people-higher-energy-accrue-greater-sense-life-satisfaction

53 Mehrabian, Albert. 1972. *Nonverbal Communication*. New Jersey. Transaction Publishers; Thompson, Jeff. 2011. "Is Nonverbal Communication a Numbers Game?" *Psychology Today*. 30 September. www.psychologytoday.com/intl/blog/beyond-words/201109/is-nonverbal-communication-numbers-game

54 Rajavanshi, Anil K. 2011. "The Three Minds of the Body—Brain, Heart, and Gut." *The Times of India*, 7 October. https://timesofindia.indiatimes.com/brain-heart-and-gut-minds/articleshow/8647137.cms

55 Felman, Adam. 2023. "Want To Know About Cardiovascular Disease" November 29. *Medical News Today*. https://www.medicalnewstoday.com/articles/257484

56 Fabiny, Anne. 2015. "Music Can Boost Memory and Mood." 14 February. *Harvard Health Publishing*. https://www.health.harvard.edu/mind-and-mood/music-can-boost-memory-and-mood

57 Tang, Yi-Yuan, Britta K Hölzel, and Michael Posner. 2015. "The Neuroscience of Mindfulness Meditation." *Nature.com*. 18 March. https://www.nature.com/articles/nrn3916

58 www.heartmath.com/science/

59 Bechara, A, H Damasio, D Trabel, and A. R. Damasio. 1997. "Deciding Advantageously Before Knowing the Advantageous Strategy" *Scence.org*. 28 February. https://www.science.org/doi/10.1126/science.275.5304.1293

60 Koontz, Alison. 2019. "The Circuitry of Creativity: How Our Brains Innovate Thinking." *Caltechletters.org*. 12 March. https://caltechletters.org/science/what-is-creativity

61 MacKenzie, Gordon. 1998. *Orbiting the Giant Hairball: A Corporate Fool's Guide to Surviving with Grace*. New York. Viking.

62 https://marekbennett.com/2020/03/23/diary-comic-4panel/

63 Phillips, David J.P. 2017. "The Magic of Storytelling." *TEDx Talks*. https://www.youtube.com/watch?v=Nj-hdQMa3uA

64 Unger, Richard. 2007. *Lifeprints: Deciphering Your Life Purpose from your Fingerprints*. Berkeley. Crossing Press.

65 Cuddy, Amy. 2023. "You are a verb, not a noun." 30 April. *Instagram*. https://www.instagram.com/p/Crq5YsCJ-h8/

66 Maister, David H, Charles H Green, and Robert M Galford. 2001. *The Trusted Advisor*. New York. Free Press.

67 Danner, Deborah D, David A Snowdon, and Wallace V Friesen. 2000. "Positive Emotions in Early Life and Longevity: Findings from the Nun Study." American Psychological Association. https://www.apa.org/pubs/journals/releases/psp805804.pdf

68 Feiler, Bruce. 2020. *Life is in the Transitions: Mastering Change at Any Age*. Penguin Random House.

69 Seligman, Martin EP. 1990. *Learned Optimism: How To Change Your Mind and Your Life*. New York. Vintage Books.

70 Kübler-Ross, Elisabeth. 1969. *On Death and Dying*. New York. The Macmillan Company.

71 McGonigal, Jane. 2012. "The Game That Can Give You Ten Extra Years of Life." TEDTalk. https://www.ted.com/talks/jane_mcgonigal_the_game_that_can_give_you_10_extra_years_of_life/transcript

72 Kaufman, Scott Barry. 2020. "Post-Traumatic Growth: Finding Meaning and Creativity in Adversity." 20 April. www.scottbarrykaufman.com/post-traumatic-growth-finding-meaning-and-creativity-in-adversity/

73 Lutz, Antoine, Daniel R. McFarlin, David M Perlman, Tim V. Salomons, and Richard J. Davidson. 2013. "Altered Anterior Insula Activation During Anticipation and Experience of Painful Stimuli in Expert Meditators." *Neuroimage*. https://www.ncbi.nlm.nih.gov/pmc/articles/PMC3787201/

74 Nhat Hanh, Thich, 2014. *No Mud, No Lotus*. Parallax Press.

75 De Bono, Edward. 2010. *Lateral Thinking: Creativity Step by Step*. HarperCollins e-books.

76 Seinfeld, Jerry. 1998. "I'm Telling You For The Last Time." Broadhurst Theatre, New York City. *YouTube*. https://www.youtube.com/watch?v=yQ6giVKp9ec

77 Science History Institute. "Alexander Fleming." https://sciencehistory.org/education/scientific-biographies/alexander-fleming/

78 Rothstien, Lori and Denise Stromme. 2017. "RAS (Reticular Activating System)" *University of Minnesota Extension*. 10 October. https://extension.umn.edu/two-you-video-series/ras

79   Grange, Dr. Pippa. 2021. *Fear Less: How to Win Your Way in Work and Life.* Vermillion.

80   Venkatraman, Rohini. 2018. "You're 96 Percent Less Creative Than You Were as a Child. Here's How to Reverse That." *Inc.com.* 18 January. www.inc.com/ rohini-venkatraman/4-ways-to-get-back-creativity-you-had-as-a-kid.html

81   Anicich, Eric M, Alice J Lees, and Shi Lui. 2021. "Thanks, but No Thanks: Unpacking the Relationship Between Relative Power and Gratitude." *Personality Social Psychology Bulletin.* https://journals.sagepub.com/doi/ abs/10.1177/01461672211025945

82   Smithsonian Institution. 2014. "George de Mestral: Velcro Inventor." 15 April. https://invention.si.edu/george-de-mestral-velcro-inventor

83   Suzuki, Shinryu. 2020. *Zen Mind, Beginner's Mind.* Boulder. Shambhala Publications, Inc.

84   Dweck, Carol. 2016. "What Having a 'Growth Mindset' Actually Means." *Harvard Business Review.* 13 January. www.hbr.org/2016/01/what-having-a-growth-mindset-actually-means

85   Daskal, Lolly. 2018. "How Improv Can Make You a Better Leader: Improvisation is a training that will change who you are." *Inc.* 3 January. www.inc.com/lolly-daskal/how-improv-can-make-you-a-better-leader.html

86   Duhigg, Charles. 2016. "What Google Learned From Its Quest to Build the Perfect Team." *The New York Times Magazine.* https://nytimes. com/2016/02/28/magazine/what-google-learned-from-its-quest-to-build-the-perfect-team.html

87   Edmondson, Amy. 2014. "Building a Psychologically Safe Workplace." *TEDxHGSE.* https://www.youtube.com/watch?v=LhoLuui9gX8

88   Walther, Anne. 2021. "What is Wabi Sabi? The Elusive Beauty of Imperfection." *Japan Objects.* 8 January. www.japanobjects.com/features/ wabi-sabi

89   Telander, Rick. 1998. "Michael Jordon on Phil Jackson." *ESPN The Magazine.* 6 April. https://www.espn.co.uk/nba/story/_/id/29050123/michael-jordan-phil-jackson-jerry-krause-one-nba-player-stand-most

90   Burton, Mary Lindley, and Richard A Wedemeyer. 1992. *In Transition: From the Harvard Business School Club of New York's Career Management Seminar.* HarperBusiness.

91   Healthy Brains. "You are your Brain." https://healthybrains.org/brain-facts/

92   Pally, Regina. 2007. "The Predicting Brain: Unconscious Repetition, Conscious Reflection and Therapeutic Change." *The International Journal of Psychoanalysis.* 88:4, 861-881. https://www.tandfonline.com/doi/abs/10.1516/ B328-8P54-2870-P703

93   Harari, Yuval Noah. 2020. *Sapiens.* New York. Harper Perennial.

94   Sowers, Katie. 2016. "When You Ignore Barriers." *LinkedIn.* 26 March. https:// www.linkedin.com/pulse/you-allow-yourself-ignore-barriers-come-along-gender-norms-sowers

95   Feltman, Charles. 2021. *The Thin Book of Trust: An Essential Primer for Building Trust at Work,* 2nd Ed. Thin Book Publishing.

96   Brown, Brené. 2018. *Dare to Lead: Brave Work. Tough Conversations. Whole Hearts.* New York. Random House.

97   Haefner, Joe. 2008. "Mental Rehearsal and Visualization: The Secret to Improving Your Game Without Touching a Basketball!" *Breakthrough Basketball.* https://www.breakthroughbasketball.com/mental/visualization. html

98 Tergesen, Anne. 2023. "For $60,000, These Colleges Help Older Workers Plot Encore Careers." *Wall Street Journal.* 17 February. https://www.wsj.com/articles/for-60-000-these-colleges-help-older-workers-plot-encore-careers-a0060b9a?page=1

99 Gibran, Kahlil. 1923. *The Prophet.* New York. Penguin.

100 Manninen, Sandra, et al. 2017. "Social Laughter Triggers Endogenous Opioid Release in Humans." *Journal of Neuroscience.* 21 June. https://www.jneurosci.org/content/37/25/6125

101 Fernandez, Rich, and Steph Stern. 2020. "Self-Compassion Will Make You A Better Leader." *Harvard Business Review.* 9 November. https://hbr.org/2020/11/self-compassion-will-make-you-a-better-leader

102 Dalai Lama, His Holiness The, and Howard C Cutler. 1998. *A Handbook for Living: The Art of Happiness.* Riverhead Books.

103 Clear, James. "Continuous Improvement: How It Works and How to Master It" *jamesclear.com* https://jamesclear.com/continuous-improvement

104 Klimecki, Olga M., Susanne Leiberg, Claus Lamm, and Tania Singer. 2012. "Functional Neural Plasticity and Associated Changes in Positive Affect after Compassion Training." *Cerebral Cortex.* 1 June. https://pubmed.ncbi.nlm.nih.gov/22661409/

105 Baraz, James and Alexander Shoshana. 2010. "The Helper's High." *Greater Good Magazine.* 1 February. https://greatergood.berkeley.edu/article/item/the_helpers_high

106 Perez, Christine. 2022. "A Global Force: Ann Mukherjee." *D Magazine.* 11 July. www.dmagazine.com/publications/d-ceo/2022/june-july/a-global-force-ann-mukherjee/

107 Wisdom 2.0. 2020. "Compassionate Management. LinkedIn CEO Jeff Weiner Interviewed by Obama CEO, David Simas." *YouTube.* 24 April. https://www.youtube.com/watch?v=HUubrI-h1ss

108 Van Bommel, T. 2021. "Remote-work Options Can Boost Productivity and Curb Burnout." *Catalyst.* https://www.catalyst.org/reports/remote-work-burnout-productivity/

109 Kennedy, Julia Taylor, and Pooja Jain-Link. 2001. "What Does It Take To Build A Culture Of Belonging?" *Harvard Business Review.* 21 June. https://hbr.org/2021/06/what-does-it-take-to-build-a-culture-of-belonging

110 Dungan, James, David M Munguia Gomez, and Nicholas Epley. 2022. "Too Reluctant To Reach Out: Receiving Social Support Is More Positive Than Expressers Expect." *Psychological Science.* 8 July. https://pubmed.ncbi.nlm.nih.gov/35802611/

111 Pink, Daniel H. 2014. "The Importance of Perspective-Taking In Leadership." *Life Science Leader.* 31 July. https://www.lifescienceleader.com/doc/the-importance-of-perspective-taking-in-leadership-0001

112 Scott, Susan. 2002. *Fierce Conversations: Achieving Success at Work and in Life. One Conversation at a Time.* New York. New American Library.

113 Greiser, Christian, Jan-Philipp Martini, Nicole Meissner, Liane Stephan, and Chris Tamdjidi. 2020. "Tap Your Company's Collective Intelligence with Mindfulness." 5 February. *BCG Global.* https://www.bcg.com/publications/2020/tap-your-company-collective-intelligence-with-mindfulness

114 Dueben, Alex. 2016. "Late Happiness." *Poetry Foundation.* 18th October. https://www.poetryfoundation.org/articles/91088/late-happiness

115 Merwin, W.S. 1998. *The Rain in the Trees.* New York. Alfred A. Knopf, Inc.

Made in the USA
Middletown, DE
15 February 2025

70924262R00173